See How They Run

ELECTING THE PRESIDENT
IN AN AGE OF MEDIAOCRACY

PAUL TAYLOR

D1039726

ALFRED A. KNOPF   NEW YORK   1990

UNIVERSITY LIBRARY
Lethbridge, Alberta

THIS IS A BORZOI BOOK
PUBLISHED BY ALFRED A. KNOPF, INC.

Copyright © 1990 by Paul Taylor
All rights reserved under International and Pan-
American Copyright Conventions. Published in the
United States by Alfred A. Knopf, Inc., New York,
and simultaneously in Canada by Random House of
Canada Limited, Toronto. Distributed by Random
House, Inc., New York.

Library of Congress Cataloging-in-Publication Data

Taylor, Paul.
    See how they run: electing the President in an age
    of mediaocracy./by Paul Taylor.— 1st ed.
        p. cm.
    ISBN 0–394–57059–6
        1. Presidents— United States— Election— 1988.
2. Political participation— United States.   3. Press
and politics— United States.   4. Electioneering—
United States.   I. Title.
JK5261988f
324.973'0927— dc20   90–32321
                                                            CIP

Manufactured in the United States of America
First Edition

UNIVERSITY LIBRARY
9032321 Lethbridge, Alberta

See How They Run

For My Family—
Stefanie, Jeremy, Ben and Sarah

Contents

Acknowledgments

THERE'S a dirty little secret about this book I might as well get off my chest right away. I had a ball writing it.

This isn't the opening note authors typically sound. It's not the way this first-time author expected to feel. In twenty years of writing for newspapers, I've always been a bleeder around deadline time. On the morning after, I'm often too embarrassed to read what I've written. If it's that much trouble to produce 750 forgettable words on the fly, I always figured that writing a book would be living hell.

Well, it wasn't. I'll get to the reasons in a minute. First I owe some thank-yous:

To Ashbel Green, my editor, and Ron Goldfarb, my agent, who had the idea that I should write a book before I did—and before they became my editor and agent.

To my editors at the Washington *Post*—Ben Bradlee, Len Downie and Bob Kaiser—who let me go for a year and kept a place for me when I got back; and Dan Balz and Ann Devroy (both since returned to the reportorial ranks), who did such a sure-footed job directing the paper's 1988 campaign coverage.

To my colleagues on the 1988 *Post* political staff: Chuck Babcock, Sid Blumenthal, Lou Cannon, Jim Dickenson, Tom Edsall, Lloyd Grove, David Hoffman, Gwen Ifill, Haynes Johnson, David Maraniss, Mary McGrory, Richard Morin, Bill Peterson, T. R. Reid, Colette Rhoney, Ed Walsh and the "unique, irreplaceable" Maralee Schwartz—all of whom make working at the *Post* so much fun.

To David Broder, the best reporter and role model I've met in journalism.

To Dave Broder, Richard Cohen, Ron Goldfarb, Ash Green, Bob Kaiser, my wife, Stefanie, and my dad, Allen, for reading the manuscript and making lots of wise suggestions. To Melvin Rosenthal, production editor at Knopf, for tenderly guiding the author and his words through many rounds of pageproofs.

To my dad and my late mom, Phoebe, for all the things that parents do. To my parents-in-law, Bea and Norm Teitel, and my brother Mark for all their love.

To my sources. Authors of books like this often list them. I'm going to skip that, mostly out of fear of leaving someone out. You know who you are, and may God bless you. I occasionally warn sources that if they say something smart, I'll quote it, but if they say something brilliant, I'll steal it. If anything in this book strikes anyone as brilliant, there's a good chance it didn't originate with me.

I have some promises to keep.

During the last four months of my leave from the *Post,* I taught an undergraduate seminar at Princeton entitled Politics and the Press. Carol Rigolot and Alison Cook of the Humanities Council and Donald Stokes and Ingrid Reed of the Woodrow Wilson School made me feel at home on campus. Princeton's premier hostess, Ginny Mason, and the whole Mason-Willig family took great care of me on the nights I stayed over. And eighteen terrific young men and women made my brief stint as a professor a time I will never forget: James Blue, Matt Bodie, Georgie Boge, Sharon Cassidy, Wendy Collins, Ann Davis, Ben Dworkin, Jon Gerber, Gautam Gode, Stig Leschly, Katie Shaver, Jason Simpson, Vanessa Taylor, Sharon Volckhausen, Jason Weinstein, Gillian Weiss, Doug Widmann, and Ken Yao.

I've put their names in because, in a sentimental moment as we were saying our goodbyes at the end of the last class, they made me swear I would. Something similar happened at a wine-soaked dinner in Philadelphia with a great bunch of friends with whom my wife and I have hailed every New Year for the last decade and a half: Barbara Beck and Larry Eichel, Libby Rosof and Murray Dubin, Rick and Marianne Edmonds, Gay and Don Kimelman, Diane and Bill Marimow, Molly and Charlie Layton. On to the millennium, gang!

And now for the secret to my happy year: I wrote this book at home. For the first time in my life, I was able to greet my kids when they returned from school each afternoon. They'd come crashing into my study and we'd fool around for a while. When they tired of me—often sooner than I thought appropriate—I could watch out the window as my sons went dribbling a basketball off to the park or my daughter played with a friend in the yard. These were stolen pleasures. Before the kids got home from school, when the house was quiet and the words sometimes wouldn't come, I could always grab a hammer and join my wife, who's been renovating our old Victorian farmhouse. We did the living room and dining room and got a start on the kitchen during my year off. She's quite a co-worker, quite a life partner and not a bad weekday companion, it turns out. You've heard of the saying: For richer, for poorer, but never for lunch? Wrong. Lunch with Stefanie was the best part.

P.T.

See How They Run

CHAPTER ONE

Campaign Follies

"A PREDICTION regarding next year's presidential election," a reader named Jeff Balch wrote the Washington *Post* in October 1987. "No Democrats will be left in the race by the time we reach primary and caucus season. George Bush will run unopposed in November and lose."

H. G. Wells once described elections as the "great feast of democracy." Balch's letter captured the tittering around the table as the meal was about to be served. In the fall of 1987, the presidential campaign was in the throes of what one wag called the Year of Living Childishly. Gary Hart and Joe Biden had already slipped out of the race, each on his own banana peel. One had an unauthorized sleepover and was gone in six days. Another was caught copying someone else's words and disappeared within a fortnight. Then the campaign manager who got the copier in trouble had to resign for being a tattletale. It was as if the proceedings had been hijacked by a team of gagwriters from *Saturday Night Live*.

During the next thirteen months, the spectacle grew less amusing but not more substantive. In the main event the following fall, George Bush and Michael Dukakis—a pair of serious, sober, well-meaning public servants running for President in a time of peace and patchy prosperity—waged a contest memorable for short sound bites, distorted attacks and hollow dialogue. The campaign was held in a world about to be shaken by the greatest rush to democracy in more than a century (an upheaval no one could foresee at the time), and in a country already falling behind in the international economic footrace (a trend everyone sensed but few wanted to talk about). In the midst of these momentous changes, our feast of democracy was devoid of adventure, mission, vitality or ideas. Its unofficial theme song was "Don't Worry. Be Happy." Its most powerful symbol was a murderer and rapist by the name of Willie Horton.

This disagreeable campaign was itself the subject of a disagreeable sneer campaign—in the press. From start to finish, the candidates were belittled as laughingstocks (Hart), lightweights (Biden), dwarfs (the rest of the Democrats), nerds (Dukakis), wimps (Bush) and bimbos (Dan Quayle) by journalists who seem to grow more cynical with each election. Did the candidates deserve it? Or did the media razzing go too far? The voters appeared to hold both views simultaneously.

On election day, they engaged in something akin to a consumer boycott. Some 91,602,291 Americans voted; another 91,050,000 in the voting-age population didn't. The 50.16 percent turnout rate was the lowest in sixty-four years, and roughly 20 percentage points lower than the average in the rest of the world's industrialized democracies.[1]

Barren and bad-mannered presidential campaigns are a tradition in this country, and so is scornful press coverage. Judged against nineteenth-century standards, the Bush–Dukakis unpleasantness was as civilized as high tea and as nourishing as a farmer's breakfast. In 1828, Andrew Jackson's mother was called a prostitute, his father a mulatto, his wife a profligate woman. All this was in the press. In 1840, William Henry Harrison's strategist, Nicholas Biddle, laid out a campaign plan that would make today's handlers green with envy: Harrison must "say not a single word about his principles or creed," Biddle insisted. "Let him say nothing—promise nothing." In 1860, Abraham Lincoln was derided as illegitimate; his wife as a traitor; his son as a war profiteer. In 1884, newspaper editorials branded Grover Cleveland a "moral leper" and a "man stained with disgusting infamy" because he had fathered an illegitimate son.

Still, however coarse and vulgar these campaigns may have been, they at least animated the masses. Turnout rates hovered around 80 percent during the final three-quarters of the nineteenth century. This was the era of the torchlight parade and the clubhouse meeting. People cared deeply about politics—it was a way to participate in the life of the community and nation before television and radio dampened appetites for such communal pastimes. The labels "Democrat" and "Republican" gave voters a sense of belonging, and issues a sense of coherence. The parties served to frame public affairs around a stable cluster of principles and policies.

Today's vestigial parties have lost their ability to articulate or defend political ideas, and it's been a generation since they've given anyone beyond a band of operatives and ideologues the feeling that they belong to something larger than themselves. Television has replaced parties as the vital link between voters and leaders; nowadays, a political rally is three people in front of a television set. But in drawing politics into the electorate's living rooms, television has driven it out of their orbit of interest. For the image of politics television presents is a montage of manipulative candidates, cynical reporters, distorted attack ads and demagogic appeals. There aren't many sympathetic figures in this picture, nor is there much room for a nourishing dialogue.

The flag-and-furlough campaign of 1988 may have been no more vacuous than the slogans and smears of a century ago. But there's an important distinction. Because they are waged in a society that lacks strong political parties and clear ideologies, today's campaigns must carry more of the burden of democracy. They must serve as the glue that connects our individualistic, disaggregated, depoliticized electorate to public life. At the moment, they are serving as a wedge.

The premise of this book is that the political dialogue is failing because the leading actors in the pageant of democracy—the politicians, the press and the voters—are bringing out the least in one another. I have no intention of assigning blame, for as I see it, all three sets of actors are trapped in a vicious circle. They have little choice but to behave as they do, given the way the rewards, penalties and incentives of their political culture are arrayed before them. The final chapter of the book offers a proposal for a modest structural change in modern media campaigns that might help everyone climb out of this rut.*

A S ANYONE who was paying even scant attention to the 1988 campaign will realize, my disinclination to point fingers is not in keeping with the original spirit of the occasion. Right from the get-go, this was a campaign where everyone was tossing furniture at everyone else.

*The book is organized as follows: an introductory chapter (1) that gives an overview of the 1988 campaign and its various dysfunctions; a series of episode chapters (2–7) that describe the interaction between candidates and reporters; a series of analytical chapters (8–10) that examine the handlers, the press and the voters; and a concluding chapter (11) that suggests a way for everyone to behave better.

In the Hart and Biden episodes, the candidates took the most punishing hits, but the press wasn't far behind. Reporters came to be known as "character cops," and it was not a term of endearment. Voters accused us of rampaging through dark alleys of the psyche, peeking beneath bedsheets, hiding in bushes, trampling over privacy rights and trivializing the quest for the presidency. When, in the summer of 1988, two scrubbed-for-rectitude nominees survived this gauntlet and were chosen by their respective parties, matters seemed ready to move toward a more elevated plane. When they didn't, the press tried to turn the tables and toss the blame at the political consultants. A *Time* cover story dubbed 1988 "The Year of the Handler." They were the ones who—according to the press indictment—polluted the airwaves with flag factories, tank rides and Willie Horton. They were the ones who had reduced media-age politics to a dismal science: take a poll, find a "hot button" issue, feed it back to the voters in the form of a picture, a symbol and a pre-masticated attack line. Repeat tomorrow. Cut down on killer gaffes by curtailing press access. Be sure the candidate shows no more spontaneity than a multiplication table. Above all, never discuss the hard realities of governance. "That's suicide," said Roger Ailes, Bush's media adviser. "If we come out with a sweeping view of how to change things, the next thirty days of stories are going to be about the flaws."

But by the end of the campaign, handlers like Ailes had their fingers pointed, too—right back at their accusers in the media. They said we had a guilty craving for artificial drama, cheap symbols and search-and-destroy pack journalism. "You get up every morning and try to figure out how to humiliate my client," Ailes told a reporter. "I get up every morning and try to figure out how to make him look good. I sleep better."

Worse, the handlers said it was we who had poisoned the well, not they. And they had some expert witnesses. "If you don't get nasty and personal in a campaign like this, the media aren't going to give you your time on television," said Georgetown University political scientist Michael Robinson, an authority on press coverage of campaigns. When candidates tried to be substantive, Robinson added, the media would reduce their nine-point programs to nine-second sound bites. "Goddamnit, Paul," Paul Brountas, Michael Dukakis' senior adviser, remembers ABC's Sam Donaldson complaining to him during the campaign, "you've got to get your candidate to stop pausing between sentences. He's taking twenty-two seconds to complete a thought."

Ailes came up with the best bumper-sticker summary of the politicians' beef with the press. "All you guys care about," he said, "are

attacks, mistakes, pictures and polls." President Reagan's chief image
maker, Michael Deaver, was out of action by 1988, but he lobbed a few
grenades from the gallery. "It always amuses me," he wrote during the
campaign, "to watch someone like Tom or Peter or Dan sitting in a
million-dollar set, his appearance the envy of every undertaker in the
nation, criticizing a politician for trying to control his or her image."

Round and round this blame game went, sound bite by ink bite,
gaffe by gambit, flag by furlough. By election day, the voters were
thoroughly fed up. The week after the election was over, a nationwide
New York Times/CBS News poll found that half of all voters surveyed
were dissatisfied with the way the candidates had discussed the
issues, and a staggering two-thirds of them wished other candidates
had run. No post-election poll had ever before tapped so deep a vein
of disaffection.

But the crowning irony was this: it was to these very voters that the
whole dreary exercise had been pitched in the first place. And it was
these very voters who had been accomplices in their own manipulation.
For all their complaints about the emptiness of the campaign, they
hadn't exactly rewarded candidates who took on the substantive
issues. For example, President Dole talked a lot about the deficit,
and so did President Babbitt, and so, in 1984, did President Mondale.
And it didn't take long for the voters to show them the door—or for
their surviving competitors to get the message. If you must talk
about the deficit (or difficult subjects of any kind), it's better to say
things like: "Read my lips—no new taxes." The voters may not
believe you, but they'll figure you're less likely to raise taxes than the
candidate who equivocates. A Washington *Post*/ABC News poll taken
a week after the election found that seven voters in every ten
disbelieved Bush's pledge not to raise taxes. This had been the
central plank of his platform, the one-liner he repeated in every
speech. America thought he was lying—and voted for him anyway.
Their behavior may have been a savvy accommodation to the casual
deceit so ingrained in the dialogue of politics. But it poses an
interesting challenge: how can candidates be expected to speak in
anything but code language if their audience punishes truth-tellers,
rewards panderers and expects to be deceived?

The signals that journalists get from the voters are no less
paradoxical. The voters say they want more substantive coverage of
the issues. But if they meant it, then the *MacNeil/Lehrer NewsHour*,
or something like it, would air on ABC, NBC and CBS—not on
PBS, where it draws a tiny fraction of the viewership of the market-
driven commercial networks.

These voters and viewers are trapped in what political scientist Walter Dean Burnham has described as a "revolution of declining expectations." The less they get from the dialogue of campaigns, the more disconnected they feel from public life, the less they expect from government—and so on. The cycle does not end on election day. It affects governance as well. President Bush assumed office in January 1989 with a Democratic majority of eighty-five in the House of Representatives and ten in the Senate—the weakest base of congressional support for any President in history. For the sixth time in the last nine presidential elections, the voters had placed the White House in the hands of one party and Congress in the hands of the other. Prior to 1956, this had happened only three times since the nation was founded. The phenomenon of a partisan division between the executive and legislative branches is the single most distinctive feature of late-twentieth-century American governance. In an age of distrust, the voters apparently aren't comfortable giving either party all the keys to the kingdom; they've added another layer to the checks and balances the Framers wrote into the Constitution. But the end product of their hedging—divided government—assures conflict, invites paralysis, diminishes accountability, compounds cynicism and reduces expectations. Whom, for example, can the public hold to account for the $400 billion savings-and-loan catastrophe? Since both parties had a hand in making the mess, neither had an interest in fixing blame. And so the nation held a presidential campaign in the middle of the worst financial scandal in our history, and neither candidate talked about it.

Those critics of the 1988 election who complained that the campaign had done nothing to prepare the nation for the governing ahead turned out to be wrong—though not in the way the complaint was generally understood. In 1989, attack politics moved from the campaign trail to the halls of Congress. For the first time in history, the Senate rejected a cabinet appointee of an incoming President—Defense Secretary–designate John Tower—and did so by waging a negative campaign against his character. Later in the session, under prodding from President Bush, Congress adopted a law that made flag desecration a crime. "We have been terrorized by the thought of negative thirty-second commercials," Senator Bob Kerrey of Nebraska lamented during the fifty-one hours of floor debate.* While Congress, the President and the Court fiddled with flag burning, educational

*In 1990, after the Supreme Court found the law unconstitutional, Congress refused to enact the constitutional amendment Bush advocated.

performance continued to decline, the family structure continued to fray, the public infrastructure continued to crumble and the nation's economic position in the world continued to erode. And Bush continued "rocking along with a 70 percent approval rating"—as his Secretary of State and former campaign chairman, James A. Baker III delighted in reminding critics.

IT MAY BE laying it on a bit thick to dump all these dysfunctions at the feet of a single disappointing presidential campaign. But that campaign is as good an observation deck as we have to study the drift and anemia of modern political life. And the first memorable event of that campaign—the undoing of Gary Hart—is as good a place as any to start the examination.

Hart obviously wasn't without blame in his sudden downfall, but press critics asked: Did his actions justify Miami *Herald* reporters snooping outside his townhouse in the dark? Did it give a Washington *Post* reporter (me!) the right to ask him under klieg lights whether he'd ever committed adultery? If we hadn't been such world-class busybodies—nosing around in places no reporters had ever ventured before during a presidential campaign—would there have been a story to begin with? How long would a President Kennedy have survived in a media culture so far removed from the see-no-evil ethic of his era? When did the nation have a more satisfying relationship with its leaders—then or now?

We replied that we were just doing our job. "Would people rather not know about these guys' flaws?" Craig Whitney, then *The New York Times*'s Washington bureau chief, asked after his paper led the assault on Biden. He captured the sense of civic guardianship we brought to our craft. "A journalist is the lookout on the bridge of the ship of state," Joseph Pulitzer wrote in 1904. "He peers through the fog and storm to give warning of dangers ahead. He is there to watch over the safety and welfare of the people." Yes, in our zeal we may sometimes help turn political campaigns into farces, but we have to go where the story takes us. We didn't charter the *Monkey Business* for a weekend in Bimini with Donna Rice. We didn't expropriate British Labour leader Neil Kinnock's words and ancestry. The candidates did. All we did was tell on them. If not us, who else would stand guard at the White House door—fending off the reckless, the shallow, the disingenuous?

By all means inspect the characters of the men who would be

President, our critics responded—just choose your looking glasses more wisely. Measure character by public performance, not private moments. Machiavelli (among others) observed long ago that private and public virtue are not synonymous. We want our friends to be loyal, truthful and empathetic; we sometimes want our leaders to be ruthless, deceitful and cold-blooded. As for the usefulness of sexual habits as a barometer of character—history is replete with great men who have fed vast egos by incessant philandering. Infidelity may make one a lesser spouse, but does it make one a lesser public figure? When we assume that it does, and on that assumption lay bare such traits for public inspection, don't we debase the currency of politics?

"My problem is that once the press starts writing about sex," said Duke University political scientist James David Barber, "it never seems to get to anything else." For years Barber had been among a group of historians, biographers and presidential scholars who had urged journalists to conduct more exhaustive probes into the backgrounds of presidential candidates. But by 1987 and 1988 he had begun to worry that a Gresham's law of character coverage had taken root, in which the sensational drove out the substantial. "There's got to be something more to this than working your way through the Ten Commandments—adultery, false witness, etc.," he said.

"Will not a culture which treats politics like a sport and lumps political figures with soap opera characters produce more celebrities than statesmen?" Hart asked in a speech he gave at Yale University after he got out of the race. "We are, in a word, trivializing our own leadership, together with the offices to which they aspire, including the presidency." The chief culprit in all this, he said, is "a media filter which demands simplicity, rewards tactics and is transfixed by personality."

Our defense at this uneasy juncture in the debate lay in the proposition that character-copping is more an effect of the political culture than it is a cause. We are reporters in an age when personality and image dominate politics the way party and ideology once did. This shift has had everything to do with the ubiquity and intrusiveness of modern communications technology. It is beside the point to argue whether the change has been for the better. One cannot uninvent television. One cannot repeal *People* magazine. Nor can one wish away the simple truth that as our culture has become more media-soaked, the way we conduct political campaigns and measure political leaders has become more personality-soaked. Journalists are not the only ones who understand this. The candidates understand

it, so do their image makers and so—often as complaining consumers, but usually as voracious ones—do the voters.

The core material of presidential campaigns has, as a result, become autobiography, authenticity, character. That's what reporters inspect because that's what candidates present. When Senator Bob Dole launched his bid for the presidency, he took the advice of his handlers and began doing something he'd conscientiously avoided throughout nearly three decades in public life. He talked about the crushing injuries he suffered as an infantryman in Italy in the final weeks of World War II, the thirty-nine months of hospitalization, the numerous operations, the way the townsfolk of his native Russell, Kansas, passed around a cigar box to solicit contributions to help him pay his medical expenses. Overcoming the war injury (along with youthful poverty) was Dole's metaphor for toughness, and toughness was Dole's presidential platform. He didn't expect to win the Republican presidential nomination with a better idea for solving Third World debt or an innovative proposal on the savings-and-loan crisis; he figured he was going to win because he was tougher than that infamous not-tough guy, George Bush.

Similarly, Jesse Jackson's platform was the story of human triumph, writ large. Here was the black son of an unwed teenage mother, a man stigmatized in childhood because his biological father lived with his own family in the house next door, a man who told audiences from coast to coast that "Jackson is my third name—I'm adopted!" (his first two names were "Jesse Burns" and "bastard")—here was this extraordinary man rising to seek the presidency. Rising, as he liked to say, "from the guttermost to the uttermost." His journey was his platform. To whites, it contained an implicit challenge: if I can make it all the way, the promise of America will be real for everyone. To blacks, it stood as vindication of the message of self-reliance, self-help and self-respect he had preached for two decades. In America, Jackson had rhymed, from pulpits and street corners and school auditoriums, "Everybody is somebody." Now he was proving it.

As candidates made biography the heart of their campaigns, the voters perked up and paid attention. They liked the stories; they related to them. Also, something in the political climate of 1988 made the "issues" seem especially distant and inaccessible.

For most of the 1980s, Americans were suspended halfway between prosperity and anxiety. People were content with today, troubled about tomorrow and confused about nearly everything. There was so much that didn't seem to compute. The national debt, for example, had soared from one trillion to three trillion in the decade. It was the symbol of our inability to keep our fiscal house in order and our willingness as a society to fob off our bills onto our children. But despite all the warnings of all the doomsayers, it hadn't stood in the way of a six-year economic boom. So could it be that bad? The Japanese were beating us in the world marketplace, buying up our real estate with dollars that used to be ours and threatening (if one believed the scare journalism) to turn us into tenants in our own country. But we were the ones who kept on voting, with our wallets and charge cards, for their products. So was the problem them, or us? The century's great struggle between democracy and communism was tipping in our favor (just how dramatically would not become clear until the year after the campaign), but did that mean it was more or less important that America remain the economic, military and political colossus of the globe? It wasn't clear.

At home, there was the scourge of drugs (with 5 percent of the world's population, we were consuming 50 percent of its illegal drugs); crime (a record 1.56 million violent crimes were reported in 1988, according to FBI figures, a 30 percent increase over 1979); a backsliding educational system (average SAT scores were 87 points lower in 1988 than they had been in 1963); an expanding underclass (the number of Americans living below the poverty line grew from 11.7 percent in 1979 to 13.1 percent in 1988, and the number of black children born into poverty grew to a staggering 50.4 percent); an epidemic of broken families (in 1987, 24.5 percent of all American babies were born out of wedlock, quadruple the 1970 figure); a growing sense of moral rot, and the gathering centrifugal forces that take hold in societies when the rich get richer, the poor get poorer and the middle stagnates.

But how did all this square with the job-creation, consumer-spending and entrepreneurial boom of the decade? In the six-year period from 1983 to 1988, the nation's 91 million households purchased an astounding 62 million microwave ovens, 57 million washers and dryers, 88 million cars and light trucks, 105 million color television sets, 46 million refrigerators and freezers, 63 million VCRs, 31 million cordless phones and 30 million telephone answering machines. There hadn't been a buying binge like it since the late 1940s, observed *Newsweek* economics columnist Robert Samuelson, when the end of the Depression and World War II had loosed an enormous pent-up demand for consumer goods.

But—once again—was this an index of health or sickness? Was this spending (and borrowing) binge, like the burgeoning federal debt, just another symptom of a cultural malady that budget director Richard Darman described as "now-now-ism." He noted that the $180 billion we spend each year to service the federal debt takes up 15 percent of the federal budget, "buys the future nothing . . . and buys the present nothing more than the ability to keep its borrowing game going . . . Collectively, we are engaged in a massive backward Robin Hood transaction—robbing the future to give to the present." Brave words for a public official—but the careful student of public affairs already knows the kicker. Darman did not sound his note of alarm during the 1988 campaign. He gave his speech nine months *after* the election.

Devoid of this kind of candor, the presidential race did nothing to dispel the electorate's confusion. The campaign was waged in a country whose psychological state philosopher Matthew Arnold had captured in a different time and place. America was caught "between two worlds—one dead, the other powerless to be born." We were mid-passage in a journey to—where? The end of Henry Luce's American century? Or the beginning of an even more glorious flowering of global democracy? And how did this affect the kids? The mortgage? Interest payments? The job?

I spent many hours in living rooms in 1987 and 1988 interviewing voters; it never ceased to amaze me how often this anxiety about national decline bubbled up to the surface—unprompted—in the musings of the middle class. "It seems like we're getting more and more into hock to Japan," said Harold Jones, a refrigerator repairman from Akron. "I just hope they don't decide to come in one day and repossess." Jones's vivid metaphor was slightly off (the Japanese already own many of the things that he presumably worries they might repossess—the skyscrapers, the banks, the factories, the real estate), but that in itself was telling. These were new and difficult concepts, and the voters often didn't seem to have a vocabulary for them, much less a reliable way to translate them into voting choices. There wasn't a Democratic or Republican answer to these questions; there were no conservative or liberal theologies about decline.

Some candidates like Representative Richard Gephardt touched a nerve by talking about trade protection and economic nationalism. His message: the enemy is without. Others, such as Jackson and the Reverend Pat Robertson, prospered for a time by speaking about moral decay, drugs, declining education standards, babies having babies, greed on Wall Street. Their message: the enemy is within. But no one made it all the way to the Oval Office with these appeals. Perhaps the fear of decline was still too great an affront to the national psyche to be safely broached in public. (Jimmy Carter had tried once, and paid a heavy price.) "America, while still No. 1 in ways that can lead to the self-hypnosis of the Reagan years, has entered a glide-down, an era of shared responsibility and mutual dependencies—and it is the whole tendency of American electoral politics to disguise this fact from the citizenry," historian Garry Wills wrote after the election. "Nothing is more identifiably destructive in a modern campaign than any touch of pessimism. Smiley-faced promises never to raise taxes are the touchstone of 'realism.' What are candidates to do but berate each other once the people have forbidden them ever to speak of serious things."[2]

While the 1980s were a particularly treacherous time for pessimists, the truth is that Americans have never looked kindly on the breed. According to a study by a pair of psychologists, presidential nominations have gone 19 out of 23 times in this century to the candidates who delivered the least pessimistic speeches.[3] That was the case again in 1988. The winning nominees were the two who, out of a field of fourteen, talked least about decline. They didn't acknowledge a problem, much less dare any solutions. "Don't worry. Be happy," said Bush. "The best America isn't behind us. The best America is yet to come," countered Dukakis.

These men won their nomination not on the nerves they touched, the hearts they moved, the platforms they offered, the visions they conjured. They won on the steadiness of their step and the soundness of their autobiographies. And the others fell, one by one, on the implausibility or inauthenticity or flamboyance or shallowness of theirs. This was a campaign in which biography trumped message; the present trumped the future; prosperity trumped anxiety.

One of the most notable victims of these dynamics was Gephardt. He turned into a fiery populist in the closing weeks of the Iowa primary campaign, shucking off his navy-blue business suits in favor of bright red parkas and farmer's caps. And his message started clicking. Until Willie Horton made his appearance later in the year, Gephardt's $48,000 Hyundai (that's how much he said the popular Korean import would cost here if we put the same tariffs on their exports as they put on ours) had been the most potent advertising icon of the campaign. But the dramatic image remake called Gephardt's authenticity into question. Wasn't he, until just yesterday, an earnest, conciliating Boy Scout who'd worked his way up the ranks to a House leadership post as "Little Dickie Do-Right"? Wasn't he a part of the very establishment he was bashing? Wasn't he funding his populist message with special-interest money? When corporate lobbyists paid for a charter flight to send forty congressmen out to Iowa to campaign for Gephardt, the inside joke on the plane had been "It's our flight, too"—a takeoff on Gephardt's populist rallying cry, "It's your fight, too."

Never mind that Gephardt had also demonstrated abundant qualities of tenacity and good humor and, most impressive of all, the capacity for political growth during his marathon quest for the presidency. The press, primed to write about the dark side of biography, found fresh evidence of opportunism in his. Down went Gephardt.

There was another reason—in addition to the political culture of *personalismo* and the conspiracy of silence on the big problems—that led the press scrutiny of character in this campaign to be so close, so harsh. Somebody had to prune the field, to "get rid of the funny ones," as one 1988 campaign manager put it. It simply wasn't practical for voters to make choices among a dozen or more contenders. There was too much information to digest. The voters couldn't wade through it, the media couldn't present it in usable fashion, the culture was too apolitical to sustain an interest in such a large field for any great length of time. Super Tuesday, the great novelty of the 1988 nomination calendar, was a disaster as a result. Twenty states held primaries on the same day—March 8, 1988—at a time when ten candidates were still in the running. The whole exercise became a blur of too many candidates, too many nasty ads, too many airport press conferences. Bob Dole's entire campaign in Oklahoma, to cite one of many such examples, lasted eighty-three minutes.

This large presidential field was a by-product of twenty years of tinkering with the nomination system. The tinkerers were Democratic party activists—most of them liberals—who concluded after the debacle of the 1968 Democratic convention that party bosses had no business choosing the party's nominee. They created a playing field tilted toward the outsider. A candidate no longer needed a national reputation or the support of political leaders to get into the game; he simply needed a handful of camp followers, access to some money and the time and willingness to spend half his waking hours for a year or two in Iowa and New Hampshire.

With the party bosses out of the equation, there was a huge vacuum at the front end of the process. Who would screen the field? The assignment fell to the press—there was no one else. And if the candidates were going to start campaigning earlier than ever, they'd have to make it past the sentries in the media earlier than ever.

The result was a campaign pre-season that was a cross between a demolition derby and a game of Trivial Pursuit. When Hart and Biden went down in 1987 through a process of trial by media ordeal, the verdicts were rendered months before voters had any chance to ratify or overrule the unsparing portraits of them drawn by newspapers and television. This pointed up an obvious malfunction in the system: a nominating process designed to assure that no elites would come between the voters and their choice of a President had left the voters out of the action altogether. The timing was out of sync—as if, in a football game, a period of sudden death had been played before the opening kickoff.

The Republicans pretty much kept to the sidelines that pre-campaign year, observing the Napoleonic dictum of not interfering with the enemy when he is in the process of destroying himself. But all was not well in their domain either. For years, the press had been making it abundantly clear that if front-runner George Bush was ever going to be elected President, he'd first have to prove he was man enough. The word that crystallized the doubts about him was "wimp." In 1987, it began working its way out of the Washington press corps' echo chamber and into their stories. It wasn't merely an invention of the press. Many voters used that word, or some variant, to describe their uncertainty about Bush's basic strength of character, depth of conviction, independence of mind. He'd climbed the ladder of political leadership as a courtesan, pleasing whoever happened to be on the rung above. He'd been a typically anonymous Vice President and—in two national campaigns—a not very impressive running mate. "He would try to maintain the status quo," one voter, Jim Reagan, thirty-one, a mid-level executive from St. Louis, said of Bush early in the campaign—making it clear that the status quo suited him just fine. "But he doesn't have a lot of backbone. It would be a risk with him."

This skepticism was weakly felt by most voters, for they didn't know enough about Bush to have worked up deep feelings. It was different with the Washington press corps. Many political reporters had watched Bush at close range over a long haul, and had come to doubt his backbone. "Everyone knowledgeable in Republican politics considered Bush incompetent to be President," Jules Witcover, one of the deans of political journalism, had written a dozen years earlier in *Marathon,* his best-selling history of the 1976 presidential campaign. During the campaign pre-season leading up to 1988, pundits of every ideological leaning, from Garry Trudeau (Bush "put his manhood in a blind trust") to George Will (Bush "emits the tinny arf of a lapdog"), seemed to go out of their way to advertise their naked contempt for the Vice President.

In October 1987, on the eve of Bush's formal announcement for the presidency, *Newsweek* ran his picture on its cover, alongside the headline: "Fighting the 'Wimp Factor.'" The Bush forces were outraged. "The first campaign school I went to—a little campaign seminar when I was growing up—said there's only one day that you're going to have good press in a campaign—that's the day you announce," recalled Lee Atwater, Bush's campaign manager. "Well, here's a guy announcing for President of the United States, and a national news magazine creates a prop. The net effect was that for the next ten days all we got at press conferences and on television talk shows and nightly news shows were reporters waving the *Newsweek* magazine cover at us. I think it was an example of something that happened this year more than I've ever seen in my twenty years of involvement. It was as if the media became a participant in the process."

Not surprisingly, some of Bush's strategists came to view 1988 as a kind of manhood rite, with the press in the role of upperclassmen at a frat hazing. Even some ordinary voters saw this as the key political dynamic for Bush. "He says 'darn' and 'heck' and 'dippity-doo' and things like that, and I get the impression that you [in the press] would like it better if he said four-letter words," Ruth Brown, a New Hampshire Bush supporter, observed just before her state's primary. "Maybe he doesn't come across as strong, but you can't call him a wimp. He was a bomber pilot."

To tease the bomber pilot out from beneath Bush's skin of preppy good sportsmanship and noblesse oblige, Ailes and Atwater goaded their candidate into pouncing all over CBS anchorman Dan Rather in a remarkably combative live TV interview in early 1988. Then, in the summer and fall, they unveiled George the Ripper, a liberal-bashing Clint Eastwood sound-alike who'd never been seen before — or since. Then, to keep this tough-guy illusion from running away with itself, they marbled the presentation with images of Kinder and Gentler George, cradling grandchildren in his loving arms.

Instead of rejecting this rank manipulation, the voters acquiesced. They intuitively knew that George the Ripper was a fraud, but they appeared to accept him as a necessary fraud. Faced with a choice between the illusion of Bush and the unvarnished reality of Dukakis, they knew what they wanted. How odd: a process designed to unmask the candidates wound up electing a masked man.

Bush could not have won easily without help from his opponent. In nominating Dukakis, the Democrats chose a candidate who had made his way to the top of the heap by the route of the remainderman. He was never the focal point of the nomination battle until he'd already won it. He was simply the last white man standing when Jackson came crashing through the gates in Michigan. Jackson's surprising victory in that caucus-like primary landed him on the cover of *Time, Newsweek* and *U.S. News & World Report* (which, like many political journalists — myself included — overestimated the significance of the event) and prompted Americans to view him for the first time as a credible candidate for his party's nomination. Unfortunately for Jackson, the birth and death of his viability were virtually simultaneous — the former triggering the latter. Once Democratic primary voters started seriously thinking about Jackson — not just about his skin color or his soaring self-help rhetoric or the glory of his journey, but about his platform and record during twenty years of protest politics—they found virtues in Dukakis that had escaped their attention earlier.

Made dangerously overconfident by the ease of his nomination victory, and the size of his lead—16 points—over Bush in late spring polls, Dukakis coasted into his party's convention believing that "competence" would carry him to the White House. His candidacy had been born, and for a time had prospered, during the period when the Iran–contra scandal hung like a cloud over the political landscape. There was Dukakis, with his umbrella, his rubber boots, his hands-on management style and his Massachusetts Miracle. But by the summer of 1988, the weather had changed. Reagan had signed an arms-control treaty with Soviet leader Mikhail Gorbachev and had reclaimed his popularity. The economy was still doing fine. Democracy was on the march around the globe. Competence was just one of many threshold tests the next occupant of the White House would have to meet; it was no longer the sine qua non. Dukakis was the last man in America to figure this out.

Bush's key strategists—Atwater, Ailes, Darman, Baker and pollster Robert Teeter—made short work of him. With the voters not ready to engage in a big conversation about the future, the Bush team decided to make it a campaign about the past. They reached back to the cultural, political, sociological and ideological divisions of the 1960s and "waved the bloody shirt," just as nineteenth-century politicians had waved it for a generation after the Civil War. They demonized Dukakis as a boutique liberal who looked for constitutional excuses not to recite the Pledge of Allegiance; a know-it-all social engineer who thought convicted murderers deserved weekend passes; a blame-America-firster who looked like Snoopy in tank and helmet. Their game plan was lifted straight out of George Wallace's and Richard Nixon's 1968 playbooks. The nation was in a different place twenty years later. But Dukakis, handcuffed by his excessive rationalism and blinded by his political parochialism (he'd never been in a campaign outside of Massachusetts; he'd never lived outside of Brookline), underestimated the force of the attacks. He never turned the conversation from the fumes of the past to the problems of the future. Even his own supporters were mystified by his fecklessness in the face of the onslaught. Some abandoned him for that reason alone, taking it as a sign that he was too insular or tone-deaf or complacent to deserve the presidency. On election day, according to exit polls, many more people voted "against" than "for"—a pattern that has become the norm in presidential elections over the past two decades. Jeane Shilling of Rock Island, Illinois, captured the "aginner" mind-set exquisitely. As Dukakis went into his post-convention swoon, she told a *Wall Street Journal* reporter: "I'm disappointed because I wanted to vote against Bush and I can't."

The dialogue of the fall campaign was widely condemned. No less an authority than Richard Nixon, who'd run for national office five times and was certainly no stranger to negative campaigns, said he found the race "trivial, superficial and inane." Walter Mondale said: "It makes me sick. All we get is attack, attack, attack." Barry Goldwater muttered: "Why don't these guys talk about the real issues?" The *Washington Post* was among the many newspapers around the country that declined to endorse either candidate. The race, it editorialized, was "not just a domestic disappointment but an international embarrassment . . . a screamingly tiresome, trivial, point-missing contest between two candidates who do not seem to be running for president so much as they seem to be having one of those headache-making fights that children are so good at staging in the back seat of the family car when everyone's nerves are pretty much gone anyway."

It makes for a pretty bleak picture. But to complete the perspective on this campaign, two competing realities need to be added to the mix. The first is that George the Ripper disappeared overnight. He was a changed man on November 9, 1988—once again the conciliating, soft-spoken, generous soul he had been brought up to be. "That was goofy time," former Representative Thomas L. Ashley (D–Ohio), Bush's old friend from Yale's Skull and Bones society, said after the campaign. "That was package and sell. He was glad to get out of that." So were the voters. They happily accorded Bush the goodwill that all incoming Presidents receive, giving the lie to predictions that the ugliness of his victory would sour his honeymoon.

The other "reality check" on 1988 is to remember that, as unhappy as everyone seemed to be with the campaign, there was actually a good deal to be happy about. As voters went to the polls on election day, unemployment stood at 5.3 percent, its lowest level in fourteen years. Inflation, the monster of the 1970s, had been tamed for nearly a decade. The Soviets were marching their troops out of Afghanistan. President Reagan and Secretary Gorbachev had just signed the first treaty ever to eliminate a whole class of nuclear weapons. The Iran–Iraq war was over. Madmen like Qaddafi and Khomeini cast a smaller shadow than they once had. There were democracies in the Philippines, Pakistan, South Korea and Argentina. Communists in

China, the Soviet Union and Eastern Europe were experimenting with freedom and market economies. America had held a race for the presidency in which a black man had advanced further than ever before, and in which a Greek-American had become the first immigrant's son in a century and a half to win his party's nomination. And he was married to a Jew—also a first. And none of this had touched off excesses of intolerance.

This brings us back to the grand paradox of 1988. If times were pretty good, if the candidates were plain vanilla, if the winner was the soul of decency (a fact he tried to hide), if the nation wasn't ready to take the leap into tomorrow, then how come it was so unpleasant getting from here to there?

Let us return to some of the leading suspects—the people in the media. Critics said our mocking tone fed the cynicism of the voters and the surliness of the candidates. Leaf through the Op-Ed pages of *The New York Times* from the fall of 1988 and pick out some of the headlines. "Bush Is Goofy." "Dukakis Smiles Like an Orthodontist." "Bentsen's Got No Elvis to Him." Dukakis–Bentsen is "A Ticket to Put Crazy Eddie to Sleep." Move on to some of the big-name columnists around the country. "It is Dole's misfortune that when he does smile, he looks like he just evicted a widow," wrote Mike Royko. "If Bob Dole says one more word about his rise from the social depths—even one—he should be sentenced to go bowling," sneered George Will. "All he wants is world peace, and his own apartment," quipped Mark Shields of the youthful Al Gore.

The condescension of the pundits flowed into other realms of journalism. "Every day there is a moment of transcendent dorkiness," *Newsweek* wrote of Bush in June 1988. "1988, You're No 1960," read the cover of *Time*'s October 24, 1988, issue. That was a takeoff on the most celebrated put-down line of the campaign, Senator Lloyd Bentsen's shot at Senator Dan Quayle in their vice-presidential debate: "Senator, you're no Jack Kennedy." Quayle jokes, of course, became a cottage industry: no vice-presidential candidate has ever been as widely ridiculed. Johnny Carson's joke about the pickup line Quayle used on Paula Parkinson before he started his National Guard tour of duty may have been the best of an enormous selection: "Honey, I'll be shipping out to Muncie in the morning."

Political humor flourishes in healthy democracies, and most of the above fell into the category of fair comment. The trouble was that the cynicism inherent in both the humor and the coverage was leavened nowhere else in the campaign, especially not on television. Robert Lichter, director of the Center for Media and Public Affairs, conducted a content analysis of the network television news coverage in the fall of 1988 and found that negative comments about Dukakis and Bush from supposedly neutral sources outnumbered positive ones by two to one. Much of this negative commentary came from the reporters themselves. "The media was largely responsible for creating what they said they abhorred—a negative campaign," said Lichter.

There was nothing new in this critique. Television "has altered the culture significantly by intensifying ordinary Americans' traditional low opinion of parties and politicians, by exacerbating the decline in their trust and confidence in government, and by helping make them even less inclined to vote than they used to be," political scientist Austin Ranney wrote in his 1983 book, *Channels of Power.* Fifteen years earlier, Spiro Agnew had scolded reporters—print and broadcast alike—for being "nattering nabobs of negativism." Around the same time, that great chronicler of modern presidential campaigns, Theodore H. White, noted that the system of rewards and incentives within the reporting craft had shifted. "The way of advancement in journalism is to attack," he said. In his *Making of the President* books, White had reported the story behind the story—all the minute details about what the adviser told the candidate on the morning of the big speech, and what brand of cigarettes they were each smoking at the time. He did so in the service of heroic journalism; he wrote of big men engaged in grand battle. A new generation of political reporters still uses White's techniques, but in the service of anti-heroic journalism. We look for the warts.

White lived to see the change and worry about what he had wrought. "It's appalling what we've done to these guys," he told Timothy Crouse, author of the best book ever written about campaign journalism, *The Boys on the Bus.* Crouse recorded White's musings in reaction to a scene in George McGovern's suite in the Doral Hotel in Miami as the 1972 Democratic convention was about to open: "McGovern was like a fish in a goldfish bowl. There were three different network crews in at different times. The still photographers kept coming in groups of five. And there were at least six writers sitting in the corner—I don't even know their names. We're all sitting there watching him work on his acceptance speech, poor bastard. He tries to go into the bedroom with Fred Dutton [an adviser] to go over the list of vice presidents, which would later turn out to be the fuck-up of the century of course, and all of us are observing him, taking notes like mad, getting all the little details. Which I think I invented as a method of reporting and which I now sincerely regret. If you write about this, say that I sincerely regret it. Who gives a fuck if the guy had milk and Total for breakfast?"

Why have we watchers changed the way we watch? There are several theories. One is technological: cameras allow us to see and know more, including the warts. Another is sociological. We are no longer the whiskey-breathed, ink-stained wretches out of *The Front Page*. A hundred and fifty years ago, Tocqueville observed that "the journalists of the United States are generally in a very humble position, with a scanty education and a vulgar turn of mind." Now we have more education, more prestige, more income—and with all this, less respect for the men and women we cover. The old saw that "there's only one way for a journalist to look at a politician— down" once captured the false bravado of craftsmen who knew their place on society's ladder was not far from the bottom. Now it comes uncomfortably close to reflecting the all-too-real attitudes of a pampered elite. When Sam Donaldson spends his free time on the Dukakis press bus chatting with his stockbroker on his cellular phone; or when a CBS producer cuts short an interview that Dan Rather is doing with a presidential candidate by advising the senator, "Sorry, Mr. Rather only has time for one more question," the craft isn't as humble as it once was.

Most reporters are neither wealthy nor famous nor powerful, of course. And no matter how comfortable our niche may have become, most of us remain, in our collective self-image, tribunes of the people. Despite our better education and breeding, our instincts remain populistic and our habits of mind are shaped by what Lionel Trilling once described as the "adversary culture." We see problems more readily than solutions; we side with the little guy against the establishment; we are progressive reformers, deeply skeptical of all the major institutions of society except our own. "Comfort the afflicted, and afflict the comfortable," reads the adage that hangs on many newsroom walls. It is a goad to anti-institutional journalism.

In addition, there is a generational component to our attack-dog instincts. Most journalists under age forty-five—the baby boomers— share a set of formative political experiences that make them distrust government. Our parents' generation watched their government win a just war, rebuild the economies of our allies and enemies, and usher in the greatest era of abundance this nation had ever seen. We saw our nation lose a war, we watched a President resign, and we began to wonder if our standard of living would ever match our parents'. It left an impression.

There is one final explanation for our anti-heroic instincts: operational necessity. Duke University's Barber once noted that "the news media's line of work is to make reality interesting." 'Twas ever thus, but the challenge hangs especially heavily over political journalists writing in an apolitical era. To grab the attention of readers, we present the campaign as a mosaic of episodes, plots, intrigues and human frailties. These dramas reflect the maxim that the world, according to journalists, is a pretty bleak place. In political coverage as in the rest of the newspaper, it isn't news when the plane doesn't crash. Gay Talese opened *The Kingdom and the Power,* his history of *The New York Times,* by observing: "Most journalists are restless voyeurs who see warts on the world, the imperfections in people and places. The sane scene that is much of life, the great portion of the planet unmarked by madness, does not lure them like riots and raids, crumbling countries and sinking ships, bankers banished to Rio and burning Buddhist nuns—gloom is their game, the spectacle their passion, normality their nemesis."

I will write about these twin flaws of journalism—cynicism and sensationalism—at more length in Chapter 10. For now, suffice it to say the first isn't entirely a flaw. It may make us less than neutral as observers, but it keeps us vigilant as watchdogs. These are journalism's two great missions—to observe and to expose. Sometimes they conflict. When they do, we generally prefer to err on the side of the watchdog. The late Alan Barth, a distinguished *Washington Post* editorial writer, once wrote of journalism: Better to bite the mailman than let the thief get by.

We bit our share of thieves in 1988. A few mailmen, too.

CHAPTER TWO

Gary Hart:
The Interview

J AMES RESTON once described journalism as "the exhilarating
chase after the Now." I can't vouch for every minute of every day,
but as I drove through a string of picturesque central New Hampshire
towns en route to an interview with Gary Hart on the night of May 6,
1987, that's just the way it felt.

My destination was the Eastgate Hotel in Littleton, where I expected
to confront Hart with information that might sink his badly listing
campaign. It would be our second encounter of an already eventful
day, and I wanted to be prepared. As I sped north in the rental car, I
kept rehearsing: "Okay now, one more time, if he says 'No comment,'
I come back with . . . "

That sort of war-gaming had me on unfamiliar terrain. Normally,
before an interview, I'll settle on an opening question, get a general
fix on the areas I want to cover, and let serendipity take over. I don't
want a rigid structure gumming up the banter and bonhomie. Former New York Mayor Ed Koch once said of interviewers like me:
"Never trust a reporter who smiles." I'm a "good cop" interviewer. I
try to ease, tease, coax and wheedle information from sources. With
body language, facial expression, tone of voice and other verbal and
nonverbal cues, I hope to let them know that I see the same world
they see; that I empathize with them; that, beneath my aloof reporter's
exterior, I may even secretly admire them.

The goodwill is both genuine and tactical. I really do like politicians.
I admire them often for their ideas, integrity, wit, drive, stamina and
extra gland of ambition, and almost always for the life they've chosen

in the great arena of public affairs. Politicians—being quick studies of human nature—know my feelings are real. But they also know I'm setting a honey trap. They know I'm hoping that in the presence of such an understanding ear they'll say too much. Sometimes, even knowing this, they do.

Although I may be an empathetic interviewer, there's some source-greasing I won't do. The legendary story told in newsrooms about a reporter who observed no such boundaries involved the late Baltimore mayor Tommy D'Allesandro. He was fighting off hostile fire at a press conference in his office when one normally friendly reporter asked a stick-it-to-'em question. The reporter, pained at the prospect of offending his good source, opened on a note of apology: "Mr. Mayor, my desk wants to know..." D'Allesandro waited for the reporter to finish, placed his head down on the giant desk in front of him, pressed his ear to the blotter and pre-tended he was straining to hear something. After a moment, he reared up. "My desk wants me to tell your desk," he announced, "to go fuck itself."

That's exactly the sort of one-upmanship I was anxious to avoid that night in Littleton. I was mapping out my moves because I hadn't had much traffic over the years with stick-it-to-'em questions and confrontation interviews. They're the stock-in-trade of investigative reporters. I'm an explainer, an analyzer, an ingratiator. Investigative reporters have a low threshold for indignation. They're quick to see high conspiracies and base motivations. I rarely see anything but nuance, and my first instinct runs toward benefit of the doubt. I find it painful to render harsh judgments about anyone in print. I find it equally difficult to praise anyone, however. I suffer from "fear of flacking," a common occupational disorder. Once a reporter ven-tures beyond the neutral zone of objectivity into the netherworld of approbation, he makes an almost tactile investment in the subject of his praise. By morning, tons of newsprint (seventy-five tons in the case of the Washington *Post*) will convey his judgment to millions of readers. It's risky. Suppose the ingrate embezzles the orphans' fund next Tuesday. Then who looks like a fool?

The media-savvy pols know that these are our darkest fears and they find our standards unreasonable. "Many journalists want us to be perfect," Hart once told Sue Casey, his 1984 New Hampshire coordinator and author of a book about his presidential race that year. "They want to see the man on the white horse. Yet their job is to prove that we're not perfect. The closer you come to that ideal, the more you disappoint them, for when they see us up close, none of us turns out to be perfect."

Sometimes I worry that my squeamishness about making sharp judgments, pro or con, makes me unfit for the slam-bang world of daily journalism. Other times I conclude that it makes me ideally suited for newspapering—certainly for the rigors and conventions of modern "objective" journalism. For I can dispose of my dilemmas by writing stories straight down the middle. I can search for the halfway point between the best and the worst thing that can be said about someone (or some policy or idea) and write my story in that fair-minded place. By aiming for the golden mean, I probably land near the best approximation of truth more often than if I were guided by any other set of compasses—partisan, ideological, psychological, whatever. I'm still wrong much of the time, and I don't kid myself about where I'm headed. Yes, I'm seeking truth. But I'm also seeking refuge. I'm taking a pass on the toughest calls I face—which may explain why I chose to be a watcher, not a doer, in the first place.

Despite these qualms, I had my foot pressed hard on the accelerator that night in New Hampshire. The Hart sex scandal story was then in its fourth day, and groaning with such delicacies of fresh detail that whatever initial claim it may have had as political tragedy had already been overtaken by the swift onrush of farce. Two days before, Donna Rice had revealed that she and Hart had taken an overnight cruise to Bimini, aboard a boat haplessly named the *Monkey Business,* a month before their fateful rendezvous in Washington. Hart's protestations that the relationship was strictly platonic were instantly rendered laughable. The only question was how long it would take him to realize it.

He wasn't there yet. The night before, in a speech to three hundred supporters in Manhattan, he'd depicted the scandal not as a burlesque of human frailty but as a conspiracy by unnamed enemies within the political establishment. "Whoever wishes to attack me is fundamentally missing the point," Hart said in a rambling speech that managed to avoid any substantive discussion of his own contribution to the mess he was in. "This is not just a political race, it's really a cause. . . . It's a crusade to move this nation forward. And if I'm right about that, it really doesn't matter if the leader is struck down in battle or with a knife in the back, because the cause goes on and the crusade continues. I have come to realize that those who practice old traditional politics are never going to understand that. . . . They'll assassinate someone's character just so they can get to the top. . . . If the system is permitted to destroy people of honor, soon that system will become dishonorable and destroy itself. March on, my friends! Our cause is our nation's future and our cause lives on! We will prevail because we love our country, and our country is going to need the very best people it can find."

That speech was Hart's second since the scandal had broken the previous weekend. He'd given his first to the American Newspaper Publishers Association, which by a stroke of luck had a long-standing commitment from him to address their annual convention. Yes, he told the publishers, "of course" he'd made a mistake in judgment in being with Ms. Rice in Washington, D.C., over the weekend while his wife was in Denver. But he insisted he "absolutely did not" do anything "immoral" and said he'd always held himself to "a high standard of public and private conduct." He acknowledged that he'd been careless about appearances, but said he'd learned his lesson. Now he understood that "even the most commonplace and appropriate behavior can be misconstrued by some to be improper."

The press, Hart said, had more to answer for than he did. He accused the Miami *Herald* of shoddy journalism, not for having placed his townhouse under surveillance the previous weekend but for mucking up the job. He was in no position to push the more obvious complaint, because a *New York Times Magazine* profile had just come out two days before in which Hart vented his frustration at the press's seeming obsession with his private life by issuing a dare: "Follow me around, I don't care. I'm serious. If anybody wants to put a tail on me, go ahead. They'd be very bored."

In one of life's delicious ironies of timing, the Miami *Herald* had acted on Hart's invitation a day and a half before the *Times* published it. Although the *Herald* political editor had an advance copy of the *Times* profile in hand when his paper decided to launch their stakeout, the invitation wasn't the spur. The *Herald* was steered toward its big scoop—and Hart toward his downfall—by a far more commonplace journalistic prod. An anonymous tipster called.

"You know, you said in the paper that there were rumors that Gary Hart is a womanizer," a woman had begun a telephone call to the Miami *Herald*'s politics editor, Tom Fiedler, four days before the paper launched its stakeout. "Those aren't rumors. How much do you guys pay for pictures?"

The caller was reacting to an article Fiedler had written in the *Herald*—a front-page news analysis which criticized newspapers and newsmagazines for making unsubstantiated references to Hart's "womanizing problem." "In a harsh light, the media reports are rumormongering, pure and simple," Fiedler wrote. He was referring principally to a *Newsweek* profile that had come out when Hart announced for the presidency two weeks before. The *Newsweek* piece noted that he had been dogged by rumors of infidelity throughout his twenty-eight years of marriage; and it quoted a former Hart political adviser, John McEvoy, observing that Hart is "always in jeopardy of having the sex issue raised if he can't keep his pants on."*

This passage triggered a run of similarly loose, fleeting references to "womanizing" in other publications. None of the stories was supported by specific allegations, much less provable facts. Hart became so exasperated that on a cross-country fly-around the day after his announcement, he challenged reporters traveling with him to redirect their curiosity toward the rival campaigns, which he'd been told—by reporters—were spreading the rumors. Hart tried retracting the advice moments after he gave it, but it was too late. He'd violated the first rule of rumor control: never give a reporter a peg to write about the rumor. His suggestion simply produced more stories. "Gary: 'I'm No Womanizer'" blared the front-page headline in the next day's New York *Post.* Other papers were more circumspect, but even stories that portrayed Hart as a victim of gossipmongering couldn't help alluding to the nature of the gossip.

Hart was furious. It wasn't just the rumors that grated; it was all forms of character scrutiny by the press. "I am an obscure man, and I intend to remain that way," he had told writer Gail Sheehy in 1984. He had his reasons to be wary. Better, perhaps, than any other politician, he knew what a fickle beast the press could be. In his first run for the presidency, he spent all of 1983 slogging across the country on a shoestring, sleeping in the homes of volunteers to save money, evangelizing about his "new ideas" before small groups—and being roundly ignored by the press. Then he finished a surprise second in the 1984 Iowa caucuses (although still far behind Walter Mondale, who received 49 percent of the vote to Hart's 16 percent), and became an overnight sensation. He got more national network television exposure the day after the Iowa caucuses than he had the entire previous year. The coverage was fawning. Here was a young, vigorous, attractive, brainy presidential contender—JFK redux. The

---

*McEvoy later claimed he had made the observation in an off-the-record conversation with a *Newsweek* reporter, in a speculative and hypothetical context. *Newsweek* stood by the quote.

race was suddenly portrayed as the Marlboro Man versus the Stolid Norwegian, whose only visible trophy from his victory in Iowa was the bags under his eyes. News clips and pictures of Hart, clad in blue jeans, red suspenders and a flannel shirt, flinging an ax to within inches of the bull's-eye at a woodsmen's competition in Berlin, New Hampshire, a few days later made the contrast more vividly than the proverbial thousand words. Not since the Beatles had stormed onto the stage of *The Ed Sullivan Show* twenty years before had any new face so quickly captivated the popular culture. Indeed, the velocity of Hart's rise in the polls was unprecedented in American political history. He shot up from 2 percent in national surveys taken in late January 1984 to the low 40s by early March. By one estimate, he was picking up 3 million new supporters a day, many of whom had no idea — beyond those red suspenders and pale-blue eyes — why he had become their man. The last time anything close to this had happened in a presidential campaign was the sudden ground swell of support for Republican Wendell L. Willkie, a businessman and internationalist who became the GOP presidential nominee in 1940. His sudden rise was triggered by the outbreak of World War II. Hart's was driven by 16 percentage points in Iowa.

That — and the media's need for a horse race. Throughout 1983, Senator John Glenn of Ohio had been expected to be Mondale's main challenger. When his campaign stalled toward the end of 1983 and ran aground in Iowa, it created the sort of vacuum journalism abhors. Hart had anticipated this. During his long year of anonymity, when funds were scarce and supporters sometimes lost faith, he had never wavered. He seemed to have had a messianic belief that he was riding the tide of history. On the evening of the Iowa caucuses, when he emerged from a shower in his New Hampshire hotel room to hear that early network projections indicated he might finish as high as second, he announced, matter-of-factly, to the staff in the room: "If I come in second in Iowa, I'm going to be President." At the time, he stood at 2 percent in the national surveys.

Hart was right that he was about to go on a wild media ride; wrong about the vehicle and destination. He got strapped onto a roller coaster, not a rocket ship. As the soar-and-swoop played out over the next few weeks, Hart's altitude seemed to have as much to do with the rhythms and needs of the press as with anything he said or did. First the press needed a fresh challenger to replace Glenn. Hart shot up. Then Hart stunned everyone by winning the New Hampshire primary the next week, and the tone of coverage started to sour. Who

is he? Does he have the steadiness, the experience, the maturity? A
skeptical profile that had been written the month before by the
Washington *Post*'s George Lardner, Jr., was recycled by the rest of the
press. Lardner's piece had been the first to note that the age Hart
used on all his campaign literature and biographical material, forty-
five, did not square with the birth certificate on file in his hometown
of Ottawa, Kansas, which made him exactly one year older. It seemed
like such a small matter, but when Hart couldn't come up with a
plausible explanation—one day he passed it off as a family joke;
another day he said it was the result of a misunderstanding with his
staff; on still another day he refused to discuss it—a seed of doubt
was planted. Soon the stories about his name change from Hartpence
to Hart were also dredged up, and once again Hart was caught
telling some needless fibs. He said it had been a family decision, but
relatives said it was Gary's, and Gary's alone. Then the newsmagazines printed samples of his signature, showing how his style of
penmanship had changed dramatically—not once but several times—
over the years. And before long these all became exhibits in the case
that Hart was some sort of Gatsbyesque figure, in flight from his
past.

Mondale, meantime, had become the underdog in the race he'd
been a prohibitive favorite to win a few weeks before, which meant he
was in a position to benefit from yet another Iron Law of Campaign
Coverage: the underdog is always right. Three weeks after New
Hampshire, the media reported it as a valiant comeback when he
won just two of the nine states contested on Super Tuesday. Hart
protested that the scorekeeping had gone berserk, but to no avail.
The media seemed to be behaving like an NBA referee. They knew
they'd missed a call earlier in the game when they hyped Hart's 16
percent showing in Iowa. Now they were evening things out.

Mondale, sensing the moment was ripe, went on the attack. At a
debate in Atlanta just before Super Tuesday, he asked, "Where's the
beef?" (a line borrowed from a popular Wendy's hamburger commercial) to question Hart's gravitas. The networks replayed the
sound bite for days. Then Mondale's campaign aired a TV ad that
used a blinking red telephone in the Oval Office to ask, in so many
words: Would you feel safe with Gary Hart's finger on the nuclear
button? The voters weren't sure, and Hart was a goner.

He hated what had happened to him. As he groped for explanations that summer, he lit on one that reflected a streak of fatalism: "I
got famous too fast," he told supporters. And another that reflected a

sense of victimhood: "I'm the only person who's bucked the system twice," Hart told Washington *Post* reporter David Maraniss on the eve of the Democratic convention in July 1984 — referring both to his own anti-establishment candidacy in 1984 and to his role as campaign manager for anti-war Democrat George McGovern in 1972. "I think there is a strong desire to punish the person who does that, to make him appear odd. That's the only reason I can figure for all the attention on my personal life. You can't find one article that did that to Walter Mondale. Anywhere in his career. I challenge you to find one article! Can you find one? The answer is no! You can't find one because they weren't written. Nobody would care about it. Do you think anybody would care if they found out Walter Mondale was a year older? Do you think anyone would care if Ronald Reagan was a year older? Of course not. The entire focus is on the person who upsets the odds."

Now Hart was running for President once again, this time starting out as the front-runner. That only seemed to have made matters worse. As his announcement date approached in the spring of 1987, he was edgy, agitated. One concern he had was that he wouldn't be able to run the campaign in the manner suited to his temperament. He'd always fancied himself a political guerrilla, storming down from the hills with his ragtag volunteer army. "He thought of himself occasionally as Kutuzov of *War and Peace* — McGovern's Kutuzov," Theodore H. White wrote of campaign manager Hart in 1972. " 'Kutuzov was under the same pressure to attack and win, to attack everywhere,' said Hart in January of 1972, 'but we're an insurgency. I believe we should attack and retreat, attack and retreat.' "

Hart's problem in the beginning of 1987, as his band of irregulars began converging on Denver for the next insurgency, was that the political universe had shifted since 1972 — and even since 1984. There was no Vietnam War to protest. Nor was there any Walter Mondale to pivot off. Hart was a rebel without a cause in the Democratic primaries. Without firing a shot, he'd won his argument with his party's old guard between 1984 and 1987. Mondale's brand of tub-thumping, press-the-flesh, old-time Democratic religion had been discredited by a forty-nine-state landslide. The party seemed ready in 1988 to turn to a new generation of political leader — stylistically cool, intellectually skeptical of the value of expensive social programs, culturally in sync with both the baby boomers and their kid brothers and sisters who'd grown up on MTV. This time, Hart wouldn't be chasing Mondale; this time, the rest of the field would be chasing Hart—

chasing and aping him. Except for Jesse Jackson, the other Democrats all more or less shared his scaled-down view of the role of government. True, none had Hart's flair for conceptual thinking on economic growth policies. True, none had ventured, as Hart had in 1986, to set forth a new foreign-policy doctrine—"enlightened engagement," as he called it—that attempted to guide America into a post-Cold War world. But it wasn't clear whether Hart could parse such farsighted ideas into the sound bites and slogans of a presidential campaign. Nor was it certain he could survive in the fishbowl of a front-runner. Hart, in short, was seen as a flawed messenger of a winning message. So Joe Biden was gearing up to run as Hart "with heart"; Mike Dukakis as Hart with competence; Dick Gephardt as Hart with a legislative record; Bruce Babbitt as Hart with executive experience.

Just as the opposition had changed, so had Hart's volunteer army. You could see it in the paraphernalia they brought to their new national command post in a squat brick building at 1600 Downing Street in downtown Denver, a mile east of the city's shimmering post-modern skyscrapers. Their Rolodexes were fatter, their computers faster, their files thicker. They weren't starry-eyed twenty-two-year-olds anymore. Some of them were doing this for the third time. Some brought along spouses and nearly grown children. All were tired of losing. Like it or not, this time they were all going to have to be more—dread word—conventional. There's no room to "attack and retreat" when the polls have your candidate 32 percentage points ahead of Jesse Jackson and more than 40 points ahead of everyone else in the Democratic field. For the next eighteen months, they knew, Hart would be thrust into the most perilous of all enviable positions in the political firmament: presidential front-runner.

Among other things, he would be expected to draw political support from the very establishment he'd spent so much of his career attacking. This presented problems. In twelve years in the Senate, he'd developed a reputation as a loner—respected for his ideas, but not for any demonstrated ability to get them enacted. In 1984, none of Hart's Senate colleagues had endorsed his long-shot candidacy; in 1987, even though the betting odds on him were much more favorable, only two or three senators were prepared to sign on. "How can you lead the country if you can't lead your peers?" one Capitol Hill insider asked shortly before Hart's announcement. Nor was insiders' unease with Hart confined to Washington, D.C. Tom Miller, the popular attorney general of Iowa and a man much wooed by presidential hopefuls, had narrowed his choice to Hart and Babbitt in early 1987 — and finally signed up with Babbitt. "I like Hart," he said in an interview. "I like the fact that he's future-oriented and not dependent on special interests. And he has a terrific mind. One of the things that did strike me, though, is that Babbitt is comfortable with himself — who he is, what he's about. He likes being Bruce Babbitt. I don't quite get that comfort level in Hart." Don Avenson, speaker of the Iowa General Assembly, was more blunt. "There's this arrogance about the guy. You always get the feeling from Gary that he'd be just as happy if politicians like me didn't exist."

In early March 1987, I asked Hart about the problems he seemed to be having with fellow politicians. We were riding together in the back seat of a car from the Maryland statehouse, where Hart had just given a speech, to a nearby private airstrip in Annapolis. "With apologies to Wilson, I'd like to ask you some questions," I had begun. The reference was to the speech Hart had just given, in which he quoted Woodrow Wilson to the effect that politics should be about principle, not personality. It drew a giggle from Hart, which I took as an invitation to proceed and a signal that he understood I had a job to do. I wasn't surprised; he was someone with whom I'd felt simpatico from our first meeting. I hadn't covered him in 1984, but in the past year we'd been together half a dozen times, including one long dinner. At least by my lights, we'd hit it off. He had a subtle mind, quick wit, easy laugh, delightful sense of the absurd, and most surprising to me — given all I'd read — he was seemingly at peace with himself. He had that rare ability to play hard in the pit one moment and shift seamlessly outside of it the next — into the observers' gallery, where he watched with a novelist's eye and a fan's delight.

"Why does everyone have you pegged as a loner?" I asked.

Hart replied that John F. Kennedy's colleagues said the same thing about him in the late 1950s.

"Yes, but they also knew that he came from a hardball political tradition in Boston. They knew, whatever his stylistic differences, that he was one of them — a pol."

After we had sparred a while, neither side scoring many points, Hart flashed some of the streak of defensiveness he'd shown to David Maraniss back in 1984. "The curiosity of 1984 was that while I was always labeled the loner, there were others in the race, who shall go nameless, who were never labeled as loners, who I have never once in twelve years seen in the private Senate dining room, which I inhabited frequently, and where many of my relationships with my colleagues were developed. Never once. This lonership question was never raised once about them. And I don't know why." Then he rattled off the names of some of his "good friends" in the Senate whom, he complained, he never got credit for having— Moynihan of New York, Johnston of Louisiana, Bumpers of Arkansas, Cohen of Maine, Harkin of Iowa. None, so far as I knew, was anywhere near endorsing him, and one, Bumpers, was thinking of running against him.

By the time he'd finished, the car had reached the airstrip and his small charter plane was waiting. But this conversation had gotten interesting. I'd hit a vein and didn't want to stop pumping. We sat in the back of the car for a few more minutes. I asked how come, with his strongest potential primary challenger, New York Governor Mario Cuomo, having announced a few weeks before that he wasn't going to run for President, Hart hadn't moved more aggressively to pick up endorsements from the politicians and fund raisers who'd been holding back, waiting on Mario. "Why not play some good, old-fashioned train-is-leaving-the-station politics," I asked, "and line up early endorsements?"

Hart was incredulous. "That's so ridiculous!" he said. "Nobody does it! Nobody does it anymore! If they do, they're either going to get a punch in the nose or a horse laugh."

I wondered: Do I know him well enough to tell him, "Cut the crap"? Or is it possible he's serious? I wasn't sure, and besides, Billy Shore, his longtime aide-de-camp, was yanking at his sleeve to get him out of the car and onto the waiting plane. So I kept quiet. But Hart, sensing my surprise and perhaps realizing he'd sounded more civics-bookish than he'd intended, lingered in the back seat and tried a different tack. "Look, I don't need to break arms now," he said in a soothing, faintly conspiratorial voice. "If the chips were down, say before the convention, I'd be perfectly capable of saying to someone, 'You don't want to be on the wrong side of this.' "

After we got out of the car and shook hands on the tarmac, there was one more parting thought. "I am not a softie," Hart said, his pale blue eyes aflame. "But I don't need to prove that to anybody now, just to prove it."

I surmised at that moment that, no matter how well he and I may have gotten along, he'd henceforth see me as a foot soldier in the palace guard of the political establishment. I covered politics for the most politics-obsessed paper in the land—a paper he'd not forgiven for its attention to his name and age change in 1984. I'd just asked some questions that exposed me, in his eyes, as a prisoner of the Washington mind-set—a small-bore, nearsighted, all-tactics political junkie. I naturally take a different view of myself, and felt a twinge of annoyance at Hart for putting me in a box too small for all my fascinating complexities (thereby getting a taste of the way politicians often feel when they read what reporters have written about them). This needs watching, I told myself—both his apparent stereotyping of me and my nascent resentment of it.

The other mental note I took from that interview was that the tranquillity of our earlier encounters was gone. Hart was uptight. It was easy enough to guess at some of the reasons. As he geared up for 1988, his leftover 1984 debt of $1.3 million had blossomed into a major embarrassment. Creditors were suing him; political opponents were distributing "Honk If Hart Owes You Money" bumper stickers; soon U.S. marshals would swoop in on one of his fund-raising events in Los Angeles and seize $29,500 that had been collected at the door. Hart the Deadbeat seemed to be pairing up with Hart the Womanizer as the name- and age-change twins of 1987—the metaphors for a disabling character flaw.

For a time, Hart had tried to head off the character cops with a charm offensive. He'd used humor to defuse the age-change issue. "Never in all my fifty years," he would tell audiences, as if he were gathering speed for some sweeping pronunciamento, "or is it forty-nine? ..." He catered to the media's curiosity about his past by writing a 5,000-word autobiographical sketch, "One Man's Luck." Its requisite handful of boyhood anecdotes only whetted the media's appetite for more. At the urging of his staff, Hart sat for long, ofttimes psychologically oriented interviews ("Is it true you used to clean your toys after you played with them?") with journalists. These were like visits to the dentist for Hart. Even worse was the trip his staff persuaded him to take to Ottawa, Kansas, his boyhood home, two weeks before his April 13, 1987, announcement. They figured it would make great human-interest footage, and give the lie once and for all to the business about Hart being a man with no roots.

They wound up getting more than they bargained for. Hart had only been back to the farming community once since burying both his parents there in 1972. He'd grown up in Ottawa as awkward, jug-eared Gary Hartpence, the son of Carl, a farm-equipment salesman, and Nina, a sickly woman of devout, fundamentalist faith. Nina took Gary each week to the town's austere, one-room Nazarene

Church, where it was hammered home to him that man is born sinful
and that his appetites and emotions must be controlled. Nina wanted
her son to become a minister; Hart grew up observing the no-dancing,
no-drinking, no-movie-shows dictates that she laid down. After he
left Ottawa in 1954, he went first to Bethany Nazarene College in
Kansas City, and then on to Yale Divinity School. But as a young
man in his twenties, Gary Hartpence changed—his name to Hart,
his worldview to secular, his degree program to Yale Law School.
Then both his parents died, within a few months of each other.
This trip back was freighted with more emotional baggage than his
staff realized.

I had been part of the press pack that went out to Ottawa with
Hart, and the story I wrote about it began:

GARY HART COMES HOME, WITH FEELING
By Paul Taylor
Washington *Post* Staff Writer
OTTAWA, Kan., April 2 — This well-kept farming town of
11,500 boasts 31 churches, no bars, no liquor stores, and one
potential president. And today, Gary Hart came home.
And home. And home. And home. And home.
In all, it turns out that Hart lived in 16 different boyhood
houses in Ottawa from 1936–54. To commemorate his homecoming, a map showing his old addresses and a story describing
the Hartpence family's constant minimigrations (mostly because
they were strapped for money) was printed on the front page of
Wednesday's Ottawa Herald.
It was but one of many morsels of biographical detail to
emerge from a campaign visit that seemed programed to unearth
nostalgia and emotion in a front-runner sometimes accused of
being too icy to be elected president. It wound up yielding less
nostalgia and more emotion than likely was intended.
The most gripping moment of the 24-hour stay came when
Hart, 50, had to struggle to hold back tears as he spoke of his
deceased parents to a town meeting of about 700 people.
Hart had visited their gravesite only a few hours before. . . . As
he spoke of them to neighbors, friends and relatives he was
seeing for only the second time since 1972, he needed to take
two long pauses (lasting 15 to 20 seconds apiece) and several
shorter ones to collect himself.
"I don't think there's anyone in the country who's ever had

better parents than I had," Hart said in an unsteady voice. "My
father was as honorable and decent a man as I think ever walked
the face of the earth. My mother loved life, loved the people
around her, loved humor. You often hear the term salt of the
earth, and I think that's what they were. Between them they
represented about the best this society has to offer. And what
they gave me, I don't think I can ever repay, except to try and
raise my children as well as they raised me."

The audience, including about 60 of Hart's relatives, sat in
the Ottawa University Chapel in transfixed silence—broken
only by the clicks of photographers' cameras—as the man known
even here for his supposedly aloof nature struggled to maintain
his composure.

"He couldn't hardly talk, could he?" Hart's uncle, Ralph
Hartpence, remarked afterward. "When you go back and touch
your roots, it can be a very intense thing," noted Wilbur Wheaton,
president of Ottawa University. "I admire him for doing it."

I wasn't sure whether Hart's reaction had been genuine or whether—
perhaps deliberately, perhaps subconsciously—he had thrown himself into an emotionally charged situation, hoping it would generate
enough of a reaction to melt the iceman image. I was a bit ashamed
of my suspicions, but that didn't keep me, a day or two after the
Ottawa trip, from calling up a source in the Denver headquarters
and testing out the theory on him. It was met by stony silence.
"We had to force him to go to Ottawa," the friend finally said. "He
hated it."

Hart's discomfort with the Ottawa trip may have accounted for his
defiance two weeks later, when he formally declared for the presidency.
His staff had prepared a conventional speech and wanted Hart to
deliver it in a conventional setting—somewhere in downtown Denver,
surrounded by the usual hordes of whooping supporters. Hart had
other ideas. His announcement speech was a sparse statement that
included an unusual concession: "As a candidate . . . I'm going to make
some mistakes." He delivered it while standing alone on a rock, in a
park outside of Denver, with his wife and daughter a few paces off to
the side and no other people or props in view. Behind him were the
craggy, snowcapped Rocky Mountains. Given Hart's awareness that
he was supposed to be on a mission to humanize himself, "the
unspoken message was: 'Back off. I need space,'" one top staffer
ruefully recalled.

Hart's campaign staff was getting antsy, too, in the weeks that preceded the April 13 announcement. Rumors, warnings, tips, threats, sightings, gossip and innuendo about their candidate's personal life had been floating like flotsam and jetsam into the Denver campaign headquarters. Bill Dixon, the campaign manager and Hart's friend since they fought together in the anti-Vietnam War movement, kept telling himself and reassuring the staff that it was all "background noise"—the sort of treachery and trivia that has a way of glomming on to any front-runner's campaign. He was determined not to let it distract him. But the buzz kept getting louder. One top staffer was told by a political friend that Hart had been socializing with coeds late at night in a campus bar in Gainesville, where he'd spent a week in late March as a guest lecturer at the University of Florida College of Law. Others in the campaign heard rumors that he'd traded phone numbers with an attractive young woman at a party aboard a yacht in Miami in early April. Dixon himself had learned secondhand from tourists in Bimini that Hart had been spotted there recently with a young woman. He also knew that Hart kept having little spats with the people in the campaign's scheduling office, insisting they leave him more time for nonpolitical weekends with Bill Broadhurst, a high-living Louisiana lawyer-lobbyist whose flourishing new friendship with Hart mystified some in the campaign, and worried others.

"Some of us [at the headquarters] thought that Gary was treating the announcement day the way some people treat their wedding day—getting everything out of his system beforehand," one Hart staffer recalled. Everyone at the Denver headquarters already knew about Hart—at least they knew to the extent that anyone ever "knows" about such things. They were aware of his reputation as a skirt chaser, and not a discreet one. On the campaign trail in 1984, they'd seen or heard about enough women finding their way into Hart's hotel rooms for nocturnal visits to surmise that, even though his marriage to Lee had been patched back together from two separations, he continued doing business on the side. Those who worked for Hart in 1972 remembered him as a shaggy-haired, cowboy-booted lothario. His name had been linked then—and ofttimes since—to Hollywood stars and starlets. When a magazine story in 1972 mentioned that Hart had a wife and children back in Denver, the joke was that half the staff at McGovern headquarters was stunned, the other half heartbroken. "Let's just say I believe in reform marriage," he said that year.

The trouble with "knowing" all this is that unless you are Billy

Shore, the loyal aide who had traveled constantly with Hart since 1984, all you really know are the rumors. Rumor upon rumor achieves a critical mass of credibility with most people; what indicts, finally, is the repetition. But even if you believe the rumors, it's not an easy subject to broach with someone you think is going to be President (or with anyone else, for that matter).

In 1984, when a different set of senior campaign staffers had similar anxieties about Hart's womanizing, they'd cobbled together some contingency plans. One top Hart aide, Washington attorney John Holum, wrote a memo to campaign manager Oliver Henkel in 1984 suggesting that someone on staff "undertake some negative research" on Hart so that "we are not surprised and set back" by whatever might be revealed. "Over the longer term, I would, in fact, recommend going further as a precaution and have a good, mature and dependable litigator carefully question Gary on further possible revelations. This may seem indelicate, but the press is doing an extremely thorough search now, and even that will pale compared to the Reagan crowd's investigative resources later."

Around the same time, a young staffer, Ken Banta, set out to try to discover how far the press was prepared to go in investigating Hart's personal life. His report to the campaign brass read in part:

GWH Character
Areas of growing doubt exist:
Personal Morality/Stability
One newsweekly has already circulated a confidential memo summarizing the Washington bureau's investigation of alleged improprieties by GWH. Other news organizations have done the same. Conclusion generally is that although the allegations are substantiated, they should not be raised publicly unless a direct connection to campaign issues arises.
Consequence: More than may perhaps be realized, editors regard the charges of impropriety as extremely serious, a reflection of possible character instability.

Henkel, a Cleveland lawyer and Hart's friend since their days together at Yale Law School, drafted a statement to be used by Hart in the event that a story came out about his extramarital activities. "We live in a generation where husband and wife from time to time have difficulties," Henkel wrote for his friend. "Lee and I have not been immune from the pressures of marriage, but we're working together to make our life stronger. I'll have nothing more to say on the subject."[1]

The statement never had to be read. No news organization ever ran a story on Hart's womanizing in 1984. Hart's fall that year had come so swiftly after his rise that by the time journalists began contemplating such stories they no longer seemed necessary or appropriate. There's a tendency in the press—as in the rest of society—not to kick a man who's on his way down.

It didn't take long for the concerns that generated a flurry of memo writing in 1984 to flare again in 1987. It wasn't just the sightings of Hart in dangerous company that troubled everyone. It was also that Dixon was being told by journalist friends that the Washington *Post* or NBC was planning to conduct a surveillance of Hart.[*] He'd also heard that former Maryland Senator Joseph Tydings, who'd campaigned for Hart in 1984, had recently hired a detective to put a tail on Hart because Tydings suspected him of having an affair with his estranged wife. Dixon had heard through the political grapevine that the detective had taken pictures of Hart leaving the apartment of a woman—not Tydings' wife, as it turned out—and that Tydings was threatening to make the information public, out of spite. Through intermediaries, Dixon had put out the word to Tydings to "come forward with whatever you have, or shut up."[†]

As if all that wasn't enough, a law-enforcement official had warned a top campaign aide that someone was planning to infiltrate the Hart campaign with a body microphone in the hope of collecting damaging information. Dixon took the warning seriously. In 1974, he had been counsel to the House committee that launched impeachment proceedings against President Nixon ("Impeach Dixon, Not Nixon" was the rallying cry of some of the President's defenders). He knew all about dirty tricks. And he knew how high the stakes could get in a presidential race. Like Hart—who wrote spy novels and served for six years on the Senate Intelligence Committee—Dixon had a conspiratorial mind-set. When he got the warning about a possible mole, he passed it along at a staff meeting. "Everyone in the office who smiles at you isn't necessarily a friend," he told them.

Dixon also told Hart about the various surveillance threats. "Yeah, I expect that," Hart replied.

On the more delicate matter of whether to tell Hart to keep his

---

*No such surveillances were ever planned by either news organization.
†Tydings has declined comment on Dixon's account.

zipper zipped, Dixon took a pass. Beneath his hard exterior, he was still very much the true believer. He admired Hart more than anyone he'd ever met. When Hart asked him at the end of the 1984 race to manage his Senate office and prepare to run his anticipated 1988 presidential campaign, Dixon hesitated for six weeks before answering. He didn't thirst for power; he thought of Washington as a den of thieves ("It's so nice to be out here in Denver," he said shortly after he moved there at the beginning of 1987, "where the air is clear and nobody has offered me a bribe all week") and he no longer craved the thrill of the chase. But finally, he did say yes. His reasoning was simple: "I felt I had to do whatever I can to keep my kids from getting blown up in a nuclear war." To anyone who didn't know Dixon, the rationale seemed melodramatic. To Dixon and his fellow crusaders, what could be more important?

Dixon wasn't comfortable confronting Hart about his private life. "I figured he's a big boy, he knows what the stakes are, he can take care of himself," he said, adding that he assumed Hart understood that he had to be on good behavior. When evidence to the contrary came in, Dixon rationalized it away. Upon hearing that Hart had been spotted with a woman in Bimini, for example, he drew comfort in learning that they'd been seen in public places. "I figured: Shit, if he's out there on the dock, having his picture taken with her, there's no problem. Gary has the ability to have a relationship with a woman without sex being involved."

Other staffers took a less benign view. Before they agreed to join the campaign, political director Paul Tully and national campaign co-chairman Charles Manatt sought and received assurances from Hart that he understood that the fishbowl of a front-runner's presidential campaign was no place to chase skirts. When reports started drifting in to Denver that Hart was up to his old tricks, finance director Eli Segal, senior adviser Hal Haddon and press secretary Kevin Sweeney all privately sought to convey their concern to Hart. But the candidate was in no frame of mind to listen. "He was told he was playing with fire, but he wouldn't even entertain the discussion — he cut everyone right off," said an aide.

The Denver staffers weren't the only ones getting tips. Down in Miami, the anonymous tipster who called Tom Fiedler after his story about gossipmongering ran in the *Herald* told him: "Gary Hart is having an affair with a friend of mine. We don't need a president who lies like that."[2]

Fiedler said he wouldn't pay money for any of her pictures and suggested she consider the gravity of her charges. He asked her to call back in the morning if she still wanted to pursue the matter. He left the office thinking he'd handled a crank call.

At 10:30 the next morning, she called back, still insisting on anonymity, but this time with more details. She said she and her friend had met Hart at a yacht party several weeks earlier. Hart initially had been attracted to her, the caller said, but she was turned off by him. Her friend, on the other hand, was smitten. Hart took the friend on an overnight cruise the next day, and the caller tagged along with a man named Bill and took some pictures. Since then, Hart had called the friend from his campaign stops all over the country.

The tipster was able to give Fiedler the dates of the telephone calls Hart had made to her friend and the states he'd called from — Georgia, Alabama, Kansas. Fiedler checked them against Hart's schedule, and everything fit. Now he assumed he might be dealing with a dirty-trickster, perhaps someone working for a rival campaign — but someone who had information worth knowing. The caller agreed to stay in touch.

In their next conversation, she told Fiedler that her friend, whom she described as an attractive blonde with shoulder-length hair and a Southern drawl, would be flying up to Washington, D.C., that Friday to spend the weekend with Hart at his townhouse. Why didn't Fiedler take the same plane, the caller proposed. "All you need to do is spot her and sit next to her on the plane. She'll tell you about Gary Hart — she's that open and proud of it."

When they hung up, Fiedler called Denver to check Hart's schedule. He was told that Hart would be in Iowa on Friday and Kentucky on Saturday for the Kentucky Derby. His source's winning streak seemed to have run out. For several days, she didn't call him — and Fiedler had no way of calling her. That Friday afternoon, still not having heard from the woman, Fiedler called Denver to double-check the schedule. There'd been a change, he was told. The Kentucky trip had been scrubbed. Hart was spending the weekend in Washington.

Fiedler rushed to his editors with the news, and they dispatched one of their top investigative reporters, Jim McGee, to Washington. With only a credit card and the clothes on his back, McGee reached the gate just in time to hear the final boarding call for Eastern flight 996. At the ticket counter, he saw what he was looking for: a woman with shoulder-length blond hair. She was carrying a big pocketbook with a distinctive pattern on it. And she was stunning.

McGee decided not to approach the woman on the plane. He was more interested in seeing who met her when she got off. But as the plane emptied its passengers into Washington's National Airport, the trail once again went cold. There was no Gary Hart to greet the blonde; nor was there anyone who looked as if he might be a campaign aide. She was met instead by a girlfriend, and the two hugged and went off. McGee assumed he'd been admiring the wrong pretty woman.

He caught a cab to Hart's Capitol Hill townhouse and began a stakeout by positioning himself halfway down the narrow residential block. Around 9:30 p.m., the front door of the townhouse swung open. Hart emerged—alongside the woman with the blond hair carrying her oversized pocketbook.

McGee rushed to the nearest pay phone and called his editors. We need more reporters and a photographer, he said. Then he called Fiedler at home.

"I can't believe it," Fiedler mumbled as he checked the flight schedule to Washington.

I N ITS Sunday edition, under the headline MIAMI WOMAN IS LINKED TO HART, the *Herald* reported that an attractive young woman had spent Friday night and most of Saturday with Hart in his Capitol Hill townhouse. The story said that a *Herald* reporter had observed the woman—who was not identified—fly to Washington from Miami Friday evening, leave the townhouse with Hart at 9:30 p.m. Friday and return to the townhouse with Hart at 11:17 p.m. that same night. It said their stakeout team—which by Saturday morning had grown to include two reporters, two editors and a photographer—saw no further traffic in or out of the townhouse until Saturday evening.

At around 8:40 p.m. Saturday, Hart and the woman emerged from a rear alley and headed for Hart's car, which was parked on the street. At the time, some members of the *Herald* stakeout team were sitting in parked rental cars; others were standing on the street; Fiedler was jogging down the block in a runner's outfit.* Hart realized that something was up. Rather than get into his car, he and the woman hurriedly returned to the townhouse. A few minutes later, Hart reemerged, this time alone. He drove his car a few blocks, parked it and walked back to his townhouse by a circuitous route. His gait was agitated. He clearly knew he was being followed.

McGee and Jim Savage, the *Herald*'s investigations editor, con-

*Contrary to claims by Hart and his supporters, the *Herald* reporters and editors did not hide in bushes, peek in windows or trespass on private property.

fronted Hart in the alley behind his townhouse. Fiedler joined them a few moments later, as did Brian Smith, a *Herald* photographer.

"Good evening, Senator," McGee began. "I'm a reporter from the Miami *Herald.*" He told Hart he had some questions about the young woman staying in his house.

"No one is staying in my house," Hart replied.

McGee explained that they had seen Hart escort the woman back into the house a few minutes earlier.

"I may or may not have," Hart replied.

They asked about the nature of his relationship with the woman.

"I'm not involved in any relationship," he said.

Then why had he and the woman just gone back into the townhouse?

"The obvious reason is that I'm being set up," said Hart in a voice the *Herald* reported as "quivering."

The awkward encounter lasted nearly twenty minutes. Hart told the reporters that the woman was a "friend of a friend"; that he had "no personal relationship with her"; that she hadn't spent the night.

How long have you known her? the reporters asked.

"Several months," Hart said.

Did you recently take a trip with her on a yacht?

"I don't remember," Hart said.

Are you denying you'd met her on a yacht?

"I'm not denying anything," Hart said.

We know you have made telephone calls to this woman from around the country, the reporters said. What did you talk about?

"Nothing," Hart said.

Did the phone calls have something to do with the campaign?

"It was casual, political," Hart said.

Throughout the encounter, Hart stood stiffly, his arms coiled around his torso. When McGee sensed the interview was about to be broken off, he asked Hart whether he had had sex with the woman.

"The answer is no," Hart snapped. He then headed up the alley toward his rear entrance. As Smith snapped pictures, Hart snapped back: "We don't need any of that."

The *Herald* spread its story—and Hart's denials—across the top of its front page the following morning.

I got a call at home that Sunday afternoon from a *Post* editor. He read me the *Herald* article and asked me to work on a follow-up. I phoned Dixon in Denver. "The story in its facts and in its inferences is totally inaccurate," he said. "Gary Hart will not dignify it with a comment because it's character assassination. It's harassment. He's offended and he's outraged. He's furious. He's a victim. Somebody has got to say at some point that enough is enough."

Dixon told me the woman's name was Donna Rice, and said she had apparently first met Hart at a New Year's Eve party in Aspen hosted by rock star Don Henley. They met again in early April at a fund-raising party on a charter boat docked in Turnberry Isle, a posh resort community just north of Miami. Rice reintroduced herself to Hart, while her friend, Lynn Armandt, struck up a conversation with Hart's companion, Bill Broadhurst. Broadhurst told Armandt he had been looking for a caretaker for his townhouse on Capitol Hill and a hostess for the entertaining he did there in connection with his lobbying business. Armandt later flew up to Washington for the job interview. She had Rice come along because she wasn't comfortable staying overnight in the home of a man she had just met. Hart, who coincidentally was in town with a rare weekend off from campaigning, joined the threesome Friday night for dinner at Broadhurst's. After dinner, all four walked the few blocks over to Hart's townhouse to see a deck that had recently been built in the back. Broadhurst, Rice and Armandt stayed only a few minutes before returning to Broadhurst's for the night.

"Bill," I said, when Dixon finished walking me through that account, "these Miami *Herald* reporters wouldn't make stuff up out of whole cloth, and they certainly understand the sensitivity of the story they're dealing with. If there was all this movement in and out of Hart's townhouse Friday night, how could they have missed it?"

"There's a back door that leads to an alley," Dixon said, "Gary goes in and out that way all the time. Those assholes must not have known about it."

"But they confronted Hart in the alley."

"But that was Saturday night. They may not have known about it Friday night."

After he talked to me and a few other reporters, Dixon hopped a red-eye to Washington to run the damage-control operation. He spent Monday calling the *Herald* story "preposterous," and he got some help when the paper had to acknowledge that its surveillance had not been airtight. Fiedler and the other reinforcements from Miami hadn't arrived until late Saturday morning. The disputed movements Friday night conceivably could have occurred at a time when Doug Clifton, a Washington-based editor who had joined McGee on the stakeout Friday night, was picking up a rental car at the airport, leaving only McGee to cover the front and back entrances. They were not both visible from any one vantage point.

On Monday afternoon, Rice held a press conference in a lawyer's office in Miami. She radiated a wide-eyed, "aw shucks, gee, it's all been one big misunderstanding" innocence. What a gloriously mixed-up profile she presented: half of her didn't seem remotely connected to the other half. She was a Phi Beta Kappa graduate of the University of South Carolina who sold pharmaceuticals and baby formula for Wyeth Labs. She was also a part-time actress and model who had silicone implants in her breasts and no compunctions about showing off her surgeon's handiwork, judging from the modeling photographs then sailing the wires into every newsroom in America. She'd partied with jet-setters; had had bit parts on episodes of *Miami Vice* and *Dallas;* and had an ex-boyfriend who was serving time on a drug charge. She faithfully corroborated Dixon's account of the comings and goings on Friday night. When a reporter asked if there was any romance in her relationship with Hart, she turned coy. "We're just pals," she said, adding that she is "more attracted to younger men." But whatever good she did Hart with that crack, she undid when she casually revealed that they had taken a cruise to Bimini the month before, and that it had unexpectedly turned into an overnight stay when there was some problem getting clearance from customs for the return trip.

As soon as he learned what Rice had said at her press conference, Dixon disappeared. The cover story in Denver was that he had taken ill. In fact, he was devastated by Rice's Bimini revelation. He'd gotten way out on the point as Hart's defense attorney, only to discover that his client (and friend and hero) hadn't breathed a word to him about something as critical to the case as the Bimini trip with Rice. Dixon flew back to Denver Monday night, let some friends in the campaign know he wouldn't be coming to work, holed up in his apartment, unplugged the phone, flipped on the television and spent the next three days watching baseball games and old movies.

Lee Hart was likewise incommunicado during much of the week. After the *Herald* broke its story, she confined herself to the small stone-and-wood cabin she and Gary had recently bought in Troublesome Gulch, west of Denver. She couldn't join her husband, a campaign spokesman announced, because she had a bad sinus cold that prevented her from flying. She didn't dare set foot outside of the cabin for fear of rousing the camera crews that were hovering about, hoping for footage of the long-suffering wife. A steady stream of women friends visited the cabin to help her keep her spirits up. Many were bitter at Hart for the way he'd treated Lee—not just that past weekend, but over the years. One afternoon, according to a source, one of them took out a large knife from the kitchen and told Lee that the next time she saw Gary she should "just cut it off. That'll take care of the problem—just cut it off." A roomful of women dissolved into mirthless laughter.

Hart also remained secluded for the first two days after the *Herald* story appeared. When he broke his silence in New York on Tuesday, he made it clear that, Bimini or no Bimini, he was sticking with his full denial. In a taut, angry tone, he told the newspaper publishers that the *Herald* story was "written by reporters who, by their own admission, undertook a spotty surveillance, who reached inaccurate conclusions based on incomplete facts, and who, after publishing a false story, now concede they may have gotten it wrong."

Late that night, I got a phone call in my hotel room in Manhattan from Ann Devroy, who was then the Washington *Post*'s political editor and my immediate boss. She said in the few days since the Rice story had appeared, the *Post* had been deluged with tips about Hart's alleged liaisons with other women. No surprise there. Capitol Hill is a small town where gossip is the drug of choice. Most of what we were getting was merely gossip, and therefore unusable. But one tip looked promising, she said. The day after the Rice story broke, a source who insisted on not being identified had given Tom Edsall, a political reporter at the *Post*, a picture of Hart leaving the townhouse of a Washington woman early one morning. The picture had been taken the previous December and was accompanied by a private detective's report detailing the time Hart arrived at the townhouse on a Saturday night and departed the following morning. The detective apparently had been hired in connection with a divorce proceeding, though Devroy said she didn't know the identity of the client who'd hired him. Nor was it clear why the detective had been following Hart around, rather than the wife who was suspected of having an affair with him. What she did know was in some ways even more delectable: the woman whose townhouse Hart was photographed leaving was not married, and therefore presumably not the woman the detective had been hired to catch. The trap sprung by a betrayed husband had caught Hart in the act—but with the wrong woman.

Devroy said the woman was a lobbyist and former staffer on Capitol Hill. According to the gossip mill, she'd had an on-and-off affair with Hart for years. She was also an acquaintance of a number of people at the *Post*, including executive editor Ben Bradlee. Devroy said that Bradlee was going to try to approach her, confirm that Hart did indeed visit her the previous December 20 and ask her about the nature of her relationship with Hart. Edsall would do what he could to find out more about the detective's report. I should stick close to Hart and await further instructions. She and the other editors hadn't yet decided what, if anything, to do with this information, but it smelled as if they would soon want me to ask Hart about it.

I hung up the phone and thought about the irony of timing. Two months earlier, I'd suggested to Devroy and several other editors that we ought to consider whether the rampant rumors about Hart's personal life were worth investigating. I gave the recommendation a touch of urgency by telling her a story I'd recently heard from a trusted political source in Texas. He said that Hart had been at a fund raiser in his state one evening, and the next day he invited the hostess of the event to his hotel for a thank-you lunch. Lunch turned into a roll in the hay. The woman, whose marriage was on the skids, had been bragging to her political friends all over Texas about her afternoon stand with the man she thought was going to be the next President of the United States. "If this stuff is still going on," I told Devroy, "this story is going to break sooner or later."

More than a month before the *Herald* story ran, we had a meeting in Bradlee's office to discuss what, if anything, to do about the Hart rumors. It was attended by Bradlee, managing editor Leonard Downie, Jr., associate editor Richard Harwood, assistant managing editor Robert Kaiser, national editor Dan Balz, columnist David Broder, Devroy and me. We kicked around the obvious questions. If a candidate for President is believed to be a womanizer, but there's no suggestion that his sexual activities have ever interfered with his public duties, is it even worth investigating, much less publishing? Is there a statute of limitations, or is screwing around in the past tense just as newsworthy as in the present? Is a series of one-night stands more reportable than a single long-term extramarital affair? Does it matter if a candidate has an open-marriage understanding with his spouse? Is Hart a special case, or if we begin looking into his mating habits, must we do the same with everyone else running for President? And how in God's name do you report a story like this? The principals aren't likely to talk, eyewitnesses tend to be rare, third-party accounts are gossip, most reporters don't want to be Peeping Toms, etc.

There was an added complication. In 1982, during one of his two legal separations from Lee, Hart had moved in briefly with *Post* reporter Bob Woodward, who was a bachelor at the time. After a short while, Hart was using Woodward's Georgetown home only as a mail drop, while he presumably was living with a girlfriend. Woodward became uncomfortable with the arrangement and asked Hart to move out, which he did. But if another newspaper were to break a story about Hart's sex life, the Woodward connection might look fishy. It might seem that we were covering for Hart.

The meeting ended when Broder—as usual, the voice of reason—suggested the paper should assign someone to do an in-depth character profile of Hart, about whom many questions lingered from 1984. If, in gathering information, the reporter concluded that the apparent lack of discretion in Hart's sex life fit into a larger context of questions about judgment, probity and honesty, the reporter should pursue these matters, within the bounds of civility. There's no reason to launch a massive sex hunt on all the other candidates, Broder continued. We're not the ones singling Hart out. If a fraction of what we've heard about him is true, he's singled himself out by his own behavior.

Broder's suggestions carried the day. The reporter assigned to write the profile was David Maraniss, who'd already done a great deal of reporting on Hart in 1984 and 1985. But Maraniss, our Southwest bureau chief and one of the paper's most sensitive writers, was tied up with another project when Kaiser telephoned him after the meeting. He wouldn't be able to start fresh reporting on the Hart story until May 4. It seemed like plenty of time. We were, after all, getting a jump on the subject. Or so we thought, right up until May 3—when the *Herald* story came out.

T HE DAY after Devroy called, Hart held a press conference at the Hanover Inn on the Dartmouth campus. The room was too small for the more than 150 reporters, photographers and cameramen straining to get in. The close quarters, the bulky equipment and the tension of approaching deadlines produced the usual jostling and frayed tempers. The start of the press conference was delayed while Hart met privately with his wife, who had finally recovered from her sinus infection and flown East to join him.

"I know Gary better than anyone else, and when Gary said nothing happened, nothing happened," she'd said in an interview at the Denver airport that morning. She conceded that "if I could have planned his weekend schedule, I think I would have done it differently." But she added defiantly: "If it doesn't bother me, I don't think it ought to bother anyone else." She also blasted the *Herald.* "I think there has been a tremendous breach of journalistic ethics in the way this story was printed in the first place. This is something that I find personally outrageous." The words were brave, but Lee's face, still swollen from the infection, was a picture of pain and betrayal.

Hart opened the press conference by calling his wife "the most extraordinary human being I have ever had the pleasure of know-ing. . . . She continues to astonish me with her strength and courage." He replayed his account of the weekend, taking pains to note that on Saturday afternoon he, Rice, Broadhurst and Armandt had gone sight-seeing in Alexandria and picnicking along the Potomac. "If I had intended a relationship with this woman, believe me—I have written spy novels, I am not stupid. . . . I wouldn't have done it this way."

A reporter promptly reminded him that, on the contrary, he had once said during a rafting trip, "I love danger." The question reflected a theory, popular among many armchair psychiatrists in the press corps, that Hart was a tormented figure who behaved recklessly because he wanted to get caught. The closer Hart got to the prize of the presidency—this theory went—the more he needed to fail. Deep down, he knew he was unworthy. He was a sybarite still at war with his Nazarene roots.

Hart would have none of it. "I don't love it that much," he replied coolly.

About halfway through the forty-minute session, Hart recognized me. I had been brooding over the speech he had given the day before to the American Newspaper Publishers Association in New York, especially the part where he talked about his morality and his high standard of public and private conduct. The nakedness of his deceit had put me in an uncharitable frame of mind. We had the following exchange:

Q. "Senator, in your remarks yesterday you raised the issue of morality and you raised the issue of truthfulness. Let me ask you what you mean when you talk about morality, and let me be very specific. I have a series of questions about it. When you said you did nothing immoral, did you mean that you had no sexual relationship with Donna Rice last weekend or at any other time you were with her?"
A. "That is correct, that's correct."
Q. "Do you believe that adultery is immoral?"
A. "Yes."
Q. "Have you ever committed adultery?"

A. "Ahh, I do not think that's a fair question."

Q. "Well, it seems to me the question of morality ... "

A. "You can get into some very fine distinctions ... "

Q. " ... was introduced by you."

A. "That's right. That's right."

Q. "And it's incumbent upon us to know what your definition of morality is."

A. "Well, it includes adultery."

Q. "So that you believe adultery is immoral."

A. "Yes, I do."

Q. "Have you ever committed adultery?"

A. "I do not know—I'm not going to get into a theological definition of what constitutes adultery. In some people's minds it's people being married and having relationships with other people, so ... "

Q. "Can I ask you whether you and your wife have an understanding about whether or not you can have relationships, you can have sexual encounters with ... "

A. "My inclination is to say no, you can't ask me that question, but the answer is no, we don't have any such understanding. We have an understanding of faithfulness, fidelity and loyalty."

Hart was standing no more than six feet from me, with no lectern or podium or stage separating us. We both had trouble keeping our voices from breaking, and neither of us spoke much above a whisper. I saw in his eyes that same wild look of hurt, bewilderment and god-awful betrayal that I'd caught on that airstrip in Annapolis. Mercifully, another reporter broke the tension by jumping in with a different question on a different subject.

A few minutes later, Tom Oliphant of the Boston *Globe* tried to revive my line of questioning, asking Hart if his relationship with Lee had been monogamous. He said he didn't have to answer that. Someone else asked Hart if he would submit to a polygraph test. "Gimme a break," he said.

Throughout these excruciating exchanges, Hart gave a gritty performance. He flashed his anger just once, briefly. "Look, folks, there is something called fairness in our society," he said. "I will answer questions. I'm doing my best, and I'll continue to do my best. But as I said yesterday, there's a broader issue here than what I did and didn't do, and that is whether our system of electing national leaders is fair or not."

Hart's plea didn't slow the inquisition. Another reporter asked about a book he'd reportedly given Rice, which bore the inscription: "In lieu of flowers, Love, Gary." Rice had apparently shown it to a woman sitting next to her on the flight up from Miami Friday night, and the inscription had found its way into the press. Hart said he didn't remember it.

"The extraordinary intimacy of the questions made Hart and the more than 150 journalists crowded into a small lounge at the Hanover Inn on the Dartmouth campus palpably uncomfortable," I wrote that evening for the next day's *Post*. "For better or worse, new ground was broken in the nature of questions put to a presidential candidate. . . ."

As I transmitted the story over the phone from my laptop computer, I got on another phone and talked to my editors. Bradlee said he had received corroboration from the Washington woman, through a mutual friend, that Hart had indeed spent the night with her the previous December 20. He said she was devastated to learn he had been under surveillance, and frightened that if her name were to be dragged into the Hart scandal, her career would be ruined. She was also distraught over Hart's liaison with Rice, for she apparently believed that she was Hart's one true love and that he was going to leave Lee to marry her.

Bradlee said he wanted me to get Hart's comments on the detective report, that night if possible. I asked if we were going to run a story. He said there had been no decision. The first thing to do was to finish reporting the story, and that meant getting to Hart.

"All we'll get is a 'no comment,'" I said. "There's no reason in the world for him to talk about it."

Bradlee said he had the impression that this woman was more than just a casual fling to Hart, and that the prospect of her getting dragged into the story might force his hand. I should let Hart know, he added, that "the phone has been ringing off the hook" with new tips about his relationships with other women. He gave me the names of two other women to pass along.

After Bradlee got off the phone, I spoke with Kaiser and Downie and raised a potentially troublesome point. "The one thing I'm not going to do is get into a negotiation," I said. "None of this 'if you do this, we won't print that' stuff." They said that they completely agreed; that everyone at the *Post* felt a negotiation would be inappropriate and that I was to avoid getting into one. If Hart pressed to know what our intentions were about printing a story, I was instructed once again to tell him we hadn't decided yet. That would keep the squeeze on. It also happened to be true.

After the press conference in Hanover, Hart headed north to hold a town meeting in Littleton, while I stayed behind to write my story and confer with my bosses. By the time I got to the Eastgate Hotel in Littleton, it was nearly 11 p.m. In a lounge just beyond the registration desk, I immediately bumped into a tableful of familiar faces: Hart press secretary Kevin Sweeney, Robin Toner of *The New York Times,* Deborah Orin of the New York *Post,* and Bill Peterson, a friend and colleague at the Washington *Post.** They were having a nightcap of popcorn and beer.

I was delighted to see Peterson. The prospect of confronting Hart in his hotel room—with his wife quite possibly at his side— had grown less appealing the closer I'd gotten to Littleton. If Peterson and I did the interview together, at least we could help each other through it. I said my hellos around the table, then motioned Bill to come out to the lobby, where I quietly filled him in on the tip we had and on my instructions for the evening. Peterson's reaction surprised me. Not only didn't he share my adrenaline rush for the assignment, he was plainly troubled by it. He thought the hour was late, the tip was weak and the story was sleazy. He worried that we were setting a precedent that could take us into the bedrooms of every other presidential candidate. I said this was a special case; the circumstances left us no choice; etc. But as I heard myself yammering, I realized— and it came as a shock—that there was more than one perspective on all this, even within my own shop. Bill and I came to a quick mutual understanding that we weren't going to settle our differences that night. We agreed to disagree. I headed back to the lounge to find Sweeney. Bill headed for his room.

Sweeney, a tall, angular, balding, bearded redhead, looked older than his twenty-nine years. With pale skin and light eyes and fine features, he had a laid-back, hippy-dippy personality that made him seem like a refugee from the 1960s. When I first met him the previous year, I'd guessed he was out of his depth in presidential politics, but in all the dealings we'd had since, he'd shown a tough hide and a delightful sense of humor. A few months earlier, he had come into the *Post* to complain about something David Broder had written in a column. Press secretaries with grievances usually call, write or let it pass: rarely do they lodge a protest in person. But Sweeney had wanted a showdown. A small group of us on the political staff received him in one

*Bill Peterson, one of the finest writers and warmest human beings ever to grace a newsroom, died of cancer July 18, 1990. He was forty-seven.

of the glass-enclosed editor's cubicles that sit suspended in the middle of the *Post*'s square-block-sized newsroom. It was all very civilized and pleasant, at first. Then, at an opening in the conversation, Sweeney squared off toward Broder and opened fire. Broder had written that Hart hadn't had a productive year, politically, in 1986. Sweeney admonished him for using too narrow a gauge. He said Hart was a different kind of candidate, who should be judged by the speeches he'd given, the white papers he'd issued and the trip to the Soviet Union he'd just taken—and not by some trivial score card of political endorsements. The subtext of the complaint was clear: just because we may be a little unconventional, that doesn't mean you, David Broder, dean of American political journalists, can mess with us. Broder understood perfectly. "It's just possible," he said with a tender smile that signaled surrender, "that columnists are sometimes wrong." I could swear, at that moment, I heard the sound of Sweeney's heart thumping.

Given my vivid memory of the encounter, it didn't surprise me that Sweeney hung tough at the Eastgate that night. I gave him a brief outline of what I had—holding back most of the details in the hope of retaining some element of surprise for the encounter with Hart. But Sweeney insisted on hearing everything before he would even consider taking my interview request to his boss. "I've got twenty-five reporters who've already put in for interviews," he said. "And you're not exactly the guy he wants to see right now."

I opened up my laptop computer and began reading him a memo I had received from Devroy earlier in the day, spelling out the details of the detective's report. Sweeney's pale complexion turned sheet-white. "I was with Hart that day!" he said, with a chilling start of recognition.

The detective surveillance had begun at a radio station in northern Virginia on Saturday afternoon, December 20, 1986, where Hart had recorded the Democratic response to President Reagan's regular weekly radio address. It tracked Hart to his own townhouse, then to a bookstore, then to the woman's townhouse, where it had him spending the night and leaving the next morning.

"I was with him," Sweeney repeated, this time in a soft, sad sigh. "After the bookstore, he told me to knock off for the night."

In a moment, he recovered his composure and began scribbling down my information. "Are you guys going with this story tomorrow?" he asked.

"I don't know what we're doing with it," I said. "We haven't decided yet. We first need to talk to Hart. And listen, Kevin. This is the best tip we have. But it's not the only one. The phone's apparently been ringing off the hook. There are other names, too."

"Gimme fifteen minutes," he said, heading off for his room.

After fifteen minutes stretched to forty-five, I knocked on his hotel room door. He let me in, apologized for the delay and explained that he'd been on the phone the whole time with the campaign high command in Denver. Hart was already asleep, he said, and the people in Denver had decided he shouldn't be awakened. He said that Hal Haddon, a lawyer, a senior adviser to the campaign and one of Hart's closest friends, would try to get in touch with Bradlee as soon as possible to discuss our story. Then the phone rang; it was Denver again. Sweeney motioned me toward the door and said he'd meet me in the lobby as soon as he could.

It was past midnight when he came out. He asked again if we were going to run the story in the morning paper. I said we weren't, and explained that everyone at the *Post* was reluctant to drag the woman into the story. This would be a concern in any case, I said, but it was made all the more palpable because a number of people at the paper, including Bradlee, were acquainted with the woman. I said we didn't know what we were going to do with the story, but we did know we needed to talk to Hart.

"Can I talk to him first thing in the morning, before he heads out on the trail?" I asked.

"He isn't even in this hotel," Sweeney said.

I was surprised, having been under the impression that the whole Hart entourage was staying at the same hotel.

"He and Lee and a few others decided to stay twenty miles from here at a hotel in Vermont," Sweeney said. "They didn't want to be in the same hotel with the press. They wanted privacy."

He told me to call him early in the morning and he'd let me know if I could interview Hart first thing.

I went to bed doubting I'd ever get the interview and feeling pretty low. Getting people to talk to you—whether by guile, threat, flattery, charm—is just about the most basic requirement of my craft. I'd failed.

Yet with that reluctant acknowledgment, the tension of a long day broke, and I began mulling over the craziness of my situation. Here I was, a child of the live-and-let-live 1960s, trying to force a presidential candidate to tell me how he had spent his private moments. Maybe Bill Peterson was seeing things more clearly than I was. . . .

A T 6:45 the next morning, I got Sweeney's groggy voice on the other end of the line. He said he didn't know anything new. "I'll get back to you as soon as I find out something," he promised.

My patience was exhausted in the time it took to shower and shave. As I headed toward Sweeney's room, I bumped into Joe Trippi in the motel parking lot.

Trippi was the deputy political director of the campaign. I didn't know how much he knew about what I'd been up to in the past twelve hours.

"What's going on?" I asked.

Trippi looked weary and sad, and he hadn't shaven. He took a deep breath.

"You're looking at the end of a candidacy here," he said. "You're looking at a family in a lot of pain. Hart's going to get out of the race tonight or tomorrow. Don't tell anybody. We're not ready to announce it for a couple of hours."

For a moment I was speechless. "Where's Hart now?" I finally asked.

"He and Lee got on a charter back to Denver in the middle of the night."

I asked him what had happened.

Trippi gave me some of the details that morning, and he, Sweeney and others filled in the rest a few days later.

After the press conference in Hanover and a town meeting in Littleton that night, Hart had had a long dinner at the Colonnade Hotel in Lyndonville, Vermont, with his wife and about ten friends and campaign staffers. The dinner conversation was full of venom at the press and war stories about surveillances and stakeouts. Hart talked about how, at the town meeting in Littleton, a three-year-old child was nearly trampled by the crush of camera crews. Lee regaled the group with stories of how their daughter, Andrea, nearly punched a reporter who tried to ask her questions while she was on her college campus.

Hart replayed the afternoon press conference, making it clear he was angry at himself for not having answered the adultery question more forcefully. "Adultery is a sin, not a crime," he said. "Questions about adultery, I answer only to Lee, and to God."

Everyone agreed that the campaign couldn't continue in such a carnival-like atmosphere. Hart wondered out loud if there was any way he could break the siege. Someone suggested he buy a half hour of network television time and appeal to the decency of the American people. Hart seemed interested, until someone else said, "The trouble is, you'll get your half hour, and then Rather and Brokaw and Jennings will get their half hour." One by one, other ideas got shot down, too. By the end of the meal, Hart's defiance had given way to dejection and resignation. No one at the table mentioned it, but everyone knew that in the few days since the scandal had broken, Hart's financial support was hemorrhaging, his poll numbers were in a free fall and the sound of silence from supporters around the country had been deafening.

Trippi said that he left the dinner thinking Hart had decided to quit the race, but that not everyone came away with the same impression. The dinner group had been seated at two tables, and there had sometimes been more than one conversation going on at once. That may have caused the confusion.

After the Harts went off to bed at about 11 p.m., the staff in Vermont made a conference call to Denver. They soon fell into a disagreement over whether Hart was planning to get out of the race, or whether they should be putting together a campaign schedule for the next two weeks. In the midst of that debate, the Denver headquarters got a call from Sweeney in New Hampshire.

"We have a new problem," Sweeney told them. "The *Post* has a story about Hart and another woman."

In Denver, Haddon, deputy campaign manager John Emerson and political director Paul Tully decided Hart needed to hear about this latest development right away. On their instructions, Billy Shore roused Hart from bed and had him call Sweeney in New Hampshire.

Sweeney told Hart about the detective's report.

"Is it a story?" Hart asked.

"Yes, it's a story," Sweeney said.

"This thing is never going to end, is it?" Hart said in a soft, low voice. "Look, let's go home."

Trippi said he and Sweeney had stayed up all night making preparations for the withdrawal. The Harts were already on a private jet heading for Denver. Haddon was going to try to talk to Bradlee that morning. He'd been authorized by Hart to propose a deal: if the *Post* didn't print its story, we'd get an exclusive account of the last days of the campaign.

I gave him Bradlee's phone number, but an exclusive was the furthest thing from my mind.* I was too busy feeling relieved, then triumphant.

The interview I never got had worked out fine. Just fine.

*We never got one.

CHAPTER THREE

Gary Hart: The Aftermath

W[HEN] I [RETURNED] to Washington that afternoon, I went over the details of the previous twenty-four hours with my editors. One reason I'd asked the adultery question at the press conference, I told them, was that I'd anticipated not being able to get to Hart privately and thought it would be good to have his response on the record.

"You were the one who asked that question?" Bradlee asked, taken aback.

"Yeah," I said, half expecting a high-five.

Bradlee rolled his eyes and said, "Sheee-yit!"

As eye rolls go, this one was ambiguous—conveying surprise more than approval or disapproval. Or so I'd like to think. I've made it a point not to ask.

Whatever he meant by it, Bradlee's reaction was my first clue that "Have you ever committed adultery?" would reverberate beyond Gary Hart. Sometimes reporters get their noses pressed up so close to the story they're working on that they have trouble seeing beyond tomorrow's headline. Over the next days, weeks and months, the Big A Question, as it came to be called, provoked so many other figurative shouts of "Sheee-yit!" with so many shades of meaning from so many quarters that the realization eventually penetrated even my thick skull. The notable journalistic deed I'd committed the previous day was not to plot an interview that never happened. It was to pose a question that had never been asked—not to a presidential candidate, in public, with the whole world watching.

At first I was baffled by the fuss, then angry, then resigned, then embarrassed for not having anticipated it. I never changed my view that the question was appropriate, given the circumstances. I also never shed my discomfort at having asked it, or my unease with some of the uses to which it was later put, or my disagreement with some of the rationales offered by its defenders as well as its critics.

It didn't take long to figure out that the latter group vastly outnumbered the former. National polls taken after Hart dropped out showed that by margins approaching three to one, people thought the press had gone too far in staking out his townhouse and asking him about adultery. Just by opening my mail over the next few weeks, I could measure the passion behind those numbers.

"To have destroyed Richard Nixon, I applauded you," one anonymous pen pal wrote, addressing his "you" not to me but to the newspaper I worked for. "For what you did to Gary Hart, I damn you all to hell, and those of you who aren't saints, I pray your dicks fall off."

"I read you were the person who asked Hart if he had ever committed adultery," wrote a man from Boston. "That's a repulsive question. You're a real sleazeball. I'm a newspaper junkie. I read four papers a day. On a recent vacation, I went down the line plunking my quarters in front of my Motel 6 and getting a big load of papers. I know newspapers. You're a sleazeball."

"Paul!" wrote one fellow, no address given. "Gary Hart gave you the wrong answer to your question about adultery. He should have responded, GET FUCKED!"

I doubt the question was much more popular in workplaces, bars, living rooms, marital beds or anywhere else it was discussed—though my mail and seat-of-the-pants poll suggested that women may have been a little less hostile to it than men. At a political event I was covering shortly after Hart withdrew, I was approached by a husband and wife who knew I was the infamous asker. "That was a miserable thing to do," he said. Before I could respond, she glared at him and interjected: "Except if you have it coming." We moved to another subject.

In the weeks after Hart got out, I must have been asked a hundred times, by inquisitors of both genders: "Have you ever committed adultery?" Bradlee and Washington *Post* publisher Donald Graham got an earful of this, too. I might have found the razzing more fun if I'd ever come up with a suitable response. "You must never have met my wife" had too much braggadocio. "Being a journalist means never having to say you're sorry" was too smug. "That's not an appropriate question except under extraordinary circumstances" was the answer I'd pick on a multiple-choice quiz in a journalism class, but it made me sound like a horse's ass. A simple "no" made me sound like a prig. I tried out a line I'd heard Dick Cavett unload on Norman Mailer years ago: "Why don't you fold that question five ways and stick it where the moon don't shine." But coming from the guy who'd started the whole business, that didn't seem very gracious. I never solved the riddle, and eventually concluded there must be some kind of biblical justice to my unease: cast an unanswerable question upon the public waters, and you will have it return a hundredfold.

While I was going through my own little hell, Hart's downfall was proving to be an irresistible subject for all takers of the cultural pulse. What did it tell us about our politics? Our journalism? Our morality? Was Hart done in by cheating (in the country-and-western lyrics sense), lying or flaunting? Or by a prurient press? Or by a puritanical press? Everyone had an opinion. Among the more provocative:

George Reedy, journalism professor and former press secretary to President Lyndon Johnson: "What counts with a candidate for president is his character, and nothing shows it like his relationship with women. Here you have a man who is asking you to trust him with your bank account, your children, your life and your country for four years. If his own wife can't trust him, what does that say? The press doesn't invent stories about the sexual peccadilloes of candidates. Hart asked to be followed around because it was already an issue."[1]

Betty Friedan, feminist: "Sexual behavior should be a private matter. But somehow flaunting it shows an arrogance toward women and all voters. There's a kind of implied denigration of women. It suggests an instability that I would not want in the President. This is the last time a candidate will be able to treat women as bimbos."[2]

Suzannah Lessard, feminist and *New Yorker* staff writer: "The reaction to the Hart episode reveals a transition in its early stages, where most of us are still confused. But it seems more or less clear that the question of a presidential candidate's philandering has a meaning that it didn't have before. And while the interpretations surely vary, they must include the growing equality of women. A feminist sensibility has seeped into public consciousness sufficiently to make philandering appear to many at best unattractive, maybe unacceptable and possibly even alarming where the candidate's emotions and psychology are concerned."[3]

Hugh Sidey, *Time*'s White House watcher: "Sex—real or imagined—is far more hazardous to the political health of a presidential candidate than to a sitting President. The man in the White House has a meticulous security system that regulates the comings and goings and the witnesses thereof. The lips of the securers are sealed until death. After that, of course, the President is always exposed to memories and diaries. But that just spices history. . . .

"The White House press corps' grand old man, UPI's Merriman Smith, used to regale the young scribes with stories of his days on Franklin Delano Roosevelt's train from Washington to Hyde Park, N.Y., how it would stop on a New Jersey siding for a rendezvous with Lucy Mercer Rutherfurd. Smith never wrote the story, never had any final facts.

"The circumstantial evidence of President Kennedy's sexual adventures during his White House years was abundant. . . . Two comely females on Kennedy's office staff, part of the traveling entourage, were known to get calls at unusual hours to report for work. Some of those requests included transcontinental flights on Air Force planes. Since the women did not have highly developed secretarial skills, imaginations were inflamed, particularly since one or the other often returned to her quarters physically spent. . . .

"It is reasonable to wonder, if Kennedy had lived and been reelected, whether he would have gotten through a second term without a devastating scandal. Judith Exner was the moll of mobsters John Roselli and Sam Giancana, and was introduced to Kennedy by Frank Sinatra. That's a deadly combination, even for those days. No president—or candidate—standing self-righteously on the great political trinity of wife, family and honor can expect to escape the judgment of the American voters on his sexual conduct. In the past, that judgment was often made posthumously. Now, it happens much sooner."[4]

David Garrow, author of *Bearing the Cross*, a Pulitzer Prize-winning biography of Martin Luther King, Jr.: "I don't think the question is monogamy or sex per se, but vulnerability. These things that are quasi-secret but known to some could make the man vulnerable in the exercise of power. It could give power and influence to those who know. King was aware that J. Edgar Hoover and the FBI were trying to record his affairs, but he was fundamentally defiant. He determined that he was not going to change his life. Hart's attitude is the same defiance. But Hart is being judged by standards that at least half our presidents would fail."[5]

James MacGregor Burns, Williams College political scientist and biographer of Franklin Delano Roosevelt: "This is a tragedy, a real loss for all of us, that a really impressive man has been brought down this way. The character of candidates and presidents is crucial. But the media aren't able to deal adequately with real and total character; their judgments are based on such old-fashioned, puritanical pieces of evidence. The character question should deal with the totality of a person. How does he treat people? Does he keep his word? Is he wise and fair? How does he handle subordinates? The real humaneness of the man."[6]

David Riesman, Harvard sociologist: "I'm against the cult of candor, of letting it all hang out. To moralize on this issue in the campaign without talking about truly important things like the arms race trivializes our society. No one can afford to be president who has no imagination, but I fear that is what we are beginning to get."[7]

Richard Cohen, Washington *Post* columnist: "Enough! In the first place, no public figure should be questioned publicly about rumors that he had an affair. . . . This amounts to a kind of sexual McCarthyism. . . . Merely to clam up, to cite personal privacy, turns the candidate into a Fifth Amendment philanderer. This is a sordid abuse of press power—demeaning to candidates and demeaning to the press as well."[8]

Hendrik Hertzberg, *The New Republic:* "Gary Hart has now become the first American victim of Islamic justice. He has been politically stoned to death for adultery. The difference is that in Iran, the mullahs do not insult the condemned prisoner by telling him that he is being executed not for adultery but because of 'concerns about his character,' 'questions about his judgment,' or 'doubts about his candor.' "[9]

Kevin Sweeney, Hart's press secretary: "The press says the story was about judgment, simply judgment. But if it was just about judgment, they wouldn't have those pictures on page one of all the papers in the country. Judgment does not wear a bikini."[10]

Meg Greenfield, Washington *Post* editorial page editor and *Newsweek* columnist: "[T]he Hart dispute was never about judgment. It was about values. It was about the way a fifty-year-old man chooses to live, about his relationships with and respect for other people, about his honesty, about whether he feels contempt or consideration for the sensibilities and values of those he aspires to lead, about achieving a right relationship between what one professes to be and what one actually is. . . . Hart was not victimized by some puritan instinct gone mad, he was found to be living a life he could neither justify nor reveal. . . .

"[T]he office of the presidency is not conducted by position papers. We do not elect opinions to public office. The presidency is conducted by human beings who, to be successful, must combine in the right way seemingly contradictory qualities: worldliness and idealism, toughness and charity, skepticism and belief, humility and self-confidence, enthusiasm and restraint. The nature of the candidate — the way these qualities are balanced in him — is the pre-eminent issue."[11]

While this debate was rippling through society at large, the journalism fraternity was engaging in one of its periodic bouts of self-criticism that occur whenever reporters become too entangled in the story they are covering. Did the Miami *Herald* and Washington *Post* act properly? Were the old rules about not reporting the private peccadilloes of public figures now defunct? Were there any new rules to replace them?

The *Herald* drew mixed reviews from the rest of the press for launching its surveillance. *The New York Times* editorialized that the *Herald*'s stakeout was "eminently justified" because of the preexisting concerns about Hart's reputation. In effect, the *Times* set forth a probable-cause standard, and ruled that it had been met in the Hart case. Its view was by no means unanimous, however. One of its own columnists, Anthony Lewis, took exception: "When I read about the Miami *Herald* story on Gary Hart, I felt degraded in my profession. Is that what journalism is about, hiding in a van outside a politician's home?" Washington *Post* columnist Edwin M. Yoder, Jr., likened the stakeout to "totalitarian journalism." Larry King, the syndicated columnist and talk show host, said, "If I worked for the Miami *Herald* and they said, 'Go sit outside someone's townhouse,' I'd quit."

The *Herald* also took flak for more mundane matters of execution. It was criticized for initially overstating the thoroughness of its surveillance and for putting a "hard" opening paragraph on its first story — stating as fact the key point that Hart so vigorously disputed. Its lead had read: "Gary Hart, the Democratic presidential candidate who has dismissed allegations of womanizing, spent Friday night and most of Saturday in his Capitol Hill townhouse with a young woman who flew from Miami and met him."

That was a conclusion, not a fact, and should have been treated as such.*

Finally, the *Herald* was second-guessed for rushing the story into its Sunday editions. By the time Fiedler, McGee and Savage had finished interviewing Hart outside his townhouse and headed over to their rooms at a nearby Quality Inn, it was nearly ten o'clock on Saturday night. As they were writing, Broadhurst reached them by telephone (having found out where they were by first calling the newspaper in Miami). He said the whole situation was innocent and offered to let them come over to his townhouse to interview the woman. But when Fiedler and then Savage pressed for details over the telephone, Broadhurst turned coy and evasive. They concluded that he was trying to stall and so they chose to finish writing the story against what was by then a very tight deadline. Once their paper was already printing, they met with Broadhurst in the early hours of the morning at a Chinese restaurant. (He did not bring along Rice.) The article that appeared in the *Herald* later that morning neither named nor carried an interview with the woman Hart allegedly had been with Friday night.

Fiedler defended the decision to go with the story Sunday by arguing that had they held back a day, Hart and Broadhurst "could have worked out an alibi, and they could have called the Washington *Post* and *The New York Times* and said, ' . . . We're not going to talk to the Miami *Herald,* we're going to talk to you.' "[12] Savage made a similar point: "Had we waited a day, I am quite sure Dixon would have mounted one hell of an offense against us, and we would have been silent. He could have called a press conference and talked about the outrage of reporters stalking Hart at his home. And we would have been sitting there for twenty-four hours, with nothing in the paper."

Every journalist sympathizes with the instinct to preserve a scoop. But, in twenty-twenty hindsight, the *Herald*'s scoop doesn't seem nearly as fragile as Fiedler and Savage made it out to be. This was the rarest of scoops — the entire story rested on the eyewitness account of the newspaper's own reporters. Even if Hart, Broadhurst and Dixon had tried to engage in preemptive damage control, it's hard to see another newspaper shooting down a story that hadn't yet been published. This was the journalistic equivalent of the tree-falling-in-the-forest riddle: it would make a noise only when the *Herald* declared it had heard something. Given the missing elements in the first-day

*Hart and Rice did leave the townhouse Saturday morning and return Saturday afternoon — movements the surveillance team managed to miss.

story, the too-muscular lead and the mistaken inference about the thoroughness of the stakeout, it seems clear the *Herald* would have profited from waiting until Monday to publish. But it's equally clear that had the story appeared a day later, it might have been tidier — but not fundamentally different. The *Herald* missed on some details. It did not — to its enduring credit — miss the story.

At the Washington *Post,* we, too, took our lumps. In a *Columbia Journalism Review* article, John Judis theorized that we had never intended to print the woman's name and accused us of engaging in "high stakes political poker rather than journalism."[13] *The New Republic*'s Hendrik Hertzberg had a different theory: we hadn't bluffed Hart, we'd blackmailed him. "Hart decided to drop out of the race, in exchange for which the *Post* agreed not to print the name of 'the Washington woman,'" Hertzberg wrote. "I'm sure there is a moral distinction between this transaction and blackmail, though it escapes me for the moment."[14]

Hertzberg's indictment is the easier of the two to dismiss. "There were no ultimatums, no negotiations," Bradlee said of his phone conversation with Hal Haddon on the morning after Hart decided to get out. No one in the Hart camp has ever disputed that. They've said it was their assumption that if Hart got out, the *Post* story wouldn't run, and if he stayed in, it would. The distinction between assuming something and being promised something may be fine, but we at the *Post* felt it was crucial, and took care to preserve it. Did we also go about reporting the story in a way that encouraged their assumptions? Guilty as charged. But what were we guilty of, besides good judgment and better luck? We had in our possession a private detective's report, confirmed by the "Washington woman," that provided readers with relevant background information they could use as they judged the competing claims in the Hart–Rice story. On the Friday that Hart withdrew, we printed the basic outlines of that information, but not the woman's name. Had Hart remained a candidate and disputed our story — the way he had disputed the *Herald*'s story of his liaison with Rice — would we have been forced to come forward with more details, including the woman's name? The easy answer is to invoke the *CJR* metaphor: in poker, when the other guy folds, you don't have to show your hole card.

I don't know what the paper would have done — I'm not sure the editors do either. I do know that when Hart stunned everyone by returning to the presidential race seven months later, there was a clamor for the *Post* to tell all. It was mostly from inside-the-Beltway types who wanted to see the town philanderer get his public flogging. Bradlee declined. "I can't ask him about every woman he ever scaboozled," he said. By then, Hart had acknowledged he was an adulterer in an appearance on ABC–TV's *Nightline,* and Bradlee argued that to continue reporting on his affairs was no longer newsworthy. It amounted to the journalistic equivalent of double jeopardy. As for the woman in the detective's report—whose relationship with Hart had been an open secret on Capitol Hill for years—we never published her name. "It really rocks me because everybody in town knows the name, but everybody's baiting me into using it," Bradlee said. "And I ain't gonna bite."

The *Post*'s ombudsman, who writes a weekly editorial page column critiquing the paper's performance, praised Bradlee's abstinence in an article headlined: A WOMAN'S HONOR KEPT. But does anybody notice a double standard? No one at the *Post* or any other newspaper in America felt compelled to protect the honor and reputation of Donna Rice by not printing her name. Is there one rule for Miami models, another for Washington lobbyists? One for one-night stands, another for long-term affairs? And how innocent, after all, was the Washington woman? With her eyes open, she had walked into a relationship with a married, public man. You play, you pay, as the saying goes.

So why protect her? We protected her—as I eventually discovered—because in the deal Bradlee had struck with their mutual friend to get confirmation of the relationship, he had agreed not to publish her name. Donna Rice was never in a position to make that kind of bargain. The story moved too fast on her. And besides, she chose to try to protect Gary Hart. Our woman had the opportunity to protect herself—and she took it. Everyone can decide for himself or herself who behaved more honorably. But at the *Post,* we can lay aside our claims to chivalry. The Faustian bargain we made with the Washington woman is a classic tool of our trade. We give a less-than-innocent party immunity from publicity in exchange for information that implicates a higher-up. It's the same deal that criminal prosecutors make all the time, freighted with the same ethical complexities. It's not pretty, it's not noble, and it's occasionally a miscalculation. But it does help us do our job.

What about the posing of the infamous "Big A" question? That, too, drew criticism from within the journalistic community. The heaviest blows came from *The New York Times*'s Op-Ed page, where I got cuffed around by four different columnists as a "titillater" who had "demeaned" the profession with a "nauseating" question. But while the paper's columnists were lobbing their grenades, the *Times*'s newsroom was busy drawing up an adultery questionnaire and distributing it to all the remaining presidential contenders. It asked how a hypothetical presidential candidate who had—and who hadn't—committed adultery should answer the question "Have you ever committed adultery?"

None of the candidates had much enthusiasm for the project, and some were openly hostile in the page-one story the *Times* ran describing their responses. Jack Kemp's spokesman told the paper it was "beneath the dignity" of a presidential candidate to answer such questions. Jesse Jackson said adultery was an "inappropriate question" in a presidential campaign "because it appears to reduce the question of moral tone to just sexuality." A spokeswoman for Michael Dukakis said: "A presidential campaign should not be about adultery. It should be about creating economic opportunity for every citizen in America. . . . " Vice President Bush, in a written response, said he wouldn't offer advice to hypothetical candidates. He added: "I believe the American people, to whom candidates and journalists are ultimately accountable, would counsel that we move with great caution and respect for privacy before we enact a new, broader journalistic test of candidate fitness based on unseemly inquiries into private behavior. For my part, I don't know how to define unseemly inquiry, but I'll know it when I see it. And so will the American public."

I was mystified by the *Times*'s behavior, as were many others in the media. The paper seemed to be taking the view that the adultery question, having been asked once, would have to be asked again and again. Its columnists wrung their hands about this unhappy prospect, even as their editors seemed to be trying to institutionalize it. I thought their premise was wrongheaded—but I also worried it might be self-fulfilling, given the *Times*'s importance as a journalistic standard-setter. So I wrote a huffy letter to the editor, which the *Times* printed a week or so later, that laid out my argument that the Hart case ought to be seen as exceptional.

To the editor:
I'm the Washington *Post* reporter who put the question to Gary Hart that offended so many *New York Times* columnists. I suspect it offended other folks, too. It's not hard to see why. The question—"Have you ever committed adultery?"—seemed to

turn me, and by extension my profession, into some kind of morals police. That's not a comfortable role for anyone.

Anthony Lewis wrote that I was responsible for the "low point" of news coverage of a story in which "reporters and editors salivated in their zeal to learn all and tell all." William Safire said that I was "demeaning" my profession and that "titillaters" in the press like me needed to be stopped. A. M. Rosenthal, quoted in another newspaper, said he found the question "nauseating."

Let's review the bidding here: Gary Hart chose to run for president and present himself as a happily married man. During the early weeks of his campaign, he also chose to spend some free time in Bimini and Washington with a woman who was not his wife. He did so despite having assured his top campaign staff that, though it was an open secret he'd conducted himself this way in the past, he understood that the fishbowl environs of a front-runner's presidential campaign was no place to engage in such behavior. When the Miami *Herald* broke the story of his relationship with Donna Rice, he criticized the paper's reporting techniques and press ethics generally, said he'd done nothing "immoral," and said he'd always held himself to a "high standard of public and private conduct."

What did Mr. Hart mean by his denial of immoral behavior? What exactly was his "high standard"? Was he telling the truth? Did his past behavior bear on his credibility this time? It seemed to me appropriate, under the circumstances, to ask whether he considered adultery to be immoral (he said he did) and then to ask whether he had ever committed adultery. Mr. Hart chose not to answer the second question—which, of course, was his right.

But what about journalists' rights, and our responsibilities? Your columnists raise questions about proportionality, civility and privacy. But by carrying their arguments to absurdity, they don't grapple with the issue at hand. Mr. Rosenthal advises us that he thinks questions about masturbation are also off limits. Mr. Safire worries that newshounds are now going to start asking questions about impotence. What in heaven's name are these guys talking about? Don't they think that political reporters know better?

It is not the job of a journalist to win plaudits for civility (though it's certainly nicer when we do). Nor is it our job to pry into the most private matters—except when public figures, in conducting or discussing their private affairs publicly, force our hand. Sometimes this job demands that we raise questions we'd rather not ask. Your columnists suggest I broke some kind of gentleman's code in this instance. I say, poppycock. What I did was ask Gary Hart the question he asked for.

After the letter appeared in the *Times,* my mailbox once again filled up with correspondence on the adultery question—this batch mostly from journalists, and almost entirely supportive. My favorite began: "Your letter to *The New York Times* was a classic. It's going in my scrapbook and it ought to be engraved and put up in newsrooms all over America." It was signed, "Heath Meriwether, executive editor, the Miami *Herald.*"

There was just one problem. My question did open a Pandora's box—not as wide as Safire and Rosenthal feared, but wide enough.

Some politicians felt pressed to take immediate defensive action. Two weeks after Hart dropped out, Representative Barney Frank (D–Mass.) announced he was gay. There was no direct connection to adultery or presidential politics. Frank, one of Congress's brightest and most effective liberal members, simply felt vulnerable in the new climate. "There was an increasing media interest in private lives," he said, "... and my guess was that someone was going to write about it, so I told them."*

On the presidential trail, Jesse Jackson, long the subject of womanizing rumors, waged an intense personal lobbying effort in the fall of 1987 to keep the Atlanta *Constitution* from publishing a story about his private life. One of the *Constitution*'s top reporters, Priscilla Painton, had spent weeks sifting through all the rumors of Jackson's liaisons, including some that had previously been published. She interviewed several women with whom Jackson was rumored to have had affairs. "For a while there, Jesse was my alarm clock, waking me up every day at 5:30 a.m. with another phone call to challenge what we were doing," said William Kovach, *Constitution* editor at the time. When Jackson sensed that his personal entreaties might not be enough, he asked a group of black business leaders to

---

*Frank was easily reelected in 1988. In 1989, however, he suffered an acute embarrassment when the Washington *Times* disclosed that he had had a relationship with a male prostitute, who used Frank's Capitol Hill apartment to run a prostitution ring. Frank confirmed the story, pleaded a combination of ignorance and stupidity, invited the House ethics committee to review his conduct and appeared to remain popular in his unusually tolerant congressional district.

fly to Atlanta and appeal to Kovach on his behalf. In the end, the paper printed nothing of a scandalous nature. Kovach said he was never certain that he had any final facts, to use Hugh Sidey's judicious phrase. How much was he influenced by Jackson's lobbying? "He was effective every time we spoke," Kovach said.

Jackson also got protective cover from his wife, Jackie. Shortly after the Hart episode, she scolded a *Life* magazine reporter: "I don't believe in examining sheets. That's a violation of privacy. If my husband has committed adultery, he better not tell me. And you better not go digging into it, because I'm trying to raise a family and won't let you be the one to destroy my family."

Toward the end of the primary campaign, the Jackson press corps became curious about the nature of Jackson's relationship with actress Margot Kidder (Lois Lane in the *Superman* movies), who traveled with the Jackson entourage for a time. The reporters gossiped about it among themselves. But except for the one reference to the "huge swallow of a kiss"[15] Kidder had been observed planting on Jackson, no one ever mentioned it in print or on the air. The closest call came on the night of the California primary, when the victorious Dukakis made a hastily arranged visit to Jackson's Los Angeles hotel suite. Kidder, riding an elevator in the hotel just before Dukakis was due to arrive, casually remarked to an ABC camera crew that happened to be in the same elevator: "I hope Dukakis doesn't go into the bedroom. It's a mess." An ABC producer who heard the remark relayed it to her bosses in New York, who instructed her to ask Jackson about the nature of his relationship with Kidder. She did the next day. Jackson declined to discuss it, and no story aired. For Jackson, at least, the traditional turn-the-other-cheek journalistic standards never budged in 1987–88.

Jack Kemp was another candidate who'd been dogged by unsubstantiated rumors—involving both women and men. "We didn't know whether our strategy would have to be to line up fifteen airline stewardesses to deny one side or twenty-five football players to deny the other side," his campaign chairman, Ed Rollins, joked after the campaign, making light of a scare he took quite seriously at the time. During Reagan's tenure as governor of California, Kemp had been acquainted with a Reagan aide who left state government under the cloud of a scandal centered on a homosexual ring. There was never any suggestion that Kemp had been involved, but the mere fact of his acquaintance had kept rumors alive over the years. After he announced for the presidency, Kemp was asked about homosexuality in a number of interviews, including one that aired on NBC's *The*

Today Show in the fall of 1987. Interviewer Nancy Collins queried him point-blank if he'd ever had any homosexual experiences. He said no, and the story quickly died. ("Not even in camp?" columnist Richard Cohen asked him in jest after the interview aired.)

The first direct casualty of the post-Gary Hart jitters was a potential presidential candidate who never got past the testing-the-waters stage—Ohio Governor Richard Celeste. A month after the Hart affair, the Cleveland *Plain Dealer* printed a page-one story, based on unidentified sources and citing unidentified women, alleging that Celeste had had three extramarital affairs. They had been gossiped about for years in the state capital, but never before reported. The day before the story ran, Celeste had been asked at a press conference if he had a "Gary Hart-type personal problem." He said no. "We at the *Plain Dealer* knew that was not true," the paper's managing editor, Thomas Greer, later wrote. "His blatant lie was tantamount to inviting us to follow him or challenge him." *Plain Dealer* executive editor William J. Woestendiek said that Celeste's denial was "another case of someone arrogantly trying to deceive the public. We feel it's something people have a right to know." Those justifications didn't stem a flood of criticism the paper received not only from readers but from other Ohio newspaper editors, who accused the *Plain Dealer* of writing a flimsy story on the flimsiest of pretenses.[16]

Around the time of the Celeste story, word raced through newsrooms across the country that a story was about to break that George Bush had once had an affair with a woman on his vice-presidential staff, Jane Doe.* For a number of days, all the major national news organizations were getting telephone calls warning them that a competitor was about to go with the Bush-Doe story.

"It was hysteria," recalled Bush campaign manager Lee Atwater, who was also getting flooded with calls. "I've never seen anything like it. The day the rumor hit the Hill, we probably got forty or fifty calls. The next day, it started melting down to the states. By the third day, we'd gotten over five hundred calls—a third from the media, a third from the Hill, a third from the states. We had the favorite game being played of *Time* calling up and saying, 'Well, we heard *Newsweek* is going with it.' Or the Washington *Post* is going with it. Or CBS is going with it. And everybody was manipulating the media. It became clear to me, number one, that no responsible news organization was going to go with it, but, number two, it was a lead-pipe cinch that

_____
*Not her real name.

some mid-level or off-the-wall paper was going to go with it. What you're afraid of then is that everybody else says, 'Oh well, we hate to do this. We didn't want to touch this story. But now it's out and so we've got to put it on the front page.' "*

Atwater and George Bush, Jr., the candidate's oldest son, decided on a preemptive strike. George Jr. called up Howard Fineman, *Newsweek*'s chief political reporter, and vouched for his father's marital fidelity. *Newsweek* reported in a June 29, 1987, "Periscope" item that Bush's oldest son had asked his father "point-blank if he ever committed adultery." After hearing the response, the younger Bush then told *Newsweek:* "The answer to the 'Big A' Question is N-O."

The phone call violated the usual rule of rumor control: denials only give the press a peg to write about the rumor. In this case, it seemed to work out fine—for a time. After the "Periscope" item appeared, the Bush rumor went into a dormancy that lasted fifteen months. But then, less than three weeks before election day, it came back with a vengeance. On Oct. 19, 1988, the stock market plunged forty points in a single hour on the rumor that the Washington *Post* was about to publish a story that Bush had committed adultery. When the Dow Jones News Service sent out a story in mid-afternoon attributing the market's sudden drop to the *Post*'s rumored story, our newsroom was inundated with calls. One editor was called by an acquaintance from the investment firm of Smith Barney who wanted to know if a story was in the works. No, the editor said. "Buy! Buy!" he heard the trader yell. Bradlee, realizing there was money being made and lost on this bad rumor, told a wire-service reporter that the *Post* had no intention of publishing a story. Trading stabilized shortly before closing time.

News organizations faced a dilemma: how to tell their readers and viewers what had happened to the market without spreading an explosive rumor that might affect the upcoming presidential election. The problem was compounded the next day when a mid-level Dukakis staffer, Donna Brazile, told the campaign press traveling with Dukakis that Bush should "fess up" to his affair. She said: "I wasn't on the stock market yesterday but I understand they got a little concerned that George was going to the White House with somebody other than Barbara." Within hours, the Dukakis campaign disavowed her comments, Brazile was forced to resign and Dukakis personally

*Even in the midst of the scare, there was some gallows humor in the Bush headquarters. "There were some of us who thought, given his reputation as a wimp, that the rumor might actually help," campaign press secretary Sheila Tate later quipped.

apologized to Bush. Some in the press thought Brazile's comments had been scripted by high-level Dukakis staffers to force the Bush rumor into print; others believed she really had gone off the reservation. Either way, the problem recurred: how to report the story—easily the most newsworthy thing that happened on the campaign trail that day—without also spreading the rumor?

Gingerly. CBS anchor Dan Rather reported that the rumors that had caused tremors on the stock market concerned "Bush's personal life." *The New York Times* wrote that the rumored article was said to be "damaging to the presidential campaign of Vice President Bush." *USA Today* was more direct, saying the rumored article would allege that "Bush had carried on an extramarital affair." No woman was named. And the story died a quick death.

Later that week, when Bush spoke at an Italian-American dinner in Washington, a dozen protesters unfurled a half-block-long banner on the sidewalk across Connecticut Avenue from the Washington Hilton Hotel. JANE DOE, it read. They spent the evening chanting through bullhorns: "George loves Jane. Jane loves George. Ladies and gentlemen, the Vice President of the United States is a hypocrite! Ladies and gentlemen, the Vice President of the United States has a mistress! George loves Jane. Jane loves George." I covered that speech and interviewed the protesters, as did several other reporters. I didn't write a single word. Neither did anyone else.

What did so many people think they knew about George Bush's private life? And why was the same press that had been so gung-ho with Hart so gentle with Bush?

In mid-October, a week before Wall Street's brief palpitation, *LA Weekly,* an alternative paper in Los Angeles, had published an article spelling out rumors about Bush that had been kicking around Washington for years. It claimed that Bush had had several affairs, the most serious with Doe, 56, who had worked for him since he served as United States envoy to China in the mid-1970s. There was no substantiation, nor were the sources of the rumors identified. The article, titled GEORGE BUSH, LOVERBOY, consisted of a series of unattributed second- or third-hand accounts of the way the two allegedly behaved in each other's company; of Bush's alleged interventions on Doe's behalf when her prickly personality caused turf battles in the office; of her allegedly open boasts of their mutual love. The author of the piece, free-lancer Richard Ryan, had shopped the information around—to *Post* reporter Walter Pincus, among others—before the *Weekly* article came out. Pincus and Bob Woodward had already tried to track down the same rumors when they were writing a five-part profile of Bush that had run in August 1988. They had spoken to many Bush friends and associates who said they were untrue. They had spoken to others who said they couldn't attest to their truth or falsity. They never put any questions directly to either Bush or Doe. "What were we going to ask them?" Pincus said. They had no final facts. And so, in keeping with the honorable standards of the craft, the *Post* printed nothing.*

With just a few exceptions, everyone else held the line on the most sensational political rumor of 1988. After the *LA Weekly* article appeared, two British tabloids, the *Evening Standard* and *Today*, bannered the rumor across their front pages. The closest thing in this country to a Fleet Street tabloid—the New York *Post*—ran a version of the *LA Weekly* account. Ryan didn't do much to enhance his credibility when he told the *National Enquirer* some weeks later that his sources were a journalist and a film director and that when you "add their rumors to all the other rumors, you know it's worth writing—even if their statements don't prove anything. . . . Anyway, all you have to do is look at a picture of Barbara and you know he would cheat on her."

Can anyone find a pattern in this zigzagging track record of reporting the private lives of public officials? Can anyone make sense of the rules of the road when they seem to have changed with every story?

The only candid place to begin is with an acknowledgment that journalism has no rules in this area. We're too unwieldy, untidy and plural a profession for rules. We aren't a profession at all—we're a craft—in part because of our aversion to rules. They strike most of us as an invitation to censorship. What we do have is a generally agreed-upon set of standard practices. It is the product of our best collective judgment, as shaped by the mores of the culture we report. For decades, these journalistic norms have held that the private life of a public official should remain private unless it impinges on public performance. Matters of health and wealth have long been treated as fair game, because they have a clear and present potential to affect public performance. Matters of sexual behavior have always been considered off limits.

*Well, nearly nothing. Even institutions of higher journalism have naughty streaks. The following item appeared in the *Post* on January 18, 1989, two days before Bush's inauguration: "Jane Doe, who has served President-elect Bush in a variety of positions, most recently running the vice-presidential Senate offices, is expected to be named deputy chief of protocol in the new administration, sources said yesterday."

The Hart case seemed to shatter that norm. For a time, the stars that guided our behavior were disturbingly in motion. The journalism craft was divided. For every *New York Times* columnist crying foul, there was a Michael Gartner, then the editor of the Louisville *Courier-Journal,* now the president of NBC News, shouting: Bravo! "I think it's one of democracy's finest hours," Gartner said of the Hart coverage. To candidates who feared that overzealous reporters were taking out a hunting license on privacy, he advised on *Nightline:* "If you don't want it in the paper, don't let it happen."

For a time, the forces of Know-Everythingism held sway. In 1987, the network newscasts devoted 132 minutes of coverage to Gary Hart and just 32 minutes to the presidential hopeful it deemed to be the next most newsworthy—Pat Robertson. Bush got 28 minutes of coverage in 1987; Dukakis, 20 minutes. Predictably, public discomfort with sensationalism eventually set in, and the norms of coverage edged back toward traditional restraint—though not always in a straight line, as Richard Celeste can attest. They never came all the way back, either. Nor could they, in a political culture which has become so steeped in personality, and in a popular culture which has gotten so much more frank and open about sex.

Even in this let-it-all-hang-out environment, however, most journalists have retained a healthy reluctance to peer into the innermost details of a politician's private life—witness their refusal to go hard after the Jackson and Bush rumors; or their willingness to let the Senate take the lead role in making public John Tower's private indiscretions. Journalists (and politicians) overcome this reluctance only when public figures leave them no choice. The tipping point is not precisely definable, and it shifts as society's standards shift. In the late 1980s, a shift toward more intrusive scrutiny was underway— not just in this country but worldwide. In 1989 alone, heads of state in nations as different from ours (and each other) as Greece and Japan were voted out of office in part because of extramarital affairs. That same year, no fewer than four members of the U.S. House of Representatives were being investigated by the House ethics committee for alleged sexual misconduct.

Once we stipulate that there are no easy or absolute rules governing journalistic behavior in these areas, are there any broad guidelines we can agree on? Several, I think. The first is that politicians are entitled to a realm of privacy. The next is that their sex life is presumed to fall within that realm. The next is that if, in the conduct of their sex life or any other aspect of their private life, they behave without discretion, all bets are off. In this formulation, being recklessly promiscuous is different from being quietly adulterous. If that is a standard which winks at discreet hypocrisies, so be it. A certain amount of hypocrisy is indispensable to social comity.

The standards I have put forth here are not new; they've been more or less in place for two decades. The precedent-setting incident in this area of journalism involved Wilbur Mills, not Gary Hart. For years, it had been an open but unreported secret that Mills, the powerful chairman of the House Ways and Means Committee, was a drunk and a womanizer. Then, at 2 a.m. one morning in the fall of 1974, the U.S. Park Police had to fish his date for the evening, a stripper named Fanne Fox, out of Washington's Tidal Basin. Mills was at the wheel of his car a few yards away, drunk and bleeding from scratches on his face. The press reported it and Mills's career was over.

Bimini was Gary Hart's Tidal Basin. Like Mills, he took too literally the invitation in the old Beatles song: "Why Don't We Do It In the Road?"

Do, if you like. Just don't expect the rest of us not to watch.

HART DID NOT see his downfall that way. In the withdrawal speech he gave in Denver on May 8, 1987—just five days after the Miami *Herald* story ran—he said he'd been stoned to death for apoliticism, not adultery. "I haven't based my campaigns on support of politicians, even though some of them are my very best friends," Hart said. "[As a result] I've become some kind of rare bird, some extraordinary creature that has to be dissected by those who analyze politics to find out what makes him tick. Well, I resist that. And so then I become cool and aloof, or elusive or enigmatic or whatnot. And then the more people want to talk about me, the more I resist it, and so on. And soon it gets to be like the cat chasing its tail . . . "

He went on to condemn a presidential selection process that "reduces the press of this nation to hunters and presidential candidates to being hunted, that has reporters in bushes, false and inaccurate stories printed, photographers peeking in our windows, swarms of helicopters hovering over our roof and my very strong wife close to tears because she can't even get out of her own house at night without being harassed.

"And then, after all that, ponderous pundits wonder in mock

seriousness why some of the best people in this country choose not to run for high office."

Hart's criticism was worth taking seriously; Hart, at the time, wasn't. He was still protesting his complete innocence. The gracelessness of his exit—he offered neither thanks nor apologies to any of his supporters—reminded a lot of people of the infamous "last press conference" that Richard Nixon had given after losing the California gubernatorial race in 1962. The comparison wasn't lost on Nixon, who wrote Hart a fan letter:

> Dear Gary: This is just a line to tell you that I thought you handled a very difficult situation uncommonly well.... What impressed me most was your refusal to quit fighting for what you believe. In politics and every other walk of life, there are more losers than winners. After all, there can be only one number one; all the rest are losers. Those who don't win must be given not just sympathy, which is in essence a degrading sentiment for whoever is its recipient, but the inspiration to fight on.
>
> You did exactly that. What you said about the media needed to be said. They demand the right to ruthlessly question the ethics of everyone else. But when anyone else dares to question their ethics, they hide behind the shield of freedom of speech. They refuse to make the distinction that philosophers throughout the centuries have made between freedom and license.
>
> We have always been political opponents and never personal friends as John Kennedy and I were when we served together on the House Labor Committee forty years ago. But as an old politician speaking to a young politician who has many good years ahead, may I say that you and your family have my respect and best wishes.

The good years Nixon envisioned for Hart certainly weren't in 1987 or 1988. A few days after his withdrawal, the *National Enquirer* ran a picture of him with Donna Rice aboard his lap, a *Monkey Business* T-shirt on his chest and a leering look in his eye. The scandal had found its level, and Hart was reduced to a farcical figure. One reason his fall had come with such breathtaking velocity was that no one had spoken up for him outside his small army of irregulars and camp followers. Now, even kindred spirits began taking potshots. Former Louisiana Governor Edwin W. Edwards, a rogue who reveled in his reputation as a ladies' man, couldn't resist offering an epicurean's critique of his friend Broadhurst's influence on the beleaguered Hart. "Billy was more careful," said Edwards, "when he was pimping for me."

Hart retreated into what he would later call an "awful" exile in Troublesome Gulch. But he did not lose his grip on the public's imagination. A Gallup poll published in *The Nation* in the summer of 1987 showed he was still the Democrats' leading choice for President. In early September, Hart appeared on *Nightline* to scotch rumors that he was getting back in the race. He apologized profusely for his conduct, confessed that during his twenty-nine-year marriage, including two separations, he had not been "absolutely faithful" to his wife, but argued that he had not been "running for sainthood." He admonished the press: "Never ask another candidate that question [about adultery]. It isn't anyone else's business." He declined to go over the disputed details of his weekends with Rice. Of the *Enquirer* photograph, he said with a shrug: "She dropped into my lap. I was embarrassed. I chose not to drop her off, and the picture was taken. . . . I was not on my watch. I let my guard down."

After spending an hour defending his right to privacy, Hart closed the show by making a personal apology to his son and daughter, saying "how sorry I am for letting them down." Did this intensely private man really need to conduct an intimate piece of family business before an audience of millions? Or had he chosen to invade his own privacy—for some good political theater?

Two and a half months later, on December 15, 1987, Hart rejoined the race. His apoliticism was in full flower. "This will not be like any campaign you've ever seen," he vowed on the steps of the state capitol in Concord, New Hampshire, "because I'm going directly to the people. I don't have a national headquarters or staff. I don't have any money. I don't have pollsters or consultants or media advisers or political endorsements. I have the power of ideas and I can govern this country. Let's let the people decide. I'm back in the race."

For a dizzy, disorienting moment, he was also back atop the Democratic field. The national polls taken immediately after his reentry had him with a two-to-one lead over his nearest rival, though the numbers appeared to be measuring empathy for an aggrieved outsider rather than support for a presidential candidate.

The Washington pundits howled that Hart was being selfish, cynical, narcissistic. "This proves you really can screw your brains out," was the insider put-down of choice. But to the rest of the country, noted political analyst William Schneider, "Hart's message is: 'Screw you. Screw the press. Screw the candidates. Screw the party.' And there's a constituency for that." Hart understood, too, there was political capital to be made from the unease everyone felt at having been eyewitnesses to his humiliation. "Are we big enough to look past the titillating details and see the big picture, the power of ideas," Garry Wills wrote of Hart's implicit challenge to the voters. "Nothing assuages the sense of being wrong like the compensating assurance of being wronged," Wills continued. "No matter what they did, the Harts felt they should not have been spied on. Whatever lies they told were an attempt at defending themselves from such unjustified spying. If their actions were wrong, so were those of the people watching the actions; and the only recompense the public can make is to stop watching and forget what it saw when it was watching."[17]

The nation's comedians wouldn't forget. "In, out, in, out—isn't that what got him in trouble in the first place?" asked David Letterman. Johnny Carson said Hart was "like Carmen Miranda asking people not to notice she's dancing with a bowl of fruit on her head." Political cartoonists took to caricaturing him in boxer shorts. "Our job has always been to point out that the king has no clothes," said David Wiley Miller, a cartoonist with the San Francisco Examiner. "With Gary Hart, it's just more appropriate."

Hart forged ahead, past the jokes. He offered something more compelling: the psychodrama of a man who seemed to be running for President as therapy for his personal and family problems. He returned with his wife at his side, their marriage tempered by adversity. "I have never wanted my husband to be President," Lee Hart said in Portland, Maine, on their second day back out on the trail together. "But I have always put my personal feelings aside, because I believe . . . he has something to offer this country. That support is deeper today that it has ever been. . . . As a family we have experienced much pain in the past several months . . . [but] we are well and strong today."

Hart broke down and wept during two different interviews he gave upon his return. "Not for me, but my country," he told Time. The man who once had said he saw politics as "an interim period in my life" was back in the race because his forced sabbatical had been "awful, just awful," he said on 60 Minutes. "I let 'em down," he said of his supporters, friends and family. "I let 'em down. That's an awful burden to bear." But even worse, he told CBS's Ed Bradley, was the prospect of living out the rest of his life haunted by the

" THE BABY, GARY... JUST THE BABY ! "

suspicion that he'd withdrawn prematurely. "See, now I will know. Otherwise I would never have known. It's that simple. How would you like to go for the rest of your life having a major unanswered question."

In his first few weeks back, he granted press access only to those who agreed to talk to him on his terms. He used the media's massive interest in him as a forum to run against the media—and the media eagerly accommodated. The week he returned, thirty-nine and a half of the fifty minutes of political coverage that aired on network newscasts were devoted to Hart.

But his crowds, sizable at first, began to thin out as the novelty of his reentry wore off. His speeches lacked resonance and bite. Aside from his complaint about the way the press had treated him, he didn't have much to say that was different from anyone else. The absence of a campaign staff quickly began to grate on both the candidate and the press; chores as rudimentary as planning and keeping a schedule became a daily adventure. Media fascination with his rebirth soon gave way to hostility. At a mid-January debate in Iowa, Hart's jaw tightened when he was asked by moderator James Gannon about adultery and judgment. In a debate the next week in New Hampshire, he flushed with anger and indignation when moderator John Chancellor introduced him by noting whimsically that his return had raised the musical question "Will you still love me in December as you did in May?"

Within a few weeks, Hart was once again verging on paranoia. "Why are my personal life, my contributor list, my campaign finances endlessly scrutinized and not those of the other candidates?" he asked in a newspaper interview in late January. (Stuart Karl, one of his key 1984 financial backers, would soon be convicted of breaking the federal election-financing laws. The story of that scandal was first published by the Miami *Herald.*) "I wonder and have wondered for a long time. And I don't know the answer. My guess is that it's mostly a combination of the fact that I'm independent and don't always play by the rules. I've always been a reformer and I don't make deals or arrangements with powerful interests and I don't take their money."

On February 8, 1988, the night of the Iowa caucuses, Hart got his answers—not to those questions, perhaps, but to the ones he said would haunt him for the rest of his life. He ran dead last in the Democratic field. He received less than 1 percent of the vote.

He remained in the race for another five weeks. His campaign days often consisted of nothing more than one speech at a college campus. At night he would go to the movies or have a leisurely dinner with his lone aide, Dennis Walto, who was under investigation by the Federal Election Commission for campaign spending violations. Lee Hart quit the campaign trail and headed back to Troublesome Gulch, exhausted. The camera crews disappeared; so, at Hart's insistence, did the expensive Secret Service protection.

At times he was lighthearted in those last days, at times bitter. "All our heroes are dead," he told *New York Times* reporter Maureen Dowd in early March. "John is dead. Bobby is dead. And I'm dead—walking dead. . . .

"I'm not a candidate, I'm a nonperson," he continued. "Can I be ignored in a smaller field? If it gets down to just two of us—me and Michael Dukakis—it would be kind of awkward if everyone kept ignoring me, wouldn't it?"

He never got there. The end had already come for Hart—a month before, in Iowa. On the night of the caucuses, he had shown up at a television studio in Des Moines for a prearranged interview. Once the returns started to come in, the producer thanked him but said they wouldn't be needing an interview after all.

And that was that. The media, which had helped create him and helped destroy him, at last were able to ignore him.

CHAPTER FOUR

Exit Joe Biden and John Sasso

O N THE FRIDAY before Labor Day 1987, Maureen Dowd of *The New York Times* telephoned John Sasso, Michael Dukakis' campaign manager. Her purpose was to gather material for a profile she was writing about Democratic pollster Patrick Caddell. But like many reporter/source conversations that begin with a specific focus, this one soon meandered into a casual exchange of news, gossip and shoptalk. In passing, Dowd brought up a news item that had recently caught her eye.

"Isn't it weird," she wondered aloud, "that Joe Biden is going around the country quoting Neil Kinnock?"

It puzzled Dowd that an American politician would borrow the words of a British Labour leader, especially one who'd just been soundly beaten in his country's national elections. She was planning to do a story about it, in the gently mocking style that's a forte of hers. The piece she envisioned would run "somewhere back around page 27" of her newspaper, land with the force of a soft elbow to Biden's ribs and be forgotten in a day or two. It was an amusing feature. It was no blockbuster.

Her question delighted Sasso. He was beginning to worry about Biden. The attractive young Delaware senator was staking a claim as the generational leader of the nation's 76 million baby boomers. He was the best stump speaker in the Democratic field, outside of Jesse Jackson. He'd overcome a slow start and was gaining fast in Iowa, where the first votes would be cast in five months. Worse—from Sasso's point of view—Biden was about to harvest precious minutes

of national network television exposure by chairing the Senate Judiciary Committee hearings on President Reagan's nomination of
Judge Robert Bork to the Supreme Court. If Bork were to be defeated,
Biden could become a hero to Iowa's likely Democratic caucus-goers—
who, according to private polls, opposed the Bork nomination by a
three-to-one margin. And if Biden were to ride that momentum to a
win in Iowa, then—who knows?

It was a good time for a brushback pitch, Sasso figured. "When
Maureen raised the question, I leaped at it," he would later recall. "I
had been looking for a way to get someone to write about it."

Yes, he told Dowd, not only was it odd that Biden had been
quoting an autobiographical passage from a Kinnock television
commercial, but did she realize he'd done it without attribution in a
recent debate in Iowa?

No, Dowd said, she hadn't known that. Did Sasso know how she
could get her hands on a transcript or tape of the debate?

I'll send you one if you'll keep my name out of it, Sasso said. This
was a routine precaution. Sasso felt he was doing nothing under-
handed, but he had a hunch the "goo-goos" (good-government types)
who attended Iowa's caucuses might not see it that way. He also
wasn't sure about his boss. Dukakis was known in his home state
as "Michael the Good." During his first term as governor, he infuriated state legislators by taking away their low-numbered car license
plates. He drove campaign contributors crazy by discriminating
against them in parceling out government jobs and contracts. In
every race he ever ran—including, now, the one for president—
he personally interviewed everyone who worked on his campaign
to tell them that he wouldn't tolerate cheap shots, shortcuts or
dirty tricks.

So Sasso needed cover, and Dowd was only too happy to oblige. As
she saw it, there would be no need to identify him anyway. He hadn't
planted a story; he was simply giving her some publicly available
information, in response to her query. Yes, he'd also steered her
in a certain direction—as sources often do. But by any reasonable
accounting, this story had germinated with her, not him. It wouldn't
need attribution.

And so a deal was struck—a routine, mutually beneficial reporter/
source transaction, the kind that's made hundreds of times a day
in newsrooms, government offices and campaign storefronts. The
stakes of this one did not seem especially high; the perils were
virtually nil. The story tickled Dowd and Sasso, but neither pre-

tended that anything much would come of it. "It was a tweak," Dowd said.

In the political cauldron of 1987, even the tweaks were lethal. Biden was gone from the race eleven days after Dowd's story appeared. Sasso succumbed after eighteen days. For several weeks after that, Dukakis staggered around the country like a man who'd been punched in the gut. Sasso, then forty, had been more than a campaign manager to him—he was a confidant, coach, strategist, alter ego. "When Dukakis lost him," said one campaign insider, "it was like losing the left lobe of his brain." It was Sasso who had cajoled Dukakis into raising his sights beyond Massachusetts and toward the Oval Office. It was he who'd talked Dukakis up to press and pols around the country; it was he who'd drafted the feasibility memos and held weekly after-hours campaign-planning sessions in the Massachusetts Statehouse, where he served as Dukakis' chief of staff. When it came to the presidency, more of the fire seemed to be in Sasso's belly than in Dukakis'.

In September 1988, eleven months after he was forced to leave the campaign for splicing together and circulating the Biden–Kinnock videotape, Sasso was brought back by a despondent Dukakis, whose presidential hopes by then were in a free fall. It was too late. Dukakis lost the presidency in the summer of 1988, not in the fall. He was done in by a provincialism that made him underestimate the symbolic force of the soft-on-crime/weak-on-defense/fuzzy-on-patriotism broadsides thrown at him. Had Sasso been around when the attacks started landing that summer—with his sharper political instincts and his unique ability to goad his reluctant warrior into battle— might the campaign have played out differently? It's one of the few interesting "what if's" of 1988.

Dowd, meantime, was horror-struck by the carnage she had wrought. She spent months wondering whether to get out of journalism. "I felt sick every day that Sasso was out of the campaign," she said. "When a source loses his job because of a story you wrote, it's about the worst thing that can happen to a reporter." Her feelings about Biden were more complicated. Like everyone else, she was astonished that her story triggered a chain of events that drove him from the race. "It was like seeing a loose thread on someone's jacket," she said. "When you pull it, you don't expect the whole thing to unravel." Over time, however, she came to feel the process had played out with a certain rough justice. "It seemed to me that Biden had lost track of who he was," she said. "He had lost track of what politics was about. He had a reputation as a great orator, which he cared about very much—

maybe too much. It sometimes seemed as if he was only in it for the applause lines. To keep those applause lines coming, he was willing to go to great lengths—even to the point of adopting another man's personality."

For all that, it still pained her to watch Biden's candidacy vaporize. "My dad was a cop," said Dowd, who, like Biden, grew up in a middle-class Irish Catholic family. "He once killed a man. He couldn't eat for a month afterward. That's what it felt like."

It felt worse for Biden.

In medieval times, people accused of crimes were forced to grab a red-hot iron or thrust a limb into boiling water. If the burns didn't heal within three days, they were judged guilty. This was known as trial by ordeal. Biden, like Hart before him, was subjected to its modern-day equivalent—trial by media ordeal.

It generally works this way: a gaffe, a misstatement, a lie, a lapse of judgment or behavior is seized upon by the media as a symbol of some larger, disqualifying flaw of character. Reporters begin rifling through the subject's closets for supporting evidence. Off balance and under great strain, the subject holds a press conference. He apologizes for some minor transgression in the hope of taking the edge off the chase, but he proclaims his basic decency and appeals for understanding from a fair-minded public. Ofttimes, he also attacks the press. The voters soak this all up the way aficionados watch a bullfight. They know everyone's lines and moves by heart; this is a spectacle they've seen over and over for twenty years. Whatever else it may be, it's become a form of popular entertainment. But it's also real life, and the voters understand they have a role to play. At some point, like Romans in the Colosseum, they will have to point their thumbs up or down. So they gauge whether or not the press is being fair. And they watch intently to see how the subject is handling the stress. They are forgiving by nature, and the recovery is frequently of greater interest to them than the transgression. Grace under pressure—or the absence of it—often becomes the spine of the drama, while the underlying offense becomes subsidiary.

These trials play out at maximum speed and cruelest efficiency when the triggering offense lands atop a preexisting set of doubts. Biden's aping of Kinnock was not an inherently big story, but it was a richly symbolic one. It gave the press a chance to disgorge its private judgment about Biden—that he was an attractive but shallow man. There's a long tradition here. When George Romney said he'd been brainwashed in Vietnam in 1968, when Edmund Muskie wept (or appeared to weep) defending his wife in 1972, when President Ford prematurely liberated Eastern Europe during a debate with Jimmy Carter in 1976, when Gary Hart danced too close to the flame with Donna Rice in 1987, the press plunged into explorations of the frailties of these presidential hopefuls as well.

Sometimes it doesn't matter what the press does or thinks: the burns heal, anyway. During the 1976 Democratic primaries, the press jumped on Jimmy Carter's comments about preserving the "ethnic purity" of neighborhoods. But Martin Luther ("Daddy") King, Sr., and other civil rights leaders said these were not the sentiments of a racist, and the momentary crisis passed. In 1980, Ronald Reagan's most memorable ad-lib—"I paid for this microphone" —was lifted straight from the movies (*State of the Union*); the details of his biography were embellished; and his encounters with fact were often befuddled, accidental or adversarial. The press pointed much of this out. None of it seemed to matter. Faced with a choice between Reagan and the out-of-favor Carter, the voters concluded that Reagan's ideology was strongly felt and his convictions sincere. Everything else was detail.

When they are functioning well, these trials unfold according to a distribution of responsibility that is both efficient and democratic. Unlike the general public, reporters have a chance to observe politicians at close range over a long haul. Like scouts in baseball, they form a "book" on the men who would be President. Many of their judgments are subjective, and this limits the interest of their readers, who place more faith in observable events and episodes. So the reporters lie in wait for some symbolic episode to come along—a gaffe, a flap, a lie—and then they empty out their notebooks to an audience that, at this newsworthy moment, is at last ready to pay attention. Now comes the democratic part: the voters can accept the judgment and let the story run, or overrule it and let the subject survive.

The problem with this model is a problem endemic to many democratic processes—there lies within it an invitation to excess. Competitive pressures and the pack mentality of reporters combine to produce coverage that is often more a feeding frenzy than a thoughtful examination of character. Perspective is lost; mistakes and misjudgments are made; nuance and subtlety and complication are chucked overboard. In theory, whenever this happens the voters should make the offenders in the media pay a price in lost credibility, lost readership, lost viewership. But that's not the way it works. The longer the spectators stay in the Colosseum, the more contempt they come to have for the accused, the accusers and the trial itself. A pox-on-all-their-houses mentality sets in. They soak up the action more for the entertainment than for the matter to be adjudicated, for their stake in those matters is low. They grow hardened and chronically cynical, like the disgruntled shopper in the story that Emanuel Celler, the late Brooklyn congressman, used to tell. She inspects the wing of a chicken she's about to buy and fires a look of disgust at her butcher. She pokes the thigh and groans. She examines the breast and announces, "Feh." The butcher looks at her, droopy-eyed. "Lady," he finally says, "tell me: could you stand that kind of inspection?"

In 1987, there were a couple of new wrinkles in the process that exacerbated its worst tendencies. The most important was timing. In the past, gaffes tended to occur in the heat of a campaign, when voters already had fully formed impressions of the candidates, and thus had a basis for judging whether the unsparing portraits drawn by the press were valid or not. But in 1987, the media ordeals kicked in long before the voters were ready to pay sustained attention to presidential politics. The campaigning had begun earlier than ever, and there was no "spring training" where the candidates could work out the kinks. And so, when the inevitable accidents happened, and when men like Hart and Biden had to stand in the dock of public opinion, they stood naked. Was Biden more than the sum of the lines he'd been fed? The public couldn't know. Their knowledge of him was minimal, their investment nil.

A year later, something similar happened to Senator Dan Quayle. He was thrown into a trial by ordeal on the very day he was introduced to the American public as the freshly minted Republican vice-presidential nominee. Once again, the voters had no prior knowledge. Once again, they resented the mean-spirited press coverage. Once again, they didn't like what they saw of the candidate either. While some of the press attacks misfired, the basic indictment against Quayle stuck: he was judged by a jury of the American people to be a lightweight. But he survived, for one simple reason. He had a benefactor in George Bush, of whom the voters by then had considerable knowledge, and in whom they had a heavy investment.

Biden and Hart had no such support structure. They were media-age candidates who believed their path to the Oval Office lay in communication skills and personal attractiveness, not in party support or institutional backing or ideological purity. This was the other wrinkle that made these trials so brutal. The nominating process is rigged to attract go-it-aloners, who are the most defenseless when trouble comes. "No one from the auto workers' union was saying, 'Joe Biden is a friend of ours, and we're putting these charges behind us because we need him,'" observed Adam Clymer, political editor of *The New York Times*. All he had were his family and a cadre of friends and political supporters. They may have been loving and loyal, but as character witnesses, they were not inherently credible. "All we could do was sit there and watch the media create a man we didn't know," said Thomas Vallely, a Biden aide. "And there was nothing we could do to stop it."

Biden was bled out of the race by a thousand small cuts. Dowd's was the first. On September 12, 1987, her piece appeared on page 1 of the *Times*—twenty-six pages ahead of her imagination. It ran beneath side-by-side pictures of Biden and Kinnock, with their faces frozen in similar open-mouthed shouts, and below a headline that read: BIDEN'S DEBATE FINALE: AN ECHO FROM ABROAD. The "soft lead" and horizontal layout on the bottom of the page framed the piece as a feature. It had bite, though. The story began:

> The Neil Kinnock commercial did not lead to an electoral success last May in Britain, but the 10-minute spot of the Labour party leader's passionate speeches, against a cool soundtrack of Brahms, raised his approval rating by 19 points and became an instant classic.
>
> On this side of the Atlantic, many Presidential campaign strategists of both parties greatly admired the way it portrayed Kinnock, who subsequently lost to Prime Minister Margaret Thatcher, as a man of character. Senator Joseph R. Biden, Jr. of Delaware, a Democratic hopeful, was particularly taken with it.
>
> So taken, in fact, that he lifted Mr. Kinnock's closing speech with phrases, gestures and lyrical Welsh syntax intact for his own closing speech at a debate at the Iowa State Fair on Aug. 23—without crediting Kinnock.
>
> In the commercial, the Briton began: "Why am I the first Kinnock in a thousand generations to be able to get to university?" Then, pointing to his wife, in the audience, he continued: "Why is Glenys the first woman in her family in a thousand

generations to be able to get to university? Was it because all our predecessors were thick?"

Senator Biden began his remarks by saying the idea had come to him spontaneously on the way to the debate. "I started thinking as I was coming over here, why is it that Joe Biden is the first in his family ever to go to a university?" he said. Then, pointing to his wife, he continued: "Why is it that my wife, who is sitting out there in the audience, is the first in her family to ever go to college? Is it because our fathers and mothers were not bright? Is it because I'm the first Biden in a thousand generations to get a college and a graduate degree that I was smarter than the rest?"

In his speech, Mr. Kinnock, an orator of great eloquence, rhetorically asked why his ancestors, Welsh coal miners, did not get ahead as fast as he. "Did they lack talent?" he asked in his lilting rhythm. "Those people who could sing and play and recite and write poetry? Those people who could make wonderful, beautiful things with their hands? Those people who could dream dreams, see visions? Why didn't they get it? Was it because they were weak? Those people who could work eight hours underground and then come up and play football? Weak?"

Senator Biden's Irish relations, it would seem, were similar, though they seemed to stay underground longer.

"Those same people who read and wrote poetry and taught me how to sing verse?" continued Mr. Biden, whose father was a Chevrolet dealer in Wilmington. "Is it because they didn't work hard — my ancestors, who worked in the coal mines of Northeast Pennsylvania and would come up after twelve hours and play football for four hours?"

Of course, the football Mr. Biden's forebears played may not have been the same game that the British refer to as football, but the Biden clan apparently was stymied by the same social forces that kept down the Kinnocks.

As Mr. Kinnock concluded, clenching both fists: "Does anybody really think that they didn't have what we have because they didn't have the talent or the strength or the endurance or the commitment? Of course not. It was because there was no platform upon which they could stand."

As Mr. Biden concluded, clenching one fist: "No, it's not because they weren't as smart. It's not because they didn't work as hard. It's because they didn't have a platform upon which to stand."

Further down in her story, Dowd noted that Biden had properly attributed the Kinnock passage on other occasions and characterized his failure to do so at the Iowa debate as an unintentional lapse. "He's under a huge amount of pressure [preparing for the Bork hearings]," Dowd quoted one unidentified Biden adviser. "He didn't even know what he said. He was just on automatic pilot." This was an unfortunate line of defense, for it seemed to concede one of Biden's perceived character weaknesses: that his mouth sometimes engaged before his brain. But the toughest line in the Dowd piece was probably the last: she closed by noting that Biden's staff was "at a loss" to come up with the name of any Biden ancestor who was a coal miner (one had been a mining engineer).

Dowd assumed she had written an exclusive. To her surprise, the same Saturday morning her story appeared, a similar one ran in the Des Moines *Register*. It was written by David Yepsen, the *Register*'s lead political reporter and an institution unto himself. In the year leading up to the Iowa caucuses, Yepsen was arguably the most influential beat political reporter in the country. His newspaper blankets its state, in both circulation and influence, as few do anywhere in the country. It takes justifiable pride in its political coverage, and it treats the presidential caucuses as an occasion to strut its stuff—both to its readers and to the visiting firemen from the national press. When out-of-state reporters ventured into Iowa on early scouting missions, their first stop was often a meal with Yepsen. He'd dish out the latest Iowa form charts; they'd feed his appetite for Washington political gossip. Even among nominal competitors on the political beat, this kind of cross-pollination goes on all the time. In 1987, it was institutionalized by a new trade publication called *Hotline,* a daily compendium of all the political reportage on television and in major newspapers around the country. *Hotline* would land on subscribers' desks or into their laptop computers by eleven o'clock each morning, to be inhaled like a junkie's fix. Many of its subscribers were themselves news organizations, eager to know what their competitors were saying and writing, and grateful for such an efficient means of monitoring it. In 1987, no reporter's work was cited more often in *Hotline* than Yepsen's. If you planted a story with him, you knew it would travel the political universe at the speed of light.

After his telephone conversation with Dowd, Sasso had instructed a volunteer in the Boston campaign headquarters to splice together a tape of Biden's Iowa speech and the Kinnock commercial. Over the Labor Day weekend, he showed it to Paul Tully, his political director, and Jack Corrigan, his field director. They agreed that it was a splendid political hit and that the similarities in gesture and intonation were much more vivid on videotape than in a transcript. Tully happened to be headed out to Iowa the next day for one of his regular field trips. He stuffed a copy of the tape into his briefcase. If the campaign was going to send Maureen Dowd a copy, he figured, why not also give Yepsen one?

The morning after Labor Day, Tully and Yepsen had breakfast at the Savery Hotel coffee shop in Des Moines. Toward the end of the meal, Tully reached into his briefcase. "I have something I think you'll want to see," he said, "but I don't want anybody to know where you got it."

Yepsen was among the many reporters* who'd missed the fact that Biden had lifted from Kinnock at the Iowa State Fair debate two weeks earlier. He barely knew who Kinnock was; he knew nothing of his campaign commercial. When he watched the tape Tully gave him on a VCR in his office later in the day, he was amused. "I thought it might be a funny column item or some kind of sidebar story," he later recalled. He described the tape, in passing, to a few editors and colleagues at the *Register*. He telephoned Biden's Iowa press secretary, who told Yepsen that Biden had properly cited Kinnock in other recent speeches in Iowa. Yepsen asked if he could produce an audio of those speeches. The press secretary said he'd get back to him. This all happened over a period of several days. There was no big hurry. It was no big story.

Late that Friday night, an editor at the *Register* noticed the Dowd piece on the Times News Service wire. It would be appearing in the *Times* the next morning. At the *Register,* as at most reputable newspapers, it's a matter of institutional pride not to run another news organization's story about something that happened in your own front yard. The editor called Yepsen at home and described the *Times* piece to him. He drove back to the office late that night and put together his own piece. It ran on page 2 as a straight news story rather than a feature. Unlike Dowd's story, Yepsen's addressed the question of attribution. In his fourth paragraph, he wrote: "An aide to one of Biden's opponents, who spoke on the condition that he would not be named, is circulating a videotape showing a Kinnock

*So was I.

commercial followed by Biden's closing remarks using some of the same lines." Yepsen referred to the tape as an "attack video," a vivid coinage that was quickly picked up by the rest of the media.

There was reason for the differences in approach between the two stories. Unlike Dowd, Yepsen had been the recipient of an unsolicited tip. Unlike Dowd, he also knew that at least one other paper—the *Times*—had gotten the same video. From his vantage point, this was a premeditated and apparently systematic effort by one campaign to undermine another. That didn't mean the substance of the attack wasn't newsworthy—he made it the lead of his piece. It merely meant the source of the attack was an element of the story as well. And so he included it, within the constraints imposed by his agreement with Tully. "I've always felt that if I can't tell the readers where something came from," he explained later, "I ought to at least let them know why I can't."

The *Times* and *Register* pieces set wheels in motion in newsrooms around the country—not all of them spinning in the same direction, however. A San Jose *Mercury-News* reporter, Phil Trounstine, dug into his notebook for an item he'd been sitting on for seven months. At a speech to the California Democratic state convention the previous February, Biden had lifted, without attribution, a couple of passages from some twenty-year-old Bobby Kennedy speeches. "Few of us will have the greatness to bend history itself," Kennedy had said at Fordham University in June 1967. "But each of us can work to change a small portion of events, and in the total of all those acts will be written the history of this generation." Biden had said in Sacramento in February 1987: "Few of us have the greatness to bend history itself. But each of us can act to affect a small portion of events, and in the totality of these acts will be written the history of this generation."

Was it a story? Initially, Trounstine thought not. Back in February, several Gary Hart supporters had tried to peddle it to reporters covering the California Democratic convention, but no one bit. In the marketplace of political oratory, a certain amount of pilferage has always been deemed acceptable. Franklin Delano Roosevelt's 1933 inaugural rallying cry—"The only thing we have to fear is fear itself"—was perhaps the most famous American sentence of the twentieth century. Yet it was linked by a trail of benign theft that ran from Henry David Thoreau's "Nothing is so much to be feared as fear" (1851) to the Duke of Wellington's "The only thing I am afraid of is fear" (1831) to Francis Bacon's "Nothing is terrible except fear itself" (1623) to Montaigne's "The thing I fear most is fear" (1580) to

the Bible's "Be not afraid of sudden fear." No one ever accused
Roosevelt of plagiarism. Nor had anyone made an issue of Kennedy's
famous "Ask not . . . " inaugural passage, which had a similarly rich
ancestry. What Biden had done with Bobby Kennedy seemed to
Trounstine to fall within this innocent tradition (ever more so because,
as Biden later explained, he had no idea that the passage, penned
for him by Pat Caddell, had originally been RFK's).

Once the *Times* and *Register* pieces ran, however, Trounstine's
thinking changed. The Kinnock passage was different: Biden hadn't
borrowed the usual proverb or paraphrased some lofty formulation
of general principle. He'd taken a declaration of identity, a cry from
the heart. Now there was a context. What had seemed insignificant
seven months before now could be summoned up to demonstrate a
pattern. Trounstine unearthed his notes and wrote the Biden–
Kennedy story. It was published two days after the Dowd and Yepsen
pieces appeared. Dowd, meantime, received a telephone call from
Jeffrey Lord, a mid-level staffer in the political office of the Reagan
White House and a one-time ardent RFK supporter. He told her how
angry he'd gotten watching Biden's California speech on C–SPAN. "I
was finishing his sentences before he was," Lord said. "I wanted to
listen to Biden because he had such a reputation as a great speaker,
but suddenly I realized the speech wasn't Joe Biden. It was Robert
Kennedy. I was really ticked."

Dowd wrote a Biden–Bobby Kennedy story—quoting Lord, among
others—on Wednesday, September 16. The Bork hearings had begun
the day before, and Biden had led off the questioning of Bork. All
three networks topped their news shows Tuesday night with a Biden–
Bork story, followed by Biden–Kinnock and Biden–Kennedy stories.
"The minute we saw the stories on TV, we knew we were in trouble,
because the juxtaposition of the speeches was so visually powerful,"
said Tim Ridley, Biden's campaign manager. For NBC, this was a
second treatment. On Saturday night, its lead political reporter, Ken
Bode, had followed up on the Dowd and Yepsen pieces by splicing
together network file tapes of Biden in Iowa and Kinnock in his
commercial. The day before, a political producer at NBC, John Ellis,
had received a copy of the pre-packaged "attack video" from Jack
Corrigan, Sasso's protégé at the Dukakis campaign. Ellis had watched
it and shown it to several others in the NBC news department, but
decided it wasn't newsworthy enough to be put on the air immediately. "Fairness to Biden dictated that I know more about the debate,"
Ellis recalled. "Plus, it just didn't strike me as a major league story."

The initial skepticism toward the story felt by virtually every reporter ran especially deep at the Washington *Post.* When the Dowd and Yepsen pieces appeared, we went into a modified "knock-down" mode—not an uncommon response throughout the trade when a competitor breaks a story whose news value is open to debate. Instead of focusing on the alleged plagiarism, the *Post*'s initial story focused on the alleged dirty trick. Biden press secretary Larry Rasky was quoted sympathetically in the *Post* piece: "What really steams me is that here we are on the eve of the Bork hearings and another Democratic candidate is deliberately trying to undermine Biden. . . . Somebody has committed an outrageous act here."

When the Kennedy story followed, the *Post* relegated it to a five-paragraph item in its "Political Notes" column. "Senator Biden and his team of speechwriters have been one of the most prolific and original in the Democratic Party," the item quoted Rasky. "We don't need to try to slip one by people to try and make our point. . . . This is a game of trivial pursuit being played by one of our opponents."

But the knock-down course carries its own risks, as the *Post* would soon discover. Tips began circulating in newsrooms that afternoon that Biden had been involved in some kind of plagiarism incident when he was a student at Syracuse University Law School. The leak apparently came from a former Syracuse Law School dean, who had mentioned the incident during a casual dinner conversation with a group of academics. A member of the dinner group tipped off a reporter for *The Legal Times,* a Washington-based trade publication.

Biden tried to head off the avalanche. The next morning he held a press conference and explained that as a freshman law student he'd been accused of copying without attribution five pages of a published law review article in a fifteen-page paper he wrote for a legal methods course. A faculty committee considered whether to expel him. Biden's defense back then was that he thought the sole point of his paper had been to show an understanding of the form of writing a legal brief, not to deal in content. The faculty failed him for the course (one of three F's he received in law school), but allowed him to take it over—he did, and got a B. No further disciplinary action was taken. When Biden graduated, his law school dean wrote to the Delaware bar that his record contained "nothing whatever of a derogatory nature."

At the press conference, Biden also said he had been mistaken not to attribute the Kennedy and Kinnock passages, but called the flap "much ado about nothing" and said it was "ludicrous" to expect a politician to attribute every thought or idea he expresses. Carl Leubsdorf of the Dallas *Morning News* asked Biden whether the real issue wasn't borrowed words but a borrowed vision. The question reflected a view—especially popular among baby-boom–aged reporters—that there was something fishy about a presidential candidate who pronounced himself the leader of a generation but who had been a bystander during the two great formative political experiences of that generation—the civil rights movement and the Vietnam War. A year later, Quayle, the Republican baby boomer, would come under fire for not fighting in the trenches of Vietnam. Now Biden, the Democratic baby boomer, was under fire for not having fought in the trenches of the anti-war movement. Everything seemed loosey-goosey back in the 1960s. Retroactively, accounts were being squared.

Biden gave a rambling answer.

"And look . . . by the time the war movement reached its peak, when I was at Syracuse, I was married. I was in law school. I wore sports coats. I was not part of that. I'm serious. What you all don't seem to understand—some of you. I think you understand it, I don't think you're really being—well, I won't characterize it. But, you know, there was a four-year period there, folks, there was light-years. When I was on the college campus—1961–65—Vietnam was like Nicaragua is now. We all said, 'That's kind of stupid, but it's going to end.' . . . So, I find you all go back and say, 'Where were you, Senator Biden?' At the time—you know I think it's bizarre. I think it's bizarre. And then, when the movement did catch up, I was a twenty-three-year-old guy, married. And look, you're looking at a middle-class guy. I am who I am. I'm not big on flak jackets and tie-dye shirts and—you know, that's not me. I'm serious."

A year and a half later, Biden remembered the press conference as one of the most maddening episodes of his political career.

"Everybody around me kept saying, 'This is big!' " he recalled of the strategy session he'd had with his advisers just before he went out to face the cameras.

"I said, 'What's the story? I'll just give them my [law school] record. There's no problem.'

"And everybody said, 'No, no, no, no. This is big.' And one in particular of my quote 'key advisers' said, 'You got to go down there, Joe, and tell 'em you plagiarized.'

"I said, 'But I didn't plagiarize.'

"They said, 'You've got to tell 'em that, Joe.'

"I said, 'Why do I have to tell 'em that?'

"They said, 'You've got to offer something up. They're going to believe it's plagiarism. So unless you say it's plagiarism, the story will never end and they'll nibble you to death and we'll never get through Bork.'

"I said, 'I won't do that. I will not do that!'

"They said, 'You gotta do that.'

"I said, 'The best I'll do, and I'm not sure I can do that, is I'll walk down there and say, here's my record—you make the judgment. Okay?'

"I came walking back up, thinking it was successful, as successful as that kind of thing can be, and walked in and this one particular heavy . . . was sitting there and said, 'You kind of blew it.'

"I said, 'Why?'

"He said, 'You didn't tell them you plagiarized.'

"I said, 'Goddamnit, I did not plagiarize.' And it was the closest I've come to picking up someone who worked for me and go—wham!

"In retrospect, I think I should have gone down and fought it out with you all. I may be wrong. Maybe the guy is right. All of the articles that were written at the time essentially said: this happened in Biden's career. No one said Biden plagiarized and none of you said that Biden plagiarized, but the headlines all said: BIDEN ADMITS TO PLAGIARISM. And, I'm thinking, the only thing that mattered to me in my whole life, the only thing, beyond my family, was that. And I thought to myself, 'How could this be happening?' I mean, it made me so-o-o-o mad! I mean, that was the toughest thing to pick up the paper and read that. I didn't care about the Kinnock stuff, because I knew that would all work. . . . But if this guy cheated in law school, then all of the rest of the stuff is more believable."

The last cut came a few days later. It was administered by C–SPAN, the Cable Satellite Public Affairs Network, which unearthed a videotape of an encounter Biden had had the previous spring with a voter in a New Hampshire living room. The clip began with a man named Frank politely asking Biden what law school he had attended and how well he had done. "I think I have a much higher IQ than you do," Biden responded, jabbing a finger at Frank. "I went to law school on a full academic scholarship . . . and wound up in the top half of my class.... I was the outstanding student in the political science department [at college].... I graduated with three degrees from college.... And I'd be delighted to sit back and compare my IQ to yours if you like, Frank."

The outburst wasn't exactly what most people have in mind when they think of presidential timber. Nor was most of it even true. A rash of new stories pointed out that Biden had graduated 76th out of a class of 85 in law school; and 506th out of 688 in college. He graduated from the University of Delaware not with three degrees but with a double major. He had received a partial scholarship to law school, based on need. "Joe exaggerates when he's angry," an aide explained.

Eleven days of this was enough for Biden. He dropped out. "In my zeal to rekindle [America's] idealism, I have made mistakes," he said, facing his second forest of microphones in less than a week. "Now the exaggerated shadow of those mistakes has begun to obscure the essence of my candidacy and the essence of Joe Biden." He said he was "angry at myself" and "no less frustrated at the environment of presidential politics that makes it so difficult to let the American people measure the whole Joe Biden and not just the misstatements I have made."

SOMEONE ONCE called Joe Biden the only twenty-nine-year-old underachiever ever elected to the U.S. Senate. He's breezy and gabby, charming and nervy, brash and passionate, sentimental, courageous and disarmingly candid, a quick study with a short attention span. He's got an infectious personality and a thousand-watt smile. For two decades, Washington hasn't quite known what to make of him.

"I would like to compliment you all on your very good judgment in inviting me," he would begin his stump speeches on the presidential trail. Pause. "Because I am one of the most important men in America." Pause. "I'd probably be President right now." Pause. "Except that I wasn't old enough to run last time."

After delivering his lines with Jack Benny–like timing, Biden would follow with a monologue on the degradations of running for President as an unknown senator from a tiny state. His best tale was of a political event early in the campaign in Cleveland, where both he and Hart spoke. He'd describe how his heart sank when the local television reporters and camera crews all raced right past him on their way over toward Hart. But then—miracle of miracles—one TV reporter finally noticed him.

"I assumed my time had come," Biden would tell his audiences, puffing his chest out.

But the reporter had mistaken Biden for Peter Ueberroth, then the commissioner of baseball, whom he resembles.

"He says, 'Commissioner Ueberroth, what are you doing here?'

"I say, 'Drug testing.'

"The reporter says, 'What?'

"I say, 'Drug testing for the media.'

"He says, 'Let's get the hell out of here. This guy isn't Ueberroth.' "

Washington *Post* columnist Mary McGrory once described Biden as "a collection of good instincts and incoherent utterances, pleasant, energetic, but not in control." He was often kidded for being verbose, but never seemed to mind. In early 1987, Bill Peterson of the *Post* covered a speech he gave at Northwestern University in Evanston, Illinois. A flyer advertising his appearance quoted a recent *People* magazine profile: "Hot, handsome Joe Biden, the Democrats' new White House hope." The talk attracted three hundred students. "There's something exciting about seeing a presidential candidate," Mike Chevalier, a sophomore, told Peterson. "Here's all this ambition, standing just five feet away from us. It's almost like going to a zoo and seeing a strange species, a rare bird." Biden spoke for two hours, then held court for another ninety minutes in front of fifty students who were too enthralled to call it a night. At 11:25 p.m., one student good-naturedly asked him what he thought about the way Brit Hume of ABC News had characterized him in a recent article in *The New Republic.* "I think he called you a windbag." Biden smiled. "I think that's a judgment for you to make," he said. At 11:45 p.m., his aides finally dragged him out of the room.

As a child, Biden had a bad stutter. The students at the private Catholic school he attended in Wilmington called him *impedimenta,* after a Latin word they'd learned in eighth grade. Biden was also a natural leader—on the ball field, in the neighborhood, at social events—and he grew up assuming, the way many such young men assume, that he just might be President one day. He decided he'd better learn to speak. To overcome the stutter, he spent long hours reciting poetry in front of a mirror. He even practiced, in the style of Demosthenes, with pebbles in his mouth. Once he stopped stuttering, his friends kid him, he never stopped talking. "My swing is a natural for me," Biden says. "I wouldn't want to tamper with it."

There are plenty of critics who share Dowd's view that, somewhere along the way, Biden came to see oratory and leadership as
synonymous. In the 1970s and 1980s, he built what reputation he had
outside of Delaware on words, not deeds. He became a popular draw
at Democratic gatherings around the country, giving a speech that
challenged the tenets of liberalism. The Democratic party, Biden
told Democrats, had squandered its vision, misjudged the national
character, wallowed in self-interest, waylaid its compassion, sur-
rendered to the status quo. It was quite a tongue-lashing—and when
Biden scolded, everyone listened.

"We [in the Democratic party] reached a point in the mid-1970s
and early '80s when we forgot we had to constantly move on. And
after fifty years of success, we stepped back and gazed with paralyz-
ing self-satisfaction at our handiwork.... We said, 'Don't change
anything.' If you attempt to alter housing programs, you are not a
true liberal. If you attempt to alter the progress of civil rights, you
are questionable. If you doubt the wisdom of anything we have
done, you are not a true Democrat. And the cost to us was more than
victory. It was our vitality. The Democratic party became a fossilized
shadow of its former self."

The path to salvation, Biden would tell audiences, lay in recon-
necting with old heroes, old values, the ideals of liberalism. "I am a
member of the baby-boom generation ... and the cynics tell us that
having reached the conservative age of mortgage payments, pedia-
trician's bills and saving for our children's education, we are ripe for
Republican picking. Well, let me tell you, folks, they have misjudged
us. ... Just because they murdered our heroes, it doesn't mean that
the dream does not lay buried in our broken hearts."

How did he reconcile his disdain for the programs of liberalism
with his championing of its ideals? He didn't say—other than to put
forth the catch-all proposition that social policy ought to meet the
"test of common sense." Biden disdained the idea of running for
President on position papers. He believed the essence of leadership
was connecting to people's values, touching their hearts. And at that,
he was a master. When he finished his stem-winders, it wasn't uncommon for eyes in the audience to be moist.

His record in the Senate was a good deal more tame. Though by
1987 his fifteen years of seniority had made him chairman of the
Judiciary Committee and ranking Democrat on the Foreign Relations Committee, he had few legislative triumphs to his credit. When
the Democrats reclaimed control of the Senate at the end of 1986,

Biden had tried to duck becoming chairman of Judiciary, fearing that, if a Supreme Court vacancy were to come up in the next two years, the hearings on a nominee would cut into his time on the presidential campaign trail. He tried to persuade Senator Edward M. Kennedy to take Judiciary, but Kennedy had his sights set on Labor and Human Resources.

When Justice Lewis Powell retired and President Reagan nominated Bork, Biden found himself in a box of his own making. "Say the administration sends up Bork," Biden had said eight months earlier in an interview with the Philadelphia *Inquirer* shortly before he became Judiciary Committee chairman. "I'd have to vote for him, and if the [liberal interest] groups tear me apart, that's the medicine I'll have to take. I'm not Teddy Kennedy."

Most politicians learn early in their careers to stay clear of "hypotheticals," for they foreclose options. When Biden's hypothetical became a reality the following summer—by which time he was running for president in an arena in which the views of liberal interest groups mattered very much—he did precisely what he had said he wouldn't. After meeting with leaders of civil rights groups, he declared: "Most certainly, I'm going to be against him." A week later, under criticism for engaging in the very pandering he'd promised to avoid, Biden said he had "made a mistake" in the timing of his announcement, but not in the substance. He said he should not have stated his opposition to Bork until he could present a fully developed legal argument—which he did, later in the summer. The Washington *Post* editorial page likened his performance to that of the Queen of Hearts in *Alice in Wonderland:* "First the punishment, then the trial." Later, when the Kinnock story broke, the conservative *National Review* gleefully suggested: "A friend of ours has a solution: Nominate Joe Biden to the court, and give him a copy of Bork's speeches."

The coincidence of the Kinnock story and the Bork hearings was devastating for Biden. It meant that he was forced to wage a two-front war to preserve his credibility, and it guaranteed that the Kinnock revelation and follow-up stories would be played on the front pages and at the top of the network news. "It's a bigger story when they find out the pitcher who is winning twenty games is on drugs," Biden said afterward. "If I were a relief pitcher who'd been sent down to the minors, you wouldn't write about it."

But it's an open question whether Biden could have survived the Kinnock story—or any bump in the road, for that matter—even had it arrived at a less pregnant moment. His campaign headquarters was a too-many-cooks operation that had been sapping Biden's energy, patience and self-confidence. "I have never been in charge of anything so weird," Tim Ridley, Biden's campaign manager, said after the election. "We were not so much a campaign as we were a confederation of non-aligned states. We each had our own strategy and our own message. I once suggested that we bring in the rival campaigns and auction off some of our surplus strategies." Biden's announcement speech in June 1987 became a focal point for the internal dissension. There were four different "message factions" within the campaign high command and each insisted on getting a piece of it. The result was a committee-written polyglot — part "Pepsi Generation," part "voice of optimism," part "save the children," and part "scold the voters" — that left everyone deflated. Biden delivered it with a scowl.

"We also tried a bunch of speeches that summer where Joe presented himself as the Senate's leading foreign-policy expert. But Joe didn't like it," Ridley said, in a tone of wry affection, "because people in the audience weren't crying."

Pat Caddell, Biden's pollster and one of his oldest friends, was a particularly disruptive force throughout this period. An intense, bearded bear of a man, he warred constantly with the others in the crowded inner circle and with the press. He flew into a rage at me the morning after Biden's announcement speech when I happened onto the same elevator he was riding at the Savery Hotel in Des Moines. My story in that day's *Post* had led with the "scold the voters" element of the speech, and noted that it resembled the much-maligned "malaise" speech Caddell had written for President Carter in 1979. Caddell thought that he'd talked me out of making that reference the day before. Furious to find it in the paper, he began firing obscenities at me on the fourth floor and didn't let up until I found refuge at the checkout desk. When word of the tirade got to Biden later that day — not from me, but from Caddell's rivals within the campaign, who were looking for a pretext to banish him — Biden was dismayed. Caddell was on the outs, for a while. But the bond between the two men was exceptionally strong, and by the end of the summer, Caddell was back. They'd been close friends for fifteen years. Biden had once told me: "It's hard to know where Pat's thinking stops and mine starts," a line which played into the suspicions of his critics that he was an empty vessel into which the brilliant misfit Caddell had poured a candidacy.

When the Kinnock story broke, Caddell gave Dowd a similar lashing over the telephone, using language so coarse that several Biden advisers left the room. On the night Biden decided to withdraw, the campaign high command conspired to make sure Caddell was left behind in Washington while they took the train up to Wilmington with Biden to make the final decision. Caddell telephoned throughout the night, hoping to make the case that Biden should stay in the race and launch a bash-the-press counterattack. But no one would put him through to Biden until the decision was irreversible. At one point in the long evening, the frustrated Caddell shouted over the phone to Larry Rasky, the press secretary: "You people have formed a vigilante group to get my candidate out of the race!"

ONCE THERE WAS a corpse, the drama swiftly changed into a whodunit. Who shot Joe? CBS News ran a piece strongly implying that Dick Gephardt's campaign had planted the "attack video." The logic seemed sound. Gephardt's two media consultants, Robert Shrum and David Doak, had broken off a business partnership with Caddell the year before and feelings were still raw. "For a while there, it got so intense that we all half suspected somebody in our campaign must have done it," recalled Joe Trippi, who joined Gephardt after Hart's demise. "People kept walking around the office saying, 'I didn't do it. Are you sure you didn't do it?'" Eventually, Gephardt's campaign manager, Bill Carrick, gathered the senior campaign staff in a room and went around the table grilling each one individually: "Did you do it?" Everyone swore innocence. Carrick ended the session by announcing that he was returning to his office. Anyone who wanted to confess privately should go to a pay phone and call him. "I told them anybody needs a quarter, I've got plenty of them." No one called.

The night Biden withdrew, the remaining Democratic candidates were in Iowa for a debate. Carrick recalled the scene: "We're all at this hotel in Davenport, getting ready for the debate. I'm on the telephone in one room, screaming at Hal Bruno at ABC that he's crazy if he goes with a story that we did it. Shrummie's on the phone with CBS, having a similar conversation. We'd just done a focus group in Sioux City, where we had some woman say that Gephardt ought to be run out of the Democratic party for doing what he did to Biden. The group leader says, 'How do you know he did it?' and she says, 'I just saw it on TV.' I've never seen Gephardt so mad. He said, 'This is insane. We didn't do a bleeping thing, and we're still getting hung.' "

The next day, Gephardt's press secretary, Mark Johnson, appealed to Craig Whitney, *The New York Times*'s Washington bureau chief, to issue a statement that the Gephardt campaign wasn't the source of Dowd's story. Whitney did so—a move that would later be second-guessed throughout the media. By helping the innocent Gephardt out of a ditch, he was adding to the peril of the source his paper had promised to protect. A short list of suspects was now one suspect shorter.

Up in Boston, Sasso began to feel the noose tighten. The political press had formed a posse to track down a killer. Three of their number—the *Times,* the *Register* and NBC—knew who had done it and had promised not to tell. Would they hold up their end of the bargain now that the stakes were higher than anyone imagined when the deals had been struck? Sasso's experience with such matters was no cause for comfort. He'd been badly burned before—on a story, ironically, that also involved a campaign tape. In the midst of a bitter 1982 rematch campaign between Dukakis and Massachusetts Governor Edward King, a Dukakis supporter sent Sasso a doctored tape of a King commercial. It made light of King's wife's polio affliction and of the couple's sex life. Sasso played it on an off-the-record basis to a couple of his friends who covered politics for the Boston *Globe.* It was the sort of tasteless joke at the expense of another politician that operatives occasionally share with reporters—as a lubricant to buddy-buddy relations. It was never intended for publication. When the King camp found out about the tape and demanded an apology, Sasso first tried to deny it existed. Eventually, he was forced to admit everything and apologize. Dukakis was furious, but the controversy receded, the campaign recovered and Sasso steered Dukakis to a hard-fought victory.

For two weeks after the Dowd and Yepsen stories appeared, Sasso was never asked by any reporter whether he had put together the Biden–Kinnock video. Tully was—and he issued a blanket denial of involvement on behalf of the entire Dukakis campaign. It's one of the enduring mysteries of this episode why the Dukakis high command stonewalled as long as it did. What was their crime? Sasso was guilty of committing an act of politics: assembling damaging but truthful information about a rival and placing it in the hands of reporters. The fact that his brushback pitch turned into a beanball was clearly beyond his control. Had he confessed immediately, there

might have been some short-term damage in Iowa, among Democrats angry that Biden was brought down on the eve of the Bork
hearings. But why not take that hit and get on with it? One theory
that circulated at the time was that Sasso was protecting Kitty Dukakis,
who, according to this theory, knew of the Biden–Kinnock tape and
had withheld that knowledge from her husband. Kitty Dukakis has
denied this; Sasso has declined to comment.

The weekend after Biden withdrew, *Time* magazine broke the
story that the Dukakis camp had been the source of the attack video.
Sasso then made his worst misjudgment of the episode: he did not
come clean to Dukakis. When the two discussed the *Time* article—
which was based on unidentified sources—Sasso simply said he
would look into the allegations. The next day, at a statehouse press
conference, Dukakis was asked about the story. Left hanging out to
dry by Sasso, he was at his most self-righteous. He proclaimed his
intolerance for negative campaigning and said he would be "astonished" and "very, very angry" if anyone in his campaign were involved.
This, from the candidate presenting himself as a hands-on manager.

By the following day, Sasso knew the jig was up. His refusal to talk
would no longer wash. He finally confessed to Dukakis, who was
heartbroken. At a press conference the following day, Dukakis accepted
full responsibility, but initially refused Sasso's offer to resign. He
said he'd concluded that the transgression, while serious, was not a
firing offense when weighed against Sasso's years of outstanding
public service. Within a few days, that would become the near-
universal judgment of the press and the political community. But in
the inferno of the moment, there was a demand for a scalp. Four
hours later, Dukakis relented. Sasso and Tully both stepped down.

Dukakis promptly got on a plane and flew to Iowa, where he made
a seventeen-city apology tour. "There is no place in American
politics for people hurting other people," Dukakis said, dejected,
downcast and cloyingly saccharine. For some, even this wasn't
enough. Dukakis was booed by angry Biden supporters at several
stops. "I like the fact that Dukakis is being contrite," Gene Freund,
Biden's co-chairman in Iowa's Pottawattamie County, grudgingly
acknowledged. "But he has to be—is there such a word?—even
contriter for me."

THE MOMENT cried out for satire. Michael Kinsley, the whimsi-
cal editor of *The New Republic*, supplied it:

Des Moines, Iowa — A tearful Senator Paul Simon announced his withdrawal from the 1988 presidential race this evening, following revelations that several of his aides had failed to wash their hands before a lemonade social and foreign-policy debate sponsored by a local elementary school PTA here last week.

This gaffe alone might have been fatal, experts say. But the Iowa political community was alive with rumors that *The New York Times* also had information it was about to publish that the aides had not brushed their teeth afterward or written thank-you notes the next day. This, say the experts, left Simon with no choice but to withdraw.[1]

The hapless departures of Hart, Biden and Sasso prompted the political coverage to take on a contemptuous can't-anybody-here-play-this-game? tone. For a time in the autumn of 1987, it seemed nobody could. The campaign became all but unspoofable, as, in rapid succession:

• Pat Robertson showed little sympathy for the fallen warriors of 1987, declaring that "anybody who cannot control his mouth or the rest of his body during a presidential campaign" is not fit to be President. He thereupon got tied up in knots defending himself against allegations that he had falsified his wedding date, his war record and assorted details of his academic and business careers.

"I have never had this kind of precision demanded of me before," he said. "I would ask a little mercy. There is something in the Bible that says, 'Judge not lest ye be judged.' "

• Pat Schroeder lost her composure and wept as she announced she was not going to run for President, fortifying a gender stereotype her candidacy was supposed to defy.

• Douglas Ginsburg removed himself from consideration as an appointee to the U.S. Supreme Court when it was revealed he had smoked marijuana in the past, prompting a scramble by presidential candidates (Gore and Babbitt) and a handful of other elected officials to hold confessional press conferences to recount their youthful encounters with controlled substances.

It was not an edifying spectacle. The two men who least appreciated the madcap humor were Sasso and Biden.

More than a year after the campaign was over, I asked both to reflect on the ordeal they'd been through. Each placed the blame primarily on himself for what had happened, but both harbored a lingering sense of betrayal at the hands of the press.

"I have come to understand that you are wasting your time if you are solicitous of the press," Sasso said. "There is no point in playing the game of 'Let's go out to dinner. Let's be friends.' If anyone in dealing with a reporter thinks that anything he says is genuinely off the record, then I would tell that person that he is foolish."

Sasso had reason to feel he'd invested his trust unwisely. The *Time* article that broke open the whodunit said its information had come from an unidentified staffer at the Des Moines *Register* "involved in preparing his paper's story." The *Time* piece also quoted a "reliable source" saying that the Dukakis campaign had given the video to *The New York Times.* Those two papers had been honor-bound to protect Sasso. Who had leaked?

Sasso's assumption, a year and a half after the fact, was that it hadn't been Dowd or Yepsen, but instead some friends or colleagues of theirs with whom each had shared the information. "I was done in by sloppiness, not maliciousness," he said. "I would never enter into an agreement like this again, unless I very carefully laid out, in advance, who in the chain of command the reporter was going to reveal his source to, and what guarantees of confidentiality the reporter was going to extract from the people he told. Because the simple truth is, when the stakes get high, the secrets don't keep." Sasso added that in the future he would not engage in such subterfuges. "If I were to face a similar situation, I would say to a reporter, 'Here, this is from me. Use it any way you want.' That would eliminate a whole range of problems."

Biden's complaint with the press went closer to the bone. He didn't feel a deal had been broken. He felt his character had been misjudged.

"I didn't understand the dynamics of the national press. . . . " he said. "I had a very simplistic view, and in retrospect it was a very unreasonable view to have. It was, jeez, you guys in the press get to know me. You'll know I'm a good guy. You'll know I have character. I mean, you'll know that, won't you? And it was an unreasonable thing to expect."

Biden brought up the Kinnock quote, reiterating that, except for the one lapse at the Iowa State Fair debate, he'd always used it with attribution. "I could never understand why—you all heard me use it, you all heard me quote him. I could never understand why nobody spoke up!"

He looked at me, plaintively. "Why was it that you didn't say something?"

I started to tell him that I'd never heard him quote Kinnock with attribution, and that I didn't think attribution was the nub of the matter anyway. But he cut me off.

"No. No. No. Let me go through this. I'm not asking the question. I think I figured it out. I think what really set people off was . . . that you, in an editorial sense, you not only thought I was using language. You thought I was trying to adopt a personality. I think it was because of Caddell. I think you guys talked yourself into, with good reason, that Caddell had found another puppet. This time it was Biden and, because unlike Hart, we know nothing about Biden, at all, it lent more credibility to the fact that Caddell was over there with a piece of clay and he was forming this thing. And then when the heat got tough and Biden kind of banished Caddell, Biden needed something, so he went out and took this guy Kinnock. He said, 'Now I'm Kinnock.' You follow me?"

I followed him.

"I think you guys had no idea who the hell I was. . . . Here's this guy, he commutes back and forth, he's never around, we don't know much about him. God, he dropped off the Budget Committee. I mean, he's on, he's off. When he's hot, he's hot. When he's not, he's not. You know. He can turn 'em on. He turns 'em off. He's gathered all these hotshots around him. Particularly, he's got Caddell. And they're all over there deciding who's going to sculpt the ear and who's going to sculpt the nose. . . . And what a performer this guy is!

"After it was all over, I put myself in the press's spot, and once I started doing that, I say to myself: Jeez, here the Paul Taylors of the world are asking why you should be President, and I'm saying: 'Watch me. I'm an orator. Watch me orate.' And then I wonder why they wonder if I have a substantive program. . . . I think I should have known a lot of things that I now know that would have saved me at that moment of my life a lot of heartache."

He paused.

"Of course, in retrospect, it would have killed me. I probably would have still been in the race, and I'd be dead. So, who knows how it works?"

Biden was talking about what happened to him in February 1988, the week of the New Hampshire primary. He was overcome by a blinding headache in a hotel room in Rochester, New York, where he had just given a speech. He went unconscious—for how long, he isn't sure. The next day, he was rushed to Walter Reed Army Hospital. Last rites were administered. The operation to repair an aneurysm in his brain lasted nine hours. The convalescence took six months—

and was interrupted by two more operations. Biden came through it all, miraculously, with no physical or mental impairment. And with the assumption that had he still been in the race, he would have tried to campaign through the pain—perhaps with fatal consequences.

This was not Biden's first close encounter with death. In 1972, a few weeks after he was first elected to the Senate, his wife and infant daughter were killed when a truck rammed into their car while they were bringing a Christmas tree home for the holiday. His two young sons were badly injured. Biden kept a vigil by their bedside and contemplated not being sworn into the Senate. He eventually took the seat, but he has commuted home to Wilmington virtually every night ever since—a distance of about 130 miles—so he could raise his sons.

Joe Biden is not without flaws. He also has a good deal more character than he was able to demonstrate in 1987. His rude initiation into national politics has made him wiser. He will not run for President in 1992. Beyond that, he will not say. Some men don't let go of their dreams, not even in extremis. When Biden was wheeled in for surgery at Walter Reed in early 1988, he's reported to have told the doctors: "Do a good job on me, boys, I'm going to be President one day."

CHAPTER FIVE

The Mario Scenario

We don't have to do what the candidates do—talk
about huge issues in thirty seconds in a field somewhere, trying to make sure cows don't urinate on our
shoes.

— Mario Cuomo, on the pleasures
of not running for President[1]

I SPENT much of 1987 and some of 1988 thinking Mario Cuomo
was going to be elected President. As you may recall, he wasn't
even running. Didn't faze me.

I figured the voters wanted someone who filled a room just by
entering it; someone who knew the lift and lilt of a metaphor;
someone whose notions of mutual obligation and civic responsibility
would be a balm for two decades of me, me, me.

I knew Cuomo doubted whether he was ready. His refusal to take
the plunge only made him more tantalizing. How many politicians
of the first rank escape the clutches of their ambition long enough to
ponder their worthiness? But I thought he'd get shoved anyway—
sooner or later, willingly or not. Given the weak Democratic field, I
envisioned a succession of split decisions in the early Democratic
primaries and caucuses, leading to talk of a brokered convention,
featuring Jesse Jackson as a lead broker. Once that prospect loomed,
I saw a posse of Democratic pooh-bahs heading up to Albany, and
Cuomo becoming the first presidential draftee since Adlai Stevenson.
("I have no ambition to be President. I have no desire for the office,
mentally, temperamentally or physically," Stevenson had declared
on the eve of the 1952 Democratic convention. What happens if we
nominate you anyway? someone asked him. "Guess I'll have to shoot
myself," Stevenson deadpanned. They did; he didn't.)

The first half of this scenario played out like clockwork. By the
end of March 1988, the Democrats were halfway through their primaries and hadn't settled much of anything. Dukakis had displayed the

wares of a nominee—money, résumé, organization, steadiness afoot—but not the soul. He didn't lift spirits or offer vision or lay out a big agenda, and the voters were beginning to notice. In mid-March, he ran a dismal third in the Illinois primary, behind Jackson, whose vote came almost exclusively from the black community, and Senator Paul Simon, a favorite son whose candidacy had been unofficially dead for a month. The following week, Dukakis suffered an even bigger humiliation in Michigan, losing to Jackson by a margin of nearly two to one in a low-turnout primary. After thirty states had cast their ballots, Jackson inched ahead of Dukakis in delegates won, 606.5 to 605.5, according to an Associated Press tally, and was slightly further ahead in votes cast.

But the bell never tolled—not for Cuomo, not for my scenario. Instead, the Democratic voters in the remaining primaries behaved precisely as I'd imagined they wouldn't—calmly, pragmatically, efficiently. They decided Dukakis would do just fine. They discovered in him such virtues as needed discovering, so as to yank the process back from the edge of the abyss. The week after Michigan—when I thought chaos and confusion would reign—Wisconsin's progressive Democrats, their concentration fixed by Dukakis' two recent hangings, chose dull but steady over thrilling but risky. The margin was wide—nearly two to one. And that was that; fun and games were over.

Rereading a personal journal I kept during the campaign, I'm struck by how passionately I'd stuck with my losing hand. I hatched the "Mario Scenario" in a piece I did for the "Outlook" section of the *Post* in March 1987. (David Broder wrote a companion piece saying that I was nuts—that the contest would winnow toward a winner, because that's the way the game is rigged. He's a comer, this guy Broder.) Over the course of the next year, I plunked down as many more bets on my theory as I could sneak into print—past editors who used to gang-tackle me whenever they caught that certain glimmer in my eye.

For a while, I had been riding high. After the disappearance of Hart and Biden, someone took a poll which showed that Donna Rice, Fawn Hall, Jessica Hahn and Tammy Faye Bakker were all better known than every Democrat running for President except Jesse Jackson. Cuomo, meantime, was engaged in what seemed to be a sumptuous tease. He was traveling around the country knocking 'em dead with rousing speeches in that rich New York Italian baritone of his—all the while shedding crocodile tears because no one took him at his word when he said he wasn't running. "I talked to my mother on the phone the other day," Cuomo used to joke, "and I said, 'Ma, they just don't believe me.' And she says, 'Hey, I don't believe you either.' "

Then the primaries began, and there was a different Democratic winner every Tuesday. The brokered convention scenario became damn near conventional wisdom. The possibilities were analyzed in all the newspapers and newsmagazines (CUOMO OR CRACK-UP, was the headline of a Mike Royko column, typical of the ilk), dissected with charts and graphs on the evening news, schmoozed about on the Sunday-morning talk shows. In London, the bookies responded to the demand of the betting public and put the odds on noncandidate Cuomo getting the nomination at 4 to 1. Draft-Cuomo committees cropped up in California and elsewhere. "Some of us just are not prepared to accept the fact that he's not running," said Representative Nancy Pelosi (D–Calif.), a longtime supporter. Even Broder's knees buckled a bit in one whispered aside to me when we both saw the Dukakis train wreck coming in Michigan.

I should have bailed out the moment I spotted the whites of the pack's eyes. But the moment was too sweet for prudence. I was drunk on the sport of it. In the old days of scoop journalism, we reporters used to measure our personal wins and losses by who got to the facts first. Now, with computers, faxes, C–SPAN, CNN, Hotline, etc., we've all grown accustomed to getting everything more or less instantaneously. Now the competition is for what University of Massachusetts journalism professor Ralph Whitehead calls "perceptual scoops"—being the first kid on the block to arrange the available facts in the most prescient way. That sure was looking like me there for a while. I'd been on this giddy romp from the start (a point I occasionally felt the need to drive home to the latecomers) and I sure as hell wasn't going to miss the glorious denouement.

But there was no denouement—glorious or inglorious. The whole Rube Goldberg fantasy simply expired, quietly, of its own improbability. The Mario Scenario had appealed to reporters like me because we're suckers for almost anything that's more interesting than reality. The wish had been father to the thought. The voters' perspective was entirely different. Their behavior called to mind the song lyric: "If you can't be with the one you love, love the one you're with." That's what they did in choosing Dukakis over crack-up.

To this day, I'm not sure if Cuomo was left high and dry in Albany or if his protestations of noninterest were sincere all along. He argues strenuously for the latter interpretation, and enjoys waving the historical record at skeptics. He said he wasn't going to run; he didn't run. He said there would be no draft; there was no draft. "I wish someone sometime would write a piece that says, 'Let's face it, he was telling the truth,'" Cuomo lamented shortly before the Democratic convention. "Nobody has. . . . You've done everything but call me a liar. You said that I was cute. You said that I misplayed the game. You said that I was really waiting for another scenario."[2]

The media did all that—me more than most. And so now it's time to square accounts. Everything you said you weren't going to do, Governor, you didn't do. But might you have behaved differently if circumstances had played out differently? As someone once said of a different New York governor—Nelson Rockefeller—in a similar context: "I believe him when he says he lost his ambition. I also believe he remembers where he put it."

What continues to intrigue me about Cuomo's noncandidacy, several years after the fact, is whether it's admissible evidence in support of the proposition that the modern presidential selection process discourages the best from getting in. I realize this is treacherous ground. One man's dream candidate is another man's bum. And one interesting man's refusal to run may inform us about nothing beyond the contours of his own psyche. That said, I still can't shake the notion that there was something wrong with a presidential campaign in 1988 that didn't include Mario Cuomo or the vision of community that he so eloquently espouses. I'll return to his contribution to this missed opportunity later in this chapter. For now, let's briefly ponder the process. What kinds of runners does it attract and repel? What kinds of incentives and obstacles must they consider? Who gets in, how and why?

W E OPEN the inquiry in February 1987. Your name is Dick Gephardt, and you've just completed yet another kaffeeklatsch in yet another New Hampshire living room. On your way to the airport, you stop at a gift shop in downtown Nashua, where you've spotted just what you've been looking for—a ceramic figurine of a German shepherd. You're delighted.

Tomorrow, you'll take it with you to Cedar Rapids, Iowa, and present it to Connie Clark, a local Democratic activist who collects such bric-a-brac. (You admired her collection the last time you paid a visit.) She is vital—or so you've calculated—to your long march on the White House. She's the head of the Cedar Rapids chapter of the

American Federation of State, County and Municipal Employees, and she's known as a big producer on caucus night. You desperately want her on your team. Your plan is to surprise her with this bauble and then don an apron and spend four hours flipping pancakes and trading small talk with the guests at a Sunday breakfast she's put together.

You began waging this all-out assault on Connie Clark's affections two months ago. Since then, you've visited her at home or spoken to her by phone a dozen times — and she's not even close to committing to your campaign. Her problem is that Joe Biden has been sending the nicest flowers and Bruce Babbitt seems so intelligent and earnest. She can't decide between the three of you. In fact, she's so torn up by the choice that she's developed her own numerical rating system to help her decide. So keep those calls and visits coming. She hopes to have a winner by May.

Meantime, you've got other irons in the fire. There's this twenty-one-year-old kid from Des Moines who did such a good job managing a city council election last year. Wasn't he surprised when you visited him at the hospital after his appendectomy? Maybe with a few more phone calls and notes . . .

These chilling scenes of a courtship — details all true — are the reverse image of Cuomo's hard-to-get routine, but the moral is the same: something's terribly out of whack with the way we ask our leaders to compete for democracy's highest prize.

It has now been two decades and five presidential elections since Democratic party reformers set out to transfer power in the nomination process from the bosses to the masses. They wanted more democracy, small "d." They got it. The system of direct-election primaries and caucuses they concocted is unlike anything practiced by any other nation. It was born of fine intentions and still has much to recommend it. It gives play to an egalitarianism (everybody gets a chance to be President) and an anti-elitism (in theory, nobody but the people get to choose their nominees) that are at the core of our political culture. But it also contains a set of tail-wags-dog distortions that grow more baroque with each campaign. It has created a new class of politicians who enhance their stature by not running for President. ("If I were to run, I'd be a dwarf like everyone else," Cuomo quipped during the heyday of his non-campaign.) And it has created its own new set of elites. One is the media, who have been thrust into the gatekeeping role once performed by the bosses. Another is the small cadre of Iowa and New Hampshire activists who keep getting better at gaming the system—at profiteering, psychologically, politically, even monetarily, from the power conferred on them by accidents of history, timing and process.

The hoary Iowa/New Hampshire joke—"How can I be sure about him for President when he's only been in my kitchen three times"—is out of date, as Gephardt's romancing of Clark attests. "These aren't primaries anymore," quipped Walter F. Mondale, speaking with the authority of someone who's been there and the security of someone who isn't headed back, "they're ambushes."

The Class of '88 campaigned exhaustively in both states, and did so even though the South, inflamed with regional grievance, tried to force the early action into its front yard by bunching fourteen of its primaries on a single day. It didn't work. Super Tuesday, the novelty of the 1988 nomination calendar, was held on March 8—a month after the Iowa caucuses and three weeks after the New Hampshire primary. It served only to increase the perceived slingshot effect of winning the two opening states. Republican and Democratic candidates spent an unprecedented combined total of 999 days campaigning in Iowa alone, according to a study by Professor Hugh Winebrenner of Drake University. Not until caucus night came and went did the winners—Gephardt on the Democratic side and Dole on the Republican—discover that fabled Iowa had been more booby trap than slingshot. There was no winner's halo for them, no fawning media coverage, no cover stories in *Time* or *Newsweek*—in short, they grumbled, "no mo" (momentum). These were the spoils they'd been competing for—far more than Iowa's cache of delegates, which amounted to barely 1 percent of the floor strength at each party's national convention. Instead, all they got for their wins was a round of skeptical scrutiny from the media and a wave of punishing attacks from their rivals. "It would have been nice," mused Bill Carrick, Gephardt's campaign manager and architect of a strategy that saw his candidate spend 148 days in Iowa, "if someone told us in advance that Iowa was going to be worth Idaho this time around."

Actually, there were warning signs. The tone of campaign coverage had been negative for the year leading up to the Iowa caucuses; it probably wasn't reasonable to expect the media to reverse instincts overnight. The belittling coverage stemmed in part from the Hart and Biden escapades and in part from the media's natural instincts. But it also seemed traceable to the presence of an impressive band of potential Presidents who'd chosen to stay on the sidelines—their disinterest implicitly mocking both the game and the players. This was the first "open seat" presidential race in twenty years; by all reckoning, it was a once- or twice-in-a-lifetime opportunity for anyone with designs on the Oval Office. Yet count the noncontestants. On the Democratic side, Cuomo, Senators Bill Bradley (N.J.), Sam Nunn (Ga.), Edward M. Kennedy (Mass.) and Dale Bumpers (Ark.), and former Virginia Governor Charles Robb all took byes. On the Republican side, so did former Senator Howard Baker, Jr. (Tenn.), Governors Thomas Kean (N.J.), George Deukmejian (Calif.), James R. Thompson (Ill.) and former Governors Lamar Alexander (Tenn.) and Richard Thornburgh (Penn.).

"This year, more than ever, if you polled people knowledgeable about national government and put together a list of the ten best candidates, not more than two or three of them actually running would be on it," Austin Ranney, a University of California at Berkeley political scientist and election expert, said in 1987.

"The system has gone crazy," agreed Norman Ornstein, a political scientist at the American Enterprise Institute. "There have been good people who have backed off before, but when you have a Mario Cuomo, who had an extraordinarily good chance of making it, get out, you ask, 'Is something amiss?' When you have not a single candidate get in from the South in a year when Democrats are all saying they need to appeal to the South, it's worrisome." (Ornstein made his observations before Senator Albert Gore, Jr., became a candidate.)

What kept these good men out? All had personal reasons unconnected to the hoops, hurdles and pitfalls of the modern nomination system. But for each of them, that system served as a deterrent. Its duration has become a self-parody. Two decades ago, the rest of the world began marveling at how long it took Americans to choose a President; since then, the length of the process has grown geometrically. In 1968, the last campaign in which the old nominating rules were more or less in place, the winning Democratic nominee announced 121 days before his party's convention. (To be fair, that was an unusual year.) In 1984, it was 511 days. In 1988, 487 days. And now more so than before, the stumping for votes, activists and financial donors (who must be rounded up in vast numbers, given the $1,000 limitation on individual contributions imposed by the campaign finance reform laws of the mid-1970s) begins long before the formal announcement.

The length of the process makes it hard for people with busy jobs to compete—big-state governors, for example. It also demands "a single-minded obsession that can distort people," said Mondale. "For four years, that's all I did. I mean, all I did. That's all you think about. That's all you talk about. That's who you're around. That's your schedule. That's your leisure. That's your luxury. That's your reading. I told someone, 'The question is not whether I can be elected. The question is whether I can be elected and not be nuts when I get there.' It can twist people."

It also induces some candidates to do things beneath the dignity of the office they are seeking. "Somehow, it's hard to imagine François Mitterrand doing living rooms in New Hampshire," mused Representative Barney Frank. "It often seems to be more at the level of running for county clerk," said Stuart Eizenstat, domestic-policy adviser to former President Jimmy Carter, adding that he and other reformers in the Democratic party ought to "plead guilty to raising exponentially the aggravation level of running for President."

That's not to say the small-state start isn't, in theory, a good idea. It levels out the playing field by reducing the importance of reputation, money and thirty-second ads. It makes intensity of support matter as much as breadth. It subjects presidential candidates to intimate review by real people, untainted by the virus of Washington insiderism. Even a lengthy campaign has some things to recommend it—certainly for a nation like ours. In a depoliticized culture, where we don't have parties to play the role of intermediaries and screeners, where we don't have fixed ideological groupings that serve as guideposts, the voters need a long time to take the measure of the men who would be President. They need the chance the marathon affords them to observe the candidates in triumph, defeat, crisis, etc.

It's just that we do all of this to wretched excess. A one-year campaign is long; a three-year campaign is beyond the pale. Having to hobnob with activists face to face is fine. But "putting such a high premium on sitting in someone's living room and being a pleasant fellow," noted Ranney, "is asking a candidate to be good at something that a President need not be especially good at."

If this is such a silly way of doing business, who thought it up? As a matter of fact, no one did. Like so much else about our political culture, the process is less a creation of the rules (though they matter some) than of political customs and folkways, tested in battle and handed down from one campaign to the next. It was Jimmy Carter who "made" Iowa. He began the 1976 campaign as an obscure ex-governor of Georgia whose chief assets were ambition, self-discipline and time. He conceived of the campaign as a marathon.

He got to Iowa before everyone else, bounced around the state in a battered-up car, camped out in living rooms and farmhouses, shook every hand on the landscape and left behind notes pinned to the barnyard door when people weren't home—"Hi, I'm Jimmy Carter. I'm running for President. Sorry I missed you." No one had ever done it this way before.

When Carter won Iowa, he unlocked a treasure chest of media goodies. Though he defeated Representative Morris Udall by 28 percent to 23 percent—a margin of just 4,500 votes—it was enough for *Time* and *Newsweek* to put his face on their covers and his story in 2,600 lines of their inside pages. Udall got 96 lines.[3] Eleven months later, Carter woke up in the White House—and the way he got there lit the fires of ambition in a generation of up-and-coming politicians who, like him, had more stamina than stature. But the lessons of his victory have been overlearned. Carter spent thirty-two days campaigning in the state; Gephardt spent nearly five times that many— and rented an apartment in Des Moines so his mother and other relatives could be there when he wasn't. "For me," Gephardt used to say, "a day without Iowa is a day without sunshine." I remember talking to him late one night in the university town of Ames, Iowa, in early 1987. He'd been on the road every weekend for a year— and there was still a year to go before the first votes would be cast in the first caucus. For his labors, he was still stuck at 1 percent in national polls. We had an 11 p.m. pizza dinner at the end of one of his typical sixteen-hour days. "I'm going to have to win this thing on the ground," he confided, as if his predicament weren't painfully obvious. "There are no long bombs for me."

There are so many degradations in this sort of campaigning that self-deprecating humor has become a kind of cottage industry along the presidential trail. Udall tells a classic of the genre. He's just approached a couple of voters in a coffee shop in New Hampshire. "I say, 'Hello, I'm Mo Udall and I'm running for President.' And they say, 'Yeah, we know. We were just laughing about that this morning.' "

But this is a misery which only afflicts willing sufferers. Udall remembers the first time someone suggested he run for President. "David Obey and Henry Reuss [Democratic congressmen from Wisconsin] came up to me in the House cafeteria over coffee one day and said I ought to think about it," Udall recalled. "I didn't run for the exit and say, 'These guys are crazy. Arrest them.' I was flattered. It's a very heady wine. You start hearing people introduce you as the next President, and you get comfortable with the idea."

Sometimes too comfortable. "There's a story out of Tolstoy," Udall continued. "Count Nikolai Rostov returns from the war on a Christmas break. He spends two weeks being toasted at parties. It's a wonderful holiday. But then he has to go back to the front. The next day, bullets are whizzing by his head.

" 'My God,' he says. 'They're shooting at me—me, who everybody loves!' "

Some men do not take the plunge. Mondale reviews the question of "why" and "why not" as an expert witness: he's made both decisions. In 1975, he backed out of running for President with a quip about not wanting to spend two years sleeping in Holiday Inns. In 1983, he got in, declaring in his announcement speech: "I'm ready to be President."

"You've got to be able to ask that most arrogant of all questions," Mondale said, explaining the distance he'd traveled over those eight years. "You have to be able to look into the mirror and say, 'I'd be the best President.' Boy, that's hard for an honest man to do."

In 1986 and 1987, Mondale, still smarting from his landslide defeat in 1984, spent time on the telephone warning his friends in the Class of '88 of the dangers ahead. "I told every one of them that you're going to get hurt unless you go at it all out, with a singleness of concentration that defies human nature," he said. "The biggest mistake people make is that they get into it willy-nilly, thinking there is no downside. But it's like a hook with a barb in it.

"Do you want to tear your life apart and get rid of everything you've known as a lifestyle? Like seeing your family? Being with your friends? A fishing trip? A hunting trip? A night's sleep? And throw it all away for this incredible vagabond's life?"

Mondale continued: "You have got a chance of losing. This country doesn't like losers. You have got a chance of losing the office you now hold. The people of your state will think you've gone high-hat once you tell them you're more interested in something else. Or you can keep the office but lose the status. After Scoop [the late Senator Henry M. Jackson of Washington] ran and lost, something came off of his authority level in the Senate."

Dukakis came to understand what Mondale's warnings were all about—but not until *after* the election. His defeat was only the beginning of a Job-like ordeal. His wife, Kitty, was hospitalized twice for alcoholism, exhaustion and depression, including one time after she ingested rubbing alcohol. His Massachusetts Miracle turned to dust. The state's budget deficit topped $1 billion, and its bond rating dropped to the level of Louisiana's while taxes were being raised and thousands of state employees were being laid off. His approval rating in Massachusetts plummeted to 19 percent. He took himself out of the running for another term as governor and became a virtual pariah on the national scene, as Democrats continued to blame him for kicking away what they thought had been a golden opportunity.

Through it all, his critics were relentless. "Truth requires that the governor of Massachusetts be described this morning as precisely what he has become: a pathetic bust-out embezzler who is incapable of adding or telling the truth," Mike Barnicle, a columnist at the Boston *Globe,* wrote on the one-year anniversary of Dukakis' acceptance speech at the Democratic National Convention in Atlanta. "The governor walks around like an unsupervised bank teller with bad habits and brings the job all the warmth and personal charm of a parking meter." Barnicle's opposite number at the Boston *Herald,* Howie Carr, weighed in with the observation that "Pee Wee" Dukakis was a "lying, incompetent, henpecked little wimp." It got so bad for Dukakis in 1989, comedian Jay Leno joked, that Willie Horton was telling fellow inmates: "Hey, I hardly knew the guy." The voters got into the act, too, as "Duke Makes Me Puke" bumper stickers became a popular item around the Commonwealth.

Still, Dukakis' miseries in the aftermath of Campaign '88 were the exception, not the rule. Out of a presidential field that started at fourteen, nearly every other candidate seemed to have grown from the experience, no matter how grueling it may have been. One of the early casualties, Bruce Babbitt, was asked in the dying days of his campaign to reflect on what he'd been through. "Sometimes, it's very tough," he said. "You wake up in another city, another strange motel. My kids I miss very much. My wife I hardly ever see. . . . They bring us together for a conjugal visit, you know, maybe once or twice a month." But was it worth it? "I got up after that last debate a couple of days ago and a shiver went down my spine as I looked at the others and said, 'What an extraordinary opportunity to stand here as a candidate for the presidency of the United States.' It is not just another horse race; it is being in the middle of a drama that I see being invested with transcendent importance." Babbitt—articulate, intelligent, deliciously ironic, a trifle gawky—was always more popular with reporters than with voters. "The press won't have Bruce Babbitt to puff up anymore!" he said, in a tone of mock vengefulness, the day he dropped out. He added: "Anyone who fears the power of the press will take great comfort from my showing." As for the psychic toll of defeat, he had a wonderfully counter-intuitive perspective. He spoke of how valuable it had been for his two young sons, who'd always known him as the all-powerful governor of Arizona, "to see me with clay feet, to learn that they could help me, buck me up, make me feel better. It brought us closer together."4

Other candidates had their own richly human reactions. No one was visibly scarred—not even Bob Dole, who seems to draw strength from the fumes of resentment. Contrary to most predictions, he returned comfortably to the Senate, where he loyally served the President he'd treated with such scorn during the campaign. Gephardt gained enough stature to wind up as House Majority Leader in 1989; Senator Al Gore gained valuable experience for his next trip to the plate; Jack Kemp got a cabinet job and a ticket to try again; Jesse Jackson won the legitimacy conferred by 7 million votes; and so on. There's always a downside to losing, but with the exception of Dukakis and early departees Hart and Biden, no one was diminished for having tried and failed. And many will try again. "Once it enters the bloodstream," Udall has said, "the disease of running for President can only be cured with embalming fluid."

This complicates the case against the process. Yes, it's flawed. No, it's not the heavy of the piece. If the shape of the playing field really did determine who played and who won, how could it, over the past two decades, have attracted candidates as dissimilar as Alexander Haig, Fred Harris, Pierre S. du Pont, Pat Robertson and Ted Kennedy? How could it have produced winners as different as Jimmy Carter, Ronald Reagan and George Bush?

EITHER A MAN wants to run for President—in which case the obstacles don't seem to matter—or he doesn't. Cuomo didn't. His disinterest remains, for me, the premier mystery of 1988.

I first explored the matter with him on the day before New Year's Eve 1986, at a time when most political insiders assumed he was going to run. Cuomo was full of himself. Early that morning he'd worked out the details of an $8.6 billion funding package for capital improvements on the New York City subway system, which had been the subject of a difficult three-week special session of the state legislature. While I was in the office with him, he got word that Warren Anderson, then the powerful Republican leader of the state senate, was prepared to sign off on the deal. This precipitated a rush of calls on his speaker phone to aides, legislators and New York City officials. Each call lasted no more than twenty or thirty seconds. Cuomo performed like a maestro. "Yes, Warren, the copy of the legislation will be over to your office right away." Click. "Jerry [Crotty, his chief aide], I just talked to Warren. I told him a copy of that legislation is on its way to his office." Click. "Warren—have you gotten it yet?" Click. "Jerry—Warren hasn't gotten it yet." This burst of micromanagement was interrupted by a call from Cuomo's youngest son, Chris, then a sophomore in high school. The discussion was of Chris's basketball game the night before, and Cuomo switched the speaker phone off, leaving me to hear only his end of the conversation. "You did good last night." Pause. "Eight points?" Pause. "Forget about the poke in the eye." Pause. "You're a baby. Every time you take a shot, you go down on one knee."

In short order, the document had made its way to Anderson's office and Crotty called back, this time to discuss how the announcement of the pact would be handled. He explained that Robert Kiley, head of the Transit Authority, would unveil the package at a press conference in New York City that afternoon.

"What's Kiley going to say?" Cuomo asked.

"We've got him lined up to say two things," said Crotty, who didn't know a reporter was sitting in the governor's office, able to hear both ends of the conversation. "He'll say how this will stabilize fares, and he'll also say how instrumental you were in pushing the whole thing through." Cuomo reached to switch off the speaker phone, but got to the button a split-second late. "Okay, enough of that," he said in an irritated voice.

His embarrassment only lasted a moment. He was too eager to describe how he'd come up with the breakthrough that made all the pieces of the funding package finally fall in place. Cuomo said he'd been at his office with a group of key aides until midnight the night before, then headed over to the governors' mansion while aides kept working through the night. When he got to the mansion—which was overflowing with relatives visiting for the Christmas holiday—he retreated to his study, stuck his head in a neck brace he occasionally wears to relieve pressure on a pinched nerve in his back, and kept working. At around 2 a.m., he put his head down on his desk for a nap. He awoke with a start at 4 a.m.—and, presto, he came up with a new idea on how to divide the funding burden for the bonds. It was the key ingredient that made the package work.

"What does the press know of any of this?" he asked combatively. "They say we should delegate. If you delegate all the time, then you've missed the chance to come up with an idea at 4 a.m. . . . If that happens to you once in your lifetime, how do you then say, 'Well, that's all right. It's better to delegate.' "

The fact that the inspiration had come to him in the depth of night, after a fitful sleep, prompted him to reflect on the physiology of thinking. "You've got to write a speech for the inaugural," he said, describing his next pressing assignment—the speech he would give the following week when he would be sworn in for a second term. (Cuomo is either the sole or principal author of all of his major speeches. He takes meticulous care with them—sometimes nursing them through a dozen or more drafts.) "You go through this terrible agonizing period of looking for an outline, looking for parameters, looking for direction, an agenda, a message. It's very, very hard. You can read a hundred books, you can read your old speeches. There are, crammed into your brain, thousands of different possibilities. You make list after list of words, key words: 'hope'; 'opportunity'; 'circle.' Then nothing happens. You move into a stagnant phase. You watch a basketball game, play the piano, read a book. You get away from it for a couple of days—that's ideal. All this time, these ideas remain in the brain. The pulses are all there, and the brain is working. The brain works while we are asleep. You'd be surprised. We have our little joke about shaving in the morning—the best ideas always coming to you then. But the truth is, you're thinking all night. I'd be surprised—maybe you haven't noticed—if many times in your lifetime you didn't wake up with a new insight. It didn't come out of nowhere. You went to sleep with the fragments of an idea, and your mind is at work."

The time allotted to our interview had long since expired. In addition to ruminating and governing, Cuomo was filibustering. He knew I had come to inquire about his interest in the presidency; I knew it was a subject he was not anxious to discuss. In one of his rare pauses for breath, I jumped in and asked if he had the fire in the belly for a presidential campaign.

"If you show me someone who has fire in the belly, I'll put seltzer in the mouth," Cuomo said. "I almost certainly wouldn't want to vote for that person. I would probably be very distrustful of anyone who had that feeling about the presidency. I would think of the presidency with awe, with vast trepidation. Not because I am not aware of my own capacities, as compared to other persons'. But because that position is the most important in the universe, and I have a dramatic sense of its significance. Just governing this state—which is a formidable task—I can imagine what it would mean to be President. One mistake and you could obliterate the known world. That is a literal fact. I don't have that kind of power as governor, thank God. . . .

"Before you would consider running for it, you would have to be able to say to yourself that there is no one more capable who could achieve it with your help. And then you would have to conclude that you could will yourself, emotionally, to exhaust yourself in the process of trying to be President. If you decide that, then you could almost convert it into a responsibility. I don't want to sound unctuous about it, but that's just the way my mind works. . . . I felt that way about the governorship. I said to myself [before deciding to get into the 1982 gubernatorial race], 'I am better than those other people out there. I am better than [Ed] Koch. I am better than [Lew] Lehrman. It gave me huge reservoirs of strength. In 1977, when I was talked into running for mayor [a campaign Cuomo lost], I started the race by saying, 'I don't think they need me. I don't believe I am as good as these other people'—and I wasn't. I could never get past that truth. In a courtroom for money, I was able to win a lot of cases for clients that people thought couldn't be won. But I have great difficulty winning cases with myself that shouldn't be won."

At the conclusion of this soliloquy on self-doubt, Cuomo introduced another subject: the strain on his family.

"Look, we went through a terrible campaign [Cuomo's 1986 reelection campaign, in which he won 65 percent of the vote, a record for a gubernatorial candidate in New York]. Maybe in a hundred years you get results like that. But what this campaign did to Andrew [his oldest son and closest political confidant, who had been accused during the campaign of using his name to attract work for his law firm], I can't tell you how frustrating that was. Nobody scarred him for life. Nobody is going to stop his progress. But what it does is bring back the price you are paying for public service. And what it makes you think about is, look, is this really an ego exercise by you? Look at what it has done to your kids. What about Madeline [one of his three daughters]? Three times she's stopped for a red light. Then she's in the newspapers. Somebody refers to her as a bleached blonde. I mean, I could strangle the guy."

I left the interview fairly certain he wasn't going to run. Over the next six weeks, however, he began for the first time publicly to explore the possibility. He accepted three speaking engagements around the country. He invited two savvy Democratic operatives— Robert Shrum, a political consultant who was a former aide to Ted

Kennedy and to Gephardt, and Kirk O'Donnell, then House Speaker Thomas P. O'Neill's chief aide—up to New York to give him a primer on the demands of running for President.

"Finally, with some reluctance, I tested the practicality of it," Cuomo recalled after the campaign was over. "I didn't even want to do that, but some people, including Andrew, said, 'Look, there's some arrogance that you're not even investigating it—whether you could do the primaries.' I talked to Shrum, and I talked to O'Donnell. They spent a total of seven hours sitting in my office, telling me how the process works. I asked each of them one question: Could I do my job as governor and still do the primaries? They didn't say if I could or couldn't, but they started talking about all the time you had to spend in Iowa. After each of them finished I said thank you very much, but concluded that I couldn't possibly do it.

"One of them said, well, you could skip all that stuff and do it at the convention. But that I ruled out. I looked around at these guys [the candidates who were already in the race or on the verge of getting in] and said, 'Look, I'm not the best.' I wasn't. I didn't feel it. I don't kid myself. I'm better, stronger, smarter than I was twenty years ago. I have no psychic impediment to admitting my own capacities. But I never really got to that ultimate test. Do they need you? That's the ultimate question. Can you honestly say you should be President because you're better than the others? I never really got to it, because, as a practical matter, it just never appeared to be something you could do."

Someone once wrote of Cuomo that he cultivates complexity while he claims he is being perfectly clear. So it seemed during that interview. "You've just given me two completely different reasons you didn't run—the practical obstacles and your sense that you weren't the best," I told him. "Which was more important?"

"I'm afraid I really can't help you, Paul," he said with a shrug. "What makes people make their important decisions? Hundreds of things . . . " His voice trailed off.

On February 19, 1987, less than two weeks after he'd visited with Shrum and O'Donnell, Cuomo announced during the last few minutes of his regular Sunday-evening radio talk show appearance that he would not seek the presidency. He hadn't discussed the matter in advance with anyone—not his wife, his family, his staff, his advisers or his friends. "The only thing I did," he recalled, "was to tell Marty [Steadman, then his press secretary] a few hours in advance to call up the reporters and make sure they were listening that night, so they wouldn't get hurt.

"I wrote the statement the night before. Actually, I wrote two statements, so that the secretaries wouldn't know," he continued, chuckling at the memory. "I wrote the one that I read and I wrote another one saying that I was running. It drove 'em crazy.

"And to Matilda [his wife] that morning I said, 'Look, we've never discussed the presidency, right?'

"And she said, 'Well, therefore I know that you're not going to do anything, because you would never do anything without talking to me.'

"I said, 'That's right. I would never think of doing anything without talking to you. Well, if I'm not going to do anything, I wouldn't have to talk to you.'

"She said, 'Yeah, okay.'

"That's what she got angry about." (Following his announcement, Cuomo was in the doghouse with his wife for not having consulted her.) "She said I set her up. She said, 'Why didn't you tell me what you were going to say?'

"I said, 'Who knows, I may have changed my mind on the way to the studio.' The truth was, I just didn't want her knowing. She would have called Andrew and who knows . . .

"I'm almost sure, on February 19 when I made that statement, I'm almost sure this bum [Andrew] was planning on doing something with the presidency. I've thought back about it and when Andrew heard I made that statement, he was shocked. I think he was working on a scheme to get me to consider the presidency. I've never gone after him on it, but I've heard from people around him." Cuomo swells with pride whenever he speaks of Andrew, who runs a non-profit company that builds low-cost housing for the poor and home-less in New York City. "He's my son, my blood, he's grown up with me, he's done all the political things with me. Can you imagine giving any serious thought to doing it and not sitting with Andrew?"

No more easily than *not* doing it and not sitting with Andrew.

Few reporters took Cuomo's February 19 declaration of non-candidacy at face value. Every time he hiccuped for the next year, we analyzed the sound for evidence of presidential intent. "The reporters loved it," Cuomo recalled. "A guy like Marc Humbert [the AP bureau chief in Albany], who I love, this was his salvation. I mean, he could write these speculation pieces and make the A wire. How else is he going to make the A wire? So he loved it. And I don't think he wanted it to end."

Did Cuomo?

He became the nation's premier political kibitzer in 1987 and early 1988, gossiping with reporters, offering free advice to the candidates, traveling to Moscow, giving terrific speeches and listening to supporters tell him he ought to be running. "It's great for non-candidates like me," he said in the midst of this romp. "We get to stand behind the batting cage and tell the players, 'Do this. Do that. Slow it down.' But we never have to go in there and make a fool of ourselves."

He loved the chase, the action, the repartee. He was constantly riding the waves of his own turbulence. And with everyone—but especially with reporters—he was always playing mind and word games.

Reporter: "Why don't you want to be President?"

Cuomo: "Who says I don't want to be President."

Reporter: "Do you want to be President?"

Cuomo: "No."

His year-long presidential tease—if it was a tease—ended badly. By the time the primaries swung into New York in mid-April, it was apparent Dukakis was going to be the nominee. The Dukakis camp wanted Cuomo to endorse him as a way to signal a party-wide closing of the ranks. He declined, mostly because he didn't want to offend Jesse Jackson and the blacks in New York. When his neutrality was read by some in the press as one last gambit to stir the pot and keep the Mario Scenario going, Cuomo was furious. For more than a year—as he saw it—the press had been using him as a prop for their professional amusement; now they were accusing *him* of dancing after the music had stopped.

One reason he had invited such skepticism was that he'd refused to make the classic Shermanesque statement of noninterest—"If nominated, I will not run; if elected, I will not serve." Cuomo felt that his declaration in February 1987 had been clear enough. If he used the formulation the media was pressing on him, it would be an acknowledgment that he'd left a crack in the door. He saw it as a matter of honor. But finally, when he sensed he was being made to look foolish, he telephoned the Albany bureau chief of *The New York Times* and managed to convey—without using the words—that he would not accept a draft. When he finally did endorse Dukakis, nearly two months later, it came as a sour footnote. "I endorse! I endorse! I endorse!" he grumbled in response to a reporter's inquiry.

There was an even more sour note yet to come. When it finally became clear to one and all that he wasn't going to get in, there was a flurry of renewed press speculation that he had backed away because of some skeleton in his closet. Cuomo still refers to this as the "Lesley Stahl syndrome."

"When Lesley Stahl [of CBS–TV] was finally convinced that I definitely wasn't going to run, she put me on that TV show [*Face the Nation*] and must have asked me four times if it wasn't true that my father-in-law or someone in my family was in the Mafia. It was so surprising to some people that I wasn't running that they figured I must have a mistress, or leprosy, or Mafia connections. Some people still believe it. I get people now — very good friends of mine, nice people — one of them said the whole Republican party knows there must be something there. They've spent a fortune trying to find out what it is. They can't find anything, but they know there must be something."

It's impossible to prove a negative in such matters, but everyone who has ever looked into the Cuomo/Mafia allegations has come away empty-handed. Veteran journalist and Mafia watcher Nicholas Pileggi wrote an exhaustive piece in *New York* magazine in 1988 that systematically shot down the rumors and identified a Republican operative in Albany who had been spreading them. The operative was subsequently fired from the GOP-controlled state senate payroll.

"They say these things about every Italian-American politician I know. . . . " Cuomo said. "I can imagine how Jesse feels. How Ron Brown [chairman of the Democratic National Committee] feels. I was not going to support Ron Brown. He was a student of mine [in law school]. He called me up [in December 1988] and he said he wanted to be national party chairman. I said, 'Hey, Ron, I'll do everything I can to help you, but I don't think I'll get too involved. People will say I'm running for President. You don't need that and I don't need that.' Then I went and had an off-the-record discussion with the editors of a magazine, and this caused me a little aggravation. It is a liberal magazine. In that discussion, the editorial board said, 'You can't make Ron Brown chairman of the party.' I said, 'Why not?' They said, 'Because he's black. He's terrific. He's really conservative, but he's black. You have Jesse. Now you'll have Ron Brown.'

"That's an atrocity. That's when I decided to support Ron Brown. I raised money right away. . . .

"Before I was elected governor, I was secretary of state and lieutenant governor. I had an identity rating of 6 percent. Then someone took a poll and asked, 'What is it you don't like about this person?' Nine percent said his Mafia connections. But only six percent knew who I was. That suggests there's something at work out there."

Cuomo's sensitivities on this front are legendary. Both his parents were immigrants, poorly educated in their own tongue as well as English, but abundantly supplied with character and mother wit. Cuomo, so fiercely proud of them as an adult, had been embarrassed by their broken English when he was a child. He was embarrassed by his own, too. "I know all about ethnic self-hate," he's told many interviewers. In the first grade, he stayed out of school thirty-eight days—not because he was sick, but because he didn't like how different he sounded. In grade school, he remembers playing at the home of a "very WASP-ish" friend, Richard Dearing. When the dinner hour came, the boy's mother said, "Tell your friend he has to go now." It's a line parents commonly use to announce dinner, but Cuomo has never forgotten the tone. "It was like they were saying, 'God forbid you should let *him* come to the table.' And I never got over it. I felt shunned. It didn't leave me with a tick, but it gave me a permanent recollection."[5]

He remembers the slights his mother suffered, too. Cuomo often tells the story of his family's move from South Jamaica, Queens, where his father owned a corner grocery store, to the slightly more affluent Holliswood section of Queens. "Three distinguished-looking women came down the hill to see my mother," he says. "She was outside sweeping the walk. They were a welcoming team of sorts, but they bore no gifts. She remembers them as 'freddo'—cold, aloof. And they said to her: 'You must be the Italian woman. Well, we want you to know you are welcome here, but please, remember to keep the tops on the garbage pails.' "

There are scores of stinging recollections imbedded in Cuomo's memory font. When he graduated from St. John's Law School, first in his class, he applied to sixty Wall Street firms. Not a single one gave him the courtesy of an interview, much less a job. Cuomo had to hang out his shingle across the East River, on Court Street in downtown Brooklyn, where he quickly made a name for himself as a trial attorney. "Mario still sees the world from Court Street," says one longtime aide and admirer. "It's all class warfare."

Some politicians surmised that he didn't run for President because he knew no one could win with a vowel at the end of his name. "There are no Marios in the South," Don Fowler, a party activist from South Carolina (and as fair-minded a man as you will find), said in 1986. The crack so infuriated Cuomo that he threatened to run just to prove that wasn't the reason he wasn't running. Another Southern Democrat, former national party chairman Robert Strauss, probably got closer to the mark on the barriers of ethnicity when he later kidded Cuomo: "We don't like Marios in Texas, and we don't like Eyetalians, and we don't like New Yorkers. But we like *cojones,* and we can hear yours clanking from a mile away."

Cuomo has always understood—in a way that Dukakis never seemed to—how to turn his immigrant roots and the outsider's imprint they'd left on his personality into a political asset. I once saw him give a speech in San Antonio, where he compared the trouble he had growing up in his Queens neighborhood to the difficulties Mexican-Americans had mastering the language of a new world where "the words sounded hard-edged and tight compared to the rolling, rounded rhythms of Mother and Father's native tongue." The audience—most of it Mexican-American—was putty in his hands. He often does a hilarious impersonation of himself as a WASP. "Can you just imagine me as Mark Conrad? Just take a look at me," he says, gesturing toward his thick nose, swarthy complexion, stubby fingers, square frame, animated hands. "Can you imagine me walking in and saying, 'Hi. I'm Mark Conrad. I play tennis. I play golf.'"

I don't think ethnicity had anything to do with his decision not to run. I take him at his word: I think some inner voice told him he wasn't ready.

"Cuomo will never, ever do something unless he feels he is as prepared as he can be," Martin Steadman, his former press secretary, told Cuomo biographer Robert McElvaine in 1987. "He prepares and prepares and prepares [thus the dozen speech drafts]. . . . He just simply will not embarrass himself or his family. He has to be as perfect as he can be, or he won't do it."[6] Fabian Palomino, Cuomo's oldest and closest friend, tells the story of Cuomo being given his first assignment as a clerk for the state Court of Appeals back in the early 1950s. It was to research the legal precedents on a simple motion. Cuomo spent weeks on it, poring over cases that reached back several centuries. He produced a stack of papers a foot high. Palomino, then the senior clerk, finally had to tell him: "You really can't spend all this time researching a simple motion. Just keep it to the existing law and give it to the judge in a couple of pages."

"Gee," Cuomo responded, "but you really have to know."[7]

To read Cuomo's two published volumes of diaries is to understand that he spends much of his inner life measuring himself against celestial standards and finding himself wanting. "Always the nagging truth is that I should be something else—a person who gives only to give, who works only to provide, who speaks only to soothe or persuade for the good, who strives only for others," Cuomo wrote in one diary entry in early 1982. "In the end, I am a man who knows what to do but knows even more sharply that he has failed by his own standards to do it as well as it can be done."[8]

Another entry, from 1980: " 'Selfish.' That's the word. As long as you think about what *you* need, *you* want, *you* feel—as long as you are selfish—you are doomed to frustration. 'Me' is a bottomless pit which cannot be filled, no matter how much in achievement, glory, acclaim, you try shoveling into it. For God's sake, you know the truth! The truth is that the only way to make anything of your life is to be what you know you're supposed to be."[9]

Another, from 1982: "When the news is best, the applause the loudest, my throttle slows things down. . . . I seem incapable of enjoying it [victory] the way people expect me to. In the moments that seem right for exultation, my head turns to analysis."[10]

Cuomo has been deeply influenced by the writings of Pierre Teilhard de Chardin, a French Jesuit theologian who argued that Christian love must embrace two elements—compassion for others and a diminution of self. Compassion for others has always come naturally to Cuomo. Diminution of self has been a harder discipline to master for a man so abundantly supplied with ego and competitive fire. Anyone who has opposed Cuomo—on a baseball diamond, in a courtroom or during a political campaign—readily identifies with the scout who watched him play outfield for the Pittsburgh Pirates' minor-league team in Brunswick, Georgia, in 1952 and noted: "He'll run over you if he gets a chance." Yet winning induces feelings of guilt in Cuomo. It also rubs against his practical philosophy of governing. On the introductory page to his first book, *Forest Hills Diary,* he quoted Edmund Burke: "All government—indeed, every human benefit and enjoyment, every virtue and every prudent act—is founded on compromise." The book is about the episode that drew Cuomo into public life in the early 1970s: he was asked by New York City Mayor John V. Lindsay to mediate a devilishly complicated, racially tinged dispute between residents of Forest Hills, Queens, and City Hall over a low-income housing project. Under Cuomo's compromise, the project was finally built, but with fewer units than originally proposed. Everybody came away with something—and everybody was angry about it. Ever since, Cuomo has governed with an instinct for the golden mean. In Albany, his most vocal critics are liberals, who complain that his incrementalist approach to public policy-making doesn't do justice to the soaring rhetoric of his speeches.

He makes no apologies. "The older I get," he once told me, "the more I try to avoid situations where in order for me to win, you have to lose."

I N THE LATE summer of 1989 I took one last stab at trying to figure out why he didn't run. Again, I interviewed him in Albany.

"Did I misunderstand my political potential? No. I mean, I know who's good in politics. And people whose judgment I respect said I'd have a good chance. I always accepted that. I didn't say, 'Oh, no, I couldn't possibly win.' Some of the people who encouraged me to run, their identity would shock you — some people from the other party. So I had some sense that, yeah, maybe I could succeed.

"But that wasn't the question. The question was whether I was the best thing for the country — whether I was better than Dukakis, better than the others. On the merits, I was not persuaded."

I pointed out that he had been a successful governor of a complex state — and before that, a lieutenant governor and secretary of state. He'd done his apprenticeship.

"Just a minute. We're talking about '86, maybe '87. That was four years as governor — a very short time. We did well in four years. We faced a $1.8 billion deficit. We did well. But I was not as sure of myself then as I am now. The test since then has been a lot tougher. The last two years we had $4.8 billion in potential deficits. The last year we had the worst challenge ever on the death penalty." Cuomo has vetoed death-penalty bills in his state in each of the last seven years; in 1989, his legislature came within one vote of overriding him. "I can't tell you how bad it was this year.* We have been tested. We know more about our capacity now than we did in '86 or '87. That's relevant. You compare yourself to a Michael Dukakis, who had three terms at that time. I had done it once. Could I do it twice? That was all part of the mix.

"Also, the keynote [at the 1984 Democratic National Convention] skewed me. I never understood the keynote. I didn't like the idea that so many people were capable of judging you on one speech. It was wonderful to receive the plaudits, but it was disconcerting to think that people might be fooled into thinking you're capable because of one speech. And so when people said, 'We think you can

---

*Cuomo's 1990 has been even worse. His state budget included $1.6 billion in new taxes, and was enacted after record delays and after the state's bond rating was lowered. But — to his credit — the budget included a fiscal reform package to wean the state from its excessive short-term borrowing habits.

do it, Mario,' I always worried, 'Well, you don't know anything. All you know is the one speech. We had one date. We were at it for five hours and I did one lousy rhumba and you think I'm Cesar Romero. Let's slow down here.'"

I asked whether he had held back because of his inexperience in foreign affairs. Cuomo has been abroad for only two brief trips in his entire life. "He knows Brooklyn but not Beirut," one of his aides once said, explaining why he hadn't run.

I was surprised by his answer.

"Foreign policy would be the easiest part of the job. The hardest part would be the economy and the budget—getting it [a grand deficit-reduction compromise] done. The easiest part would be foreign policy. I have no doubt in my mind. Does it require you to learn things? Oh yeah. Facts. But foreign policy, negotiating, dealing with people who are different, reaching them, projecting to them, dealing with leaders, making deals, making understandings—no, I don't think foreign policy is the hard problem. It certainly requires that you learn a lot of facts, but I have been learning facts all my adult life. There's nobody I know better than I am at learning new facts."

Cuomo sounded to me like a man whose doubts were in full retreat. Will he try in 1992? I've long since learned not to hazard guesses. Suffice it to say that his comments made me think back to a crack he'd made the day after he took himself out of the presidential race in 1987.

I'd asked him then if he thought he'd have any regrets. He answered wistfully: "I can't promise I won't look at the next President and say, 'Gee, he has a big nose. I have a big nose, too.'"

CHAPTER SIX

Jesse Jackson: The Never-Ending Campaign

It ain't over till it's over—and even then it's not over.
—Jesse Jackson, July 15, 1988, eve of the Democratic
National Convention in Atlanta

A FEW DAYS before Super Tuesday, Jesse Jackson was approached in Beaumont, Texas, by a middle-aged white couple.

"Mind if my wife takes a picture of me with you?" the man asked. "I marched in Selma."

"Glad to be with you again, friend," Jackson replied.

"No, you don't understand," the man said. "I marched with the Klan. I don't want to be on the wrong side of history again."

Multiply the moment by thousands and thousands. At some point, it measures the grandeur of Jesse Jackson's 1988 campaign. Everywhere he went, every time he spoke, he touched hearts, stirred hopes, broke barriers, changed minds.

The French writer Madame de Staël once said of Rousseau: "He invented nothing, but he set everything on fire." Jackson's campaign invented nothing—at least not by the hard calculus of winning and losing. The coalition of liberals, social justice activists and economic "outs" he cobbled together never got him to within shouting distance of his party's nomination, much less the presidency. Nor did Jackson's 1988 candidacy invigorate political participation among his core constituency: black voter turnout in the general election declined from 1984 to 1988 by roughly the same proportion that overall participation did, and it continued to lag 5 or 6 points behind white turnout. Nor were there any public-policy initiatives or landmark bills that bore his stamp. Nor did his campaign trigger any detectable outbreak of racial harmony. In the late 1980s, incidents of racial violence were on the rise, and blacks and whites were seemingly more estranged from one another than at any time since before the civil rights era.

Yet alongside this roster of "didn'ts" stands a list of a different color. In 1989, a black man was elected governor of a state; another was elected mayor of the nation's largest city; another was elected chairman of the Democratic National Committee; another was elected Majority Whip of the U.S. House of Representatives. These were all firsts.

One needn't sentimentalize. These electoral breakthroughs may well have occurred had there never been a Jesse Jackson. Indeed, some probably occurred *despite* Jesse Jackson, who is sufficiently polarizing that Douglas Wilder of Virginia, for one, took pains to keep him at arm's length throughout his history-making campaign for governor. Yet there are some figures who, by pushing at the boundaries, make space for others. It is difficult to calibrate their impact, but, Madame de Staël notwithstanding, they do "invent" something. What they invent is new possibilities.

Jackson is such a figure—and at the still-youthful age of forty-eight, he's likely to remain one for a long time. Figures of this kind rarely win elections, but Jackson will probably seek the presidency again. He believes he is "still on a growth curve" with the American people, and he has discovered that, even when he loses, running for President is compatible with—if not indispensable to—the mission he has set for himself as a pioneer for peace, civil rights and social justice.

When Jackson measures his own accomplishments, he makes a distinction between what he calls the "small p" of politics and the "big H" of history. Here's how he did in the "small p" department: Out of an initial field of fourteen presidential hopefuls in 1988, Jackson racked up the third-highest vote total in the primaries—behind only the two eventual nominees, Bush and Dukakis. He doubled his overall vote total from the 1984 primaries, tripled his white vote total and tripled his delegate total. He gained more votes in 1988 (6.7 million in the primaries and another 260,000 in the caucuses) than Walter Mondale did in winning the Democratic nomination in 1984. He achieved more votes than any black has ever won in any campaign in this nation's history. And unlike in 1984, when his support was largely monochromatic, he did so in 1988 by getting a third of his support from whites.

The political explanation for this base expansion is not complicated. Jackson ran in a year when the rest of the Democratic field was running away from liberalism—leaving behind orphaned chunks of the McGovern, Kennedy and Mondale constituencies. He appealed to them by deemphasizing his Third World foreign policy agenda, dropping his complaints against the party rules, cutting his ties to Nation of Islam minister Louis Farrakhan and other black separatists and offering himself as an economic populist. He called for taxing the rich, making the poor take more responsibility for their lives, cutting the military budget and waging an all-out war on drugs.

Jackson's white support was heavily concentrated among liberal elites. His populist vision of a political alliance of working-class blacks and whites may have been a set piece of his speeches, but it never materialized on election day. In primary after primary, the poorer a white voter, the less likely he or she was to be a Jackson supporter. Seventy percent of Jackson's white voters had attended college; 25 percent had gone to graduate school. Expressed another way, nearly a quarter of all whites who attended graduate school and voted in the Democratic primaries voted for Jackson. These people, by and large, were the very ones whose taxes Jackson wanted to raise.[1]

Jackson's success among whites had another notable feature: it was inversely related to the geographic proximity of whites to blacks. That is, Jackson received his greatest percentage of white votes in states where the black population was lowest, and vice versa. He received 33 percent of the white vote in Oregon; 32 percent in Vermont; 31 percent in California; 24 percent in Nebraska; 23 percent in Wisconsin; 22 percent in Connecticut and New Mexico. The black population in these states ranged from 1 percent to 7 percent. In primaries where Jackson did worst among whites—Louisiana (5 percent of white vote), Alabama (6 percent), Georgia (6 percent), Mississippi (6 percent)—the black population ranged from 23 percent to 31 percent. (All data is from ABC and CBS exit polls.)

One last pattern in Jackson's 1988 vote is instructive. He fared much better in the first half of the primary season than in the second. At the end of March 1988, when thirty states had held primaries or caucuses, Jackson was the leading Democratic vote-getter, with 3.15 million votes to Dukakis' 2.95 million. But from then until the convention, when the multi-candidate field winnowed down to three and finally to two, Dukakis won 6.7 million votes to Jackson's 3.5 million. Some of the shift occurred because the white vote was no longer being split among three or four white candidates. But much of it was a reaction to Jackson, whose surprising early successes had forced many voters for the first time to visualize him in the Oval Office. At that point, a whole new set of doubts came into play:

Was his platform too radical? His style too flamboyant? His personality too self-serving? His lack of credentials too troublesome? Jackson was tripped by his own rising star. As swiftly as his base had expanded, it found a ceiling. He never got above the middle 30 percent range in any major primary.

For a few upside-down days in early spring, though, Jackson seemed to have the Democratic party by the throat. I vividly remember an off-the-record conversation I had the day after the Michigan primary with one of the top Democratic leaders in Congress. "Jesse's going to be the nominee," he whispered, off the record, as we snaked through the lobby of the Capital Hilton Hotel following the Sunday afternoon performance of the Gridiron Dinner, an annual tribal bonding of the Washington press and political establishments. "It's not going to be worth the pain of denying him—we'd have to turn our backs on everything we claim to stand for as a party. We might as well just let it happen gracefully." Two things about his analysis shocked me. The first was that he seemed to believe every word of it. The second was that so did I.

My misperception passed in a matter of days, but I'll forever keep it in my memory bank as a cautionary tale about the danger of extrapolating too much from the passions of the moment. I'd spent a good deal of time traveling with Jackson in Michigan. I'd seen the way he was drawing crowds ten times bigger and a hundred times more animated than Dukakis'. I'd interviewed white auto workers in Flint and white truck drivers in Lansing and white flight attendants in Detroit who were close to tears after his speeches. And I'd thought: if he can reach them . . .

In all the excitement, I'd made a rookie mistake. The crowds that show up at political rallies—Jackson's, anybody's—aren't cross-sections of America, even though they may resemble cross-sections of America. They're self-selecting subgroups. In Jackson's case, they came from many walks of life, but they all belonged to the same secular church. They were the congregation of the aggrieved. They had a fundamental beef with the system—be it economic, racial or cultural—and cheering Jesse was their way of expressing it. That didn't necessarily mean he was their choice for President.

In the final stage of the primaries, while he kept losing states to Dukakis by margins of two to one, the crowds kept cheering and Jackson kept assuring them: "We are winning. We are winning every day." By that he meant: judge me as a runner in a greater race—a catalyst, a motivator, a vivifier of hope. Earlier, Jackson had considered it patronizing when pundits hung an asterisk beside his name and asked, "What does Jesse want?" But when his candidacy was on the downslope, no one was more vocal than he in pleading special status.

Give him back his asterisk and Jackson wasn't a loser in 1988, he was a marvel. He had a soaring impact on people, unlike anything I've ever seen in politics. Some voices from his audience:

• "He's going to bring a halt to drugs and crime," said Gary Bushell, twenty-nine, a black car-service driver from Brooklyn. "It's going to be astonishing! He's going to get us to wake up in the morning and say, 'I don't want no more of this stuff.' And then they can't sell the stuff."[2]

• "[His success] makes me feel each day as I go out to battle that I can win," said Betty Williams, forty-three, a black lawyer from Brooklyn.[3]

• "The guy is a poet," said Tim Malone, a white paper-company sales manager from Eugene, Oregon. "I voted for Reagan the first time for the same reason I came to see Jesse today: he makes me feel good about myself and my country."[4]

• "I'm twenty-four and mine is the generation of apathy," said Kathleen Krause, a white college student from Lansing, Michigan. "Half the kids I know from high school aren't even registered to vote. Maybe, just maybe, he can get us out of this apathy."[5]

Political correspondents more experienced than I say the only presidential candidates in their lifetimes who generated this kind of electricity on the campaign trail were Robert Kennedy and George Wallace, both of whom ran in 1968. That was a year of war, assassination, urban riots and student sit-ins. The political seas would have been heaving no matter who ran for President. Jackson's 1988 campaign was waged on calm waters. Yet below a tranquil surface, he found millions of people who were worried about moral and social rot and economic dislocation. He found that these anxieties came in black and white, and he discovered that he could minister to them in both colors.

This last discovery had a mellowing effect on Jackson. "Jesse always knew he could get through to people in a black church," observed Ann Lewis, a white woman who was one of his closest advisers. "The breakthrough for him was finding out he could get through to whites, too."

"Whites all over the country have opened their hearts to me," Jackson said midway through the primaries. "They know there has been this separation, and now they have been willing to say, 'Let's call it even.' They know my message is authentic. They know I have stood for them—at the plant gate and the farm auction. And now they are starting to stand with me. You can't help but be moved by that. You can't help but grow from that."

Nor could the nation. When Jackson won the Michigan primary at the end of March, triggering what *The New York Times* aptly called "Ten Days That Shook the Campaign," *Time* senior writer Walter Shapiro caught the meaning of the moment in a cover story. "Any American child can grow up to be president," the piece began. "That idealistic sentiment began as part of the catechism of democracy, but through generations of rote it has degenerated into a kindergarten fable. Adults, of course, know the truth. The presidency is reserved for white men who have held high office and who have almost always avoided embracing a cause or expressing a sentiment that is far outside the mainstream of established opinion. But there are rare moments when the truths that seemed self-evident begin to be reexamined. The recalibration is a slow process, and it does not always immediately lead to dramatic consequences. Still, just the act of toying with a previously unimaginable possibility leaves an indelible mark. Even if the surface of life goes on pretty much as before, a seed has been planted that may someday bloom."[6]

Jackson planted his seed in a society that, by the late 1980s, had made one black man, Bill Cosby, its national daddy, and another, Colin Powell, the keeper of its most sensitive national-security secrets. These breakthroughs were all the more heartening because they'd come about naturally, in the course of things, and evoked precious little comment. They were emblematic of the journeys of millions of blacks who had climbed into the American middle class, through doors thrown open by the civil rights struggles of the 1950s and 1960s. In 1940, there were 300 black engineers; in 1980, there were 36,109. In 1970, there were 3,000 black lawyers; in 1982, there were 18,000. In 1970, there were 14,000 black school administrators; in 1982, there were 48,000. In 1988, there were 7,226 black elected officials. A decade earlier, there had been one-third fewer. From 1967 to 1987, the percentage of black families with annual incomes over $35,000 (in constant 1987 dollars) nearly doubled, to 22.2 percent.

Yet there was another set of figures that told a much different story. From 1967 to 1987, the percentage of black families with incomes under $10,000 (again, in constant dollars) also rose, from 28.3 percent in 1967 to 30 percent in 1987. In 1987, the median income for blacks was 57.1 percent of the median income for whites, lower than it had been in any year of the 1970s. The fraction of black men aged 18 to 24 in college dropped from 35.4 percent in 1976 to 27.8 percent in 1987. In 1986, more young black males (aged 20–29) were either in jail or on probation or parole (609,690) than in college (436,000). At the end of the 1980s, blacks made up 46 percent of the nation's prison population, and owned 2 percent of its businesses. They accounted for 50 percent of the nation's murder victims, and held 1 percent of the nation's family wealth. In 1987 and 1988, black life expectancy actually decreased—the only time in this century it did so while white life expectancy was going up. The main reason was the sharp increase in homicides, now the leading cause of death among black males aged 15–24. A black male born today (if present homicide rates continue) has a 1-in-23 chance of being murdered before he reaches age twenty-five. A staggering 62.2 percent of all black babies born in 1987 were brought into the world out of wedlock (nearly double the 1970 percentage), and 45 percent will be raised in poverty.

As the numbers make achingly clear, the black community has traveled down two separate paths in the twenty-five years since the apex of the civil rights era. Roughly two-thirds of all blacks have made it into the economic mainstream; roughly one-third are officially classified as poor, and perhaps half of that group are chronically poor, mired in what has come to be called the underclass. But today's poor are even worse off than the poor of a generation ago, in part because of the way that relatively inexpensive drugs and the attendant criminal culture have gripped the ghetto; in part because the migration of upwardly mobile blacks out of the inner city has removed churches, role models, the work ethic and other socializing forces from the places where they are most desperately needed. "You make $150 a week at Roy Rogers, but $150 a minute on the street," says the 17-year-old black youth jailed on drug charges.[7] Meantime, the middle-class two-thirds may have escaped the slums, but not the stigma. For when much of white America thinks about blacks, it's still the one-third they see in their mind's eye.

In the early days of his campaign, Jackson chose to find the glass two-thirds full, not one-third empty. He frequently scolded reporters for underestimating Americans on matters of race. "Racism is not genetic; it is not irredeemable," he told them, invoking the examples of Cosby and Powell. When reporters would ask him, "Do you think a black man can be elected President?" he would throw the question back at them.

"What do you think?" he asked a young Hispanic reporter who put the question to him at a press conference in Santa Fe in the spring of 1987.

"I—I'm asking you," the reporter stammered.

"No. No. I'm asking you," Jackson persisted, tenderly. "Because what you think matters."

"No," the reporter finally said.

"Well," Jackson said. "I hope the day has come when people can consider politicians the same way they consider baseball players. On the baseball diamond, the only thing that matters is hitting and pitching and fielding and making the plays with the fewest errors. Forty years ago, America wasn't ready to be color-blind on the baseball field. Now it is color-blind as a matter of course. This year, I'm getting invitations to talk to the state legislatures in Mississippi, in Montana, in Nebraska. I'm getting invited to talk to Kiwanis Clubs and Rotary Clubs in the most rural, whitest parts of the country. Four years ago, America wasn't ready for that—but America is getting better."

When he was losing week after week toward the end of the primary season, Jackson began sounding more like the tribune of black aggrievement he'd been for his previous twenty years in the public life. He felt that press scrutiny had been too tough on him after his Michigan victory. And he complained that Bush and Dukakis were being allowed to skate along, making never-never-land promises about how they would balance the budget, while he wasn't getting credit for presenting the most detailed deficit-reduction plan put out by any candidate in either party. (Jackson's budget called for freezing military spending for five years, doubling spending on education, welfare and social services and raising taxes on the wealthy and corporations.)

It rankled him all the more when commentators claimed the double standard was operating in reverse. "If he were white, you would not take Jesse Jackson seriously, based on his record—he doesn't have a record," said Jack Nelson, the Washington bureau chief of the Los Angeles *Times*.[8] The Center for Media and Public Affairs, a media monitoring group, found that Jackson's television coverage was the most extensive and the most positive of all candidates running in the primaries. His 74 percent positive coverage rating was 17 points above the average of all Democratic primary contenders, 20 points above the average of all Republicans, and more than double the score that Bush and Dukakis would get in the fall campaign. "Jesse may not have gotten a free ride from the media," Jon

Margolis of the Chicago *Tribune* cracked, "but he certainly had a cut-rate fare."

Jackson did not see it that way. "They say if I was not black, I wouldn't have gotten where I am," he said on a flight from Albuquerque to Los Angeles in May 1988, speaking in a slow cadence. "Well, if Bush was not white, he'd be waiting on tables. . . . And when Dukakis started talking about [southern Africa] at that debate the other day, he sounded like a basketball player, but ya'll don't call them on it.

"For me, it's always uphill," he continued. "I get no momentum. I get no normal roll. I have to fight for everything I get. I have to keep earning my votes, Dukakis keeps inheriting his [from the other white candidates]. I have to be superior to be equal. I can live with it, though. The only gratification I get from paying the double dues is that I may not get credit but I know what I know what I know."

My guess is that most blacks see their lives in white America in much the same way, while most whites believe blacks ought to lose the self-pity and start climbing the ladder. This chasm in perception is part of what makes the race problem so intractable. Two decades ago, there was a national consensus—abstained from only by white bigots—about what held blacks back. Now it is neither agreed upon nor openly discussed, for the implications of each race's worst suspicions—black inferiority; white collective guilt—are too raw to broach in public. One effect of this unhealthy silence has been a rising tide of racial intolerance among the young—the supposedly enlightened, post–*Brown v. Board of Education* generation. "This is one of the most significant trends of the last few years," said Janet Caldwell of the Center for Democratic Renewal, an Atlanta organization that monitors hate groups. "Young people are out of touch with history. They don't have a connection to the civil rights movement and they don't have that kind of ideal."9

The late 1980s saw an increase in white-on-black racial violence among youths in working-class communities like Howard Beach, Queens; Bensonhurst, Brooklyn; Forsyth County, Georgia. It was not merely a class phenomenon, however. A total of 175 campuses— including some of the nation's most elite—experienced some kind of racial incident from 1985 to 1988, according to a survey by the National Institute Against Prejudice and Violence, which had not monitored so many episodes since the 1960s. They ranged from a black student being beaten at the University of Massachusetts at Amherst, to racist jokes being aired on a campus radio station at the University of Michigan, to members of a fraternity at the University of Wisconsin holding a mock slave auction, to a swastika with the words "white power" being hung at Yale's Afro-American Cultural Center, to freshmen defacing a poster of Beethoven, giving the composer thick lips and placing it on a black student's door in a dormitory at Stanford, to graffiti with the inscription "Niggers, Spics and Chinks quit complaining or get out" turning up on campus at Smith College.

None of this was discussed during the presidential campaign. The view of most Americans seemed to be that "we did blacks" in the 1960s. Racial issues had been off the national agenda ever since. Jackson gained in popularity in 1988 in part because he shelved the black portion of his rhetoric. After the campaign was over, however, as passions were inflamed by the brutal rape and assault of a white jogger in Central Park by a gang of blacks who were out "wilding," and a few months later by the murder of a black teenager in Bensonhurst, Brooklyn, by a gang of whites who mistakenly thought their victim was on his way to visit a white girlfriend, there were the stirrings of a national dialogue. Television documentaries aired; Op-Ed pages filled up; magazine articles were published. One of the cutting edges of the new debate centered on affirmative action — a set of policies launched in workplaces and classrooms in the late sixties and early seventies to help victims of past discrimination make up for lost time. In the ensuing two decades, affirmative action had triggered a flood of lawsuits, stirred predictable resentments among a generation of whites and stigmatized many blacks who would have advanced without special help. Now some of its former defenders — black as well as white — were beginning to wonder if it had done more harm than good.

Several thoughtful writers brought unusual texture to this discussion. Excerpts from four essays:

"Of the eighteen black students (in a student body of 1,000) who were on campus in my freshman year [1964], all graduated, though a number of us were not from the middle class," Shelby Steele, an associate professor of English at San Jose State, wrote in February 1989, "At the university where I currently teach, the drop-out rate for black students is 72 percent, despite the presence of several academic support systems: a counseling center with black counselors; an Afro-American studies department; black faculty, administrators, and staff; a general education curriculum that emphasizes 'cultural pluralism'; an Education Opportunities Program; a mentor program; a black faculty and staff association; and an administration and faculty that often announce the need to do more for black students.

" . . . I don't congratulate my generation. I think we were advantaged. We came along at a time when racial integration was held in high esteem. And integration was a very challenging social concept for both blacks and whites. We were remaking ourselves—that's what one did at college—and making history. We had something to prove. . . .

"There is much irony in the fact that black power would come along in the late Sixties and change all this. Black power was a movement of uplift and pride, and yet it also delivered the weight of pride—a weight that would burden black students from then on. . . . In the name of pride, it required the denial of black anxiety. Without a frank account of one's anxieties, there is no clear direction, no clear challenge. Black students today . . . are not filled with the same urgency to prove themselves, because black pride has said, You're already proven, already equal, already as good as anybody.

"The 'black identity' shaped by black power most powerfully contributes to racial tensions on campuses by basing entitlements more on race than on constitutional rights and standards of merit."[10]

Leon Wieseltier wrote in *The New Republic:* "In the memory of oppression, oppression outlives itself. The scar does the work of the wound. That is the real tragedy: that injustice retains the power to distort long after it has ceased to be real. It is a posthumous victory for the oppressors, when pain becomes a tradition. And yet the atrocities of the past must never be forgotten. That is the unfairly difficult dilemma of the newly emancipated and the newly enfranchised: an honorable life is not possible if they remember too little and a normal life is not possible if they remember too much. A black man or woman who did not look for racism among the causes of his or her misfortune would be mad. But a black man or woman who found racism everywhere he or she looked would also be mad."[11]

Joe Klein, a self-described guilt-ridden white liberal, wrote in *New York* magazine: "Integration seems an impossibly romantic notion now. Even to propose it as the solution to the racial morass raises derisive hoots in the black community and patronizing smiles from whites. Serious talk of integration ended when 'black power' began to flourish and equal rights was supplanted by affirmative action as the rally cry of the movement. Aggrievement—the notion that blacks deserved special compensatory treatment—replaced assimilation at the top of the activists' agenda. . . . Liberals quickly, romantically—and quite irresponsibly—acceded to the new black demands; conservatives were quietly relieved that blacks no longer wanted in. Only a few brave souls raised the obvious question: How could blacks be included in American society if they insisted on separating themselves from it?"[12]

Ernest van den Haag, a conservative law professor at Fordham University, wrote: "The greatest harm currently suffered by blacks is done by those who want to favor them. Indeed, a vested bureaucratic interest in affirmative action has grown up, and unfortunately many black political leaders benefit from this policy.... Leaders benefit from the advantages of being 'spokesman' and from being able to mobilize the guilt feelings of whites profitably, while telling their supporters that they can procure advantages without effort. In the long run blacks will have to pay for this demagogic leadership."[13]

Van den Haag's observations go to the heart of what bothers many people about Jackson. So did Bush's description of him during the campaign as a "hustler from Chicago." Behind all of that lofty language, critics have always wondered: Isn't Jesse just in it for himself?

The question doesn't yield a simple answer, for Jackson has always operated in the fuzzy area where idealism and opportunism overlap. In 1968, as a maverick young lieutenant to Martin Luther King, Jr., he outraged fellow civil rights leaders by falsely claiming that he had cradled the dying King in his arms—this in a ham-handed (but ultimately successful) effort to anoint himself as King's heir. During the 1970s and early 1980s, Jackson used his Chicago-based economic self-help organization, PUSH, to lead (or threaten) black consumer boycotts against corporate targets. The boycotts would be called off when the corporations signed compacts pledging to hire more black employees and recruit more black franchise owners. The chief beneficiaries were a handful of black car dealers and fast-food store owners—who would immediately become a source of financial contributions to PUSH. Jackson had no apologies for his modus operandi. He had apprenticed in Chicago under, among others, Saul Alinsky, the community organizer whose motto was: "The hell with charity; you'll only get what you're strong enough to take."

Before he began running for President, Jackson's sole experience in public life had been in mobilizing protest, venting grievance, demanding compensatory treatment—not in building consensus. A Chicago politician tells the story of young Jackson's relationship with one of his first political adversaries, the late Mayor Richard J. Daley. "He'd march on City Hall, make all sorts of wild demands, call the mayor all sorts of names. The next day he'd come in alone and settle for a fraction of what he was asking for out on the streets. 'That was all for leverage,' he'd tell the mayor."

At every important decision point in his career, Jackson has sought to position himself the way he did with Daley—one foot on the inside, one foot in the streets. He believes this tactical straddle maximizes his leverage from a position of disadvantage. Even more, he believes it has made him what he is today—a self-invented missionary for change with a burgeoning national and international portfolio, operating without an office, title or a formal set of responsibilities.

This is a man who began life—quite literally—as a poor bastard. Now, even with a Republican administration in power, he confers regularly—on matters ranging from drugs to education to justice to housing to labor policy—with a half-dozen Cabinet members. As often as not, they initiate the calls. Foreign dignitaries and dissidents on every continent receive him. International peace organizations seek his leadership. The economically aggrieved in this country— including more and more predominantly white groups, such as farmers, miners, airline pilots, autoworkers, textile workers, telephone technicians—seek his help.

"I suppose you could say I'm sort of an entrepreneur," Jackson said in an interview in December 1989. "I've made up my own plays. If I had run the conventional play, I wouldn't be here. . . . Maybe I'd be a congressman from Chicago, something like that. But a lot of people who spend all their time trying to get to the inside are like giants on the island of Lilliput. Anyone who would be a political change agent cannot do it with both feet on the inside."

The interview turned to whether Jackson should seek the mayoralty of Washington, D.C., his new base of operations after a move from Chicago. He said he was "rasslin' with" a decision. The argument for it was that he could do good in a city that desperately needed new leadership, and at the same time fill a gaping hole in his presidential résumé. Jackson was skeptical. "The people who keep saying, come over here now to get credentials—many of them got their credentials because I was over there. Credentials have never been about ability. They have always been about leverage. The question is, where is the most leverage for change, and does the mayor's office in Washington increase that leverage?"

Two months after we spoke, Jackson took himself out of the running for mayor—even though, in the interim, Washington Mayor Marion Barry had been busted in a drug sting operation. Pundits from across the political spectrum excoriated him for not seizing the opportunity. "Jackson's decision is part of his descent into triviality, bounding around the world to wherever television cameras are gathered, being parasitic of the achievement of others," wrote George Will. "He's made it far too easy for people to conclude that Marion Barry was right when he [said]: 'Jesse don't wanna run nothing but his mouth,'" wrote David Broder. "Jackson calls that a cheap shot. But when he had a chance to disprove it, he ducked." The critics were mostly white. Most of Jackson's black supporters saw the situation the way Jackson saw it: the mayoralty was a snare urged on him by white "friends" who wanted to coax him off the presidential playing field, where his continued participation was inconvenient to the Democratic party. They resented the idea that Jackson should be asked to prove himself in a job where he'd be dealing with "street lights and that kind of junk," in the words of Hazel F. Obey, a board member of Jackson's National Rainbow Coalition, Inc.

I suspect Jackson shares Obey's contempt for the minutiae of government. I also suspect that somewhere hovering near his decision not to run for mayor was a dimly acknowledged specter of self-doubt. Years ago, Jackson used to describe himself as a "tree shaker, not a jelly maker." When he started running for President, he said he'd outgrown the metaphor. But it seems to me that it still captures his shrewd sense of his own strengths and weaknesses. He knows he can motivate. He doubts he can administer. Running for President is mostly about the former. Being President is about both. The voters understand the difference.

E VEN DURING his giddy season of success in 1988, Jackson showed little appetite for making the transition from movement leader to mainstream administrator. No other presidential contender, for example, raised money the way he did. He would call the congregation forward at the end of his political sermons and ask them to give witness by giving money. First he'd have those willing to donate $1,000 march to the front, then $500, then $100, then $50, and so on—down to a dollar. Willie L. Brown, Jr., the canny speaker of the California General Assembly who served as Jackson's 1988 campaign chairman, used to complain to Jackson that it wasn't presidential to raise money that way. "I'll tell you what's not presidential," Jackson once shot back. "Not having gas money to get to the next town." Though he was always pleading poverty, he raised and spent

$26 million in 1988, second only to Dukakis' $31 million among the Democrats.

Jackson was equally unconventional in the way he handled another key campaign activity—scheduling. In 1984, reporters and staff used to joke that the Jackson campaign operated on J.S.T. (Jesse Standard Time), whose hours were anybody's guess. He took it on as a personal challenge to be more punctual in 1988, but he still had trouble giving up his autonomy over scheduling. When Gerald Austin, a Democratic consultant and streetwise Bronx native, was named campaign manager in 1988, he was asked what he thought his biggest problem would be. "Getting control of the schedule away from Jesse," he said. Jackson knew the country better than anyone on his staff, and he had the best nose for publicity. The trouble was, he also liked to preserve maximum flexibility, which wasn't possible when his campaign entourage sometimes numbered two dozen, the traveling press was another fifty and the Secret Service maintained a round-the-clock detail of eight. Though Jackson's schedule did become somewhat more orderly in 1988, there was some backsliding at the end. The worst lapse was on the eve of the California primary, when he showed up seventeen minutes late for a live half-hour television broadcast that had cost his campaign $135,000, leaving disc jockey host Casey Kasem to kill time as he assured puzzled viewers that the candidate was expected any minute.

Jackson was unconventional in more consequential ways. The day after the primary season ended with the voting in California and three other states, he began publicly lobbying to be Dukakis' running mate. This is virtually never done by mainstream politicians. He knew from the first that he wasn't going to be asked (though he may have gotten swept up by his own campaign for a short while). It was all tactical: he wanted to force the issue, to make it easier for a black (perhaps him) to make it onto the ticket the next time. He was once again marching on City Hall, demanding one thing in the hope of coming away with something else. When Dukakis picked Lloyd Bentsen—and failed to notify Jackson in advance with a phone call—Jackson had the effect he wanted. He was the aggrieved party. He spent the week before the convention elaborately milking his grievance as he kept up a running commentary about whether he would enthusiastically campaign for the ticket in the fall. His antics had Democrat regulars in Atlanta complaining bitterly (though almost always privately) that he'd hijacked the convention. He was getting two or three times the coverage of the nominee. "What does

Jesse want?" went one joke that circulated in Atlanta. "The same thing as any terrorist: $5 million and an airplane." On the first morning of the convention, he and Dukakis had a three-hour private meeting—they were joined at the end by Bentsen—where they aired their differences and reached a chilly agreement to cooperate. Jackson campaigned for the ticket in black neighborhoods in the fall, but not with much enthusiasm.

What he had wanted for his leverage—more than jobs for his campaign staff, more than any promise of a high-level position in a Dukakis administration, more than "$5 million and an airplane" with which he would campaign for the ticket in the fall—was the simple dispensation to stay in the limelight. The problem for Jackson is that the end of a presidential campaign arrives like Cinderella's midnight. It's not merely the moment of defeat; it's the time when the klieg lights go out; the camera crews stop following him; the Secret Service disappears; the charter plane is leased to a new customer. With no base other than his wits, his throat and his reputation, he must do whatever he can to keep the gig going—including making demands that, when unfilled, reinforce his supporters' sense of grievance.

In short, Jackson's quests for the presidency are all but scripted to start in hope and end in recrimination. And not just for Jackson, but for his party. Why did Dukakis squander a 17-point lead after the convention and lose to Bush by 7.5 percentage points? There are lots of explanations, many treated elsewhere in this book. One of them may have been Jackson's domination of coverage in Atlanta. Shortly before the convention, Congressman Robert Michel (R–Ill.) had predicted, with a candor he instantly regretted, that Jackson's heavily black delegation in Atlanta would leave an indelible mark on television viewers. "I think a lot of people are going to be surprised when they look at the convention this summer," Michel said in late June, "and see that one-third of the delegates are black."

Michel's only mistake was saying out loud what most politicians privately believed. The fall campaign began with Republicans portraying the Democratic ticket as a three-headed hydra—Dukakis/Bentsen/Jackson—and ended with them making Willie Horton a household name. They never mentioned race explicitly; they never had to. Mutely, race occupied the same ground in 1988 it has held for the past quarter-century: one of the most important factors in determining party loyalty and presidential vote choice.

When President Johnson signed the Civil Rights Act on July 2,

1964, he reportedly told his aide Bill Moyers: "I think we just delivered the South to the Republican party for a long time to come." He was prophetic. In every presidential election since 1968, the Republican candidate has carried a majority of the white vote— not just in the South, but nationwide. Working-class Northern Catholics and Southern Protestants, especially the male of the species, have defected in droves from the Democratic fold in the past quarter-century. Both groups remain natural Democrats on most economic issues. They have been driven to vote Republican in presidential races by national-security issues (though by the late 1980s these had waned in importance as the Cold War wound down), by their cultural conservatism and by a set of domestic concerns that are either directly related to race (busing, affirmative action, civil rights) or have racial overtones (welfare, crime, drugs).

"These white Democratic defectors express a profound distaste for blacks, a sentiment that pervades almost everything they think about government and politics," Democratic pollster Stanley Greenberg wrote in 1985 after conducting an extensive round of focus-group discussions with former Democratic voters. "Blacks constitute the explanation for their vulnerability and for almost everything that has gone wrong in their lives; not being black is what constitutes being middle-class; not living with blacks is what makes a neighborhood a decent place to live." Likewise, Harry MacPherson, a lawyer, author, party graybeard and former LBJ adviser, attributed the Democrats' five-out-of-six presidential losing streak to "the white man's view that the Democratic Party had cast their lot with black Americans, to the ultimate disadvantage of whites."[14]

On the other hand, there are those who believe that only a Democratic Party led by a Jackson can exorcise the demons of race. Norman Mailer, writing an Op-Ed piece in *The New York Times* that appeared in the midst of the racially inflamed New York primary, observed: "The fundamental problem facing America today is not our sagging spasmodic economy (although that is bad enough), nor the abyss of our drug population, which contributes to economic lassitude vis-a-vis the Japanese. No, the problem beneath other problems is that the gulf between blacks and whites has not begun to close. It is an incubus upon the energies of this nation. . . . Jesse Jackson is not perfect . . . [but] what does count for me is that Jackson offers a cogent sense of sympathy for human suffering. He can appreciate the paucity of identity among the underprivileged. Of all of our candidates, he speaks to our powerful passion for human promise and improvement. . . . Jesse Jackson, elected as president and growing in stature, could illuminate our lives and give us dignity again as Americans. I want to believe in that. I am tired of living in the miasma of our indefinable and ongoing national shame."

Ever since the association in the public mind between "Democrat" and "black" has grown so strong, black support for Democratic presidential candidates has risen from the 2–1 and 3–1 ratios of the 1950s and 1960s to the 10–1 ratios of the 1980s. The size of the black vote has grown, too. Jackson claimed credit for registering 2 million new blacks in his first run for the presidency in 1984. (It's debatable how much credit he personally deserved and how much belonged to the unprecedented activity of scores of grass-roots voter registration groups.) Enough of these new black voters returned to the polls in 1986 to help tip five close Senate campaigns that year over to the Democrats, helping them recapture control of the chamber they lost in 1980. Jackson now argues that his party's path back to the White House lies with reaching out to the more than 11 million blacks who still do not vote. He appears to greatly overestimate the possibilities here, however. As voter-turnout analyst Ruy Teixeira has pointed out, had blacks voted at the same turnout ratio as whites in 1988, Bush would have defeated Dukakis by 6.1 million votes instead of 7.0 million; had black turnout exceeded white turnout by 10 percent (this has never happened), Bush's winning margin would have fallen to "only" 4.7 million.[15] "Our problem in presidential campaigns is not that we aren't getting enough blacks to vote Democratic," said Democratic Senatorial Campaign Committee chairman John Breaux (D–La.), one of the Southerners who owed his 1986 election to a strong black vote. "It's that we aren't getting enough whites."

While Jackson rejects that analysis, he also knows how to count. He did his best to "whiten" his appeal in 1988: his message was tailored to cut across racial barriers, and his staff at the topmost levels was almost all white. Then, in the ragged endgame, he fell back into a mode of aggrievement. He was once again the black candidate, the tribune of resentment. "He went from black to white to black again," said campaign manager Austin, measuring Jackson's political journey from 1984 to 1988.* Whites became less interested in what he had to say, and some of the magic was gone.

*Austin was relieved of his responsibilities in the final weeks of the campaign, as Jackson brought in Washington lawyer-lobbyist Ronald H. Brown, Jr., to run his convention operation. Brown subsequently became the party's national chairman.

SOME OF the magic Jackson will never lose. His effect on his audiences—his rhymes, his cadences, his voice that starts in a whisper and rises to a roar, his call-and-response of the black church—is nothing short of mesmerizing.

"What do I want?" Jackson would ask audiences in 1988, taunting the doubting pundits with the question he so disliked. "I want to stop drugs. What do I want? I want to wipe out malnutrition. What do I want? I want to end ghettos, save jobs, secure farms, invest in people, raise the minimum wage, build affordable housing, make America better, then let the sun shine on everybody!"

As Jackson's pace would quicken and his majestic voice would climb the decibel scale, the shouts of his audience would swell with him, loud and fervent.

He had the same kind of transforming effect each time he delivered what came to be known as his ode to the working poor.

"No matter what Reagan and Bush say, most poor people are not on welfare. They work every day.

"They take the early bus. They work every day.

"They care for other people's babies and can't watch their own. They cook other people's food and carry leftovers home. They work every day.

"They are janitors running the buffing machines, and orderlies in the hospital. A loaf of bread is no cheaper for them than it is for the doctor. They work every day.

"They put on uniforms and are considered less than a person. 'Hey, you, maid.' They work every day.

"They change the beds in the hotels. Sweep our streets. Clean the schools for the children. They're called lazy, but they work every day.

"They are nurses who wipe the fevered bodies of those who are sick. They clean out the commodes. No job is beneath them.

"And yet when they get sick"—Jackson is shouting now—"they cannot afford to lie in the bed they have made up every day!

"That's not right. That's not right. America is a better nation than that."

Jackson visited at least one high school per week during the campaign, as he has for the last fifteen years. The routine rarely changed, no matter whether he was in a slum, a suburb or a farm town. Near the end of his lecture to the students about taking responsibility for one's life, he would lower his voice and shush the audience.

"How many of you, in this room, know somebody who is dead because of drugs? Please stand."

Typically, a handful of students would stand.

"How many of you know someone who is in jail because of drugs? Please stand." Often a quarter to a half of the student body would stand.

"How many of you know somebody who uses drugs? Please stand." Virtually the entire audience would stand.

"Please be seated.

"Now, be honest and be fair to yourselves. How many of you have tried drugs?"

Usually, only a few students would stand at first. Eyes would quickly scan the room, necks would crane. Then a few more students would stand. Then up to a third or a half of the room. Then Jackson would make the altar call.

"If you have the will to say no to dope, please come forward." Dozens would—some nervously giggling, some grimly silent. Jackson would congratulate them for their courage, then direct them to join hands and repeat: "I've fallen beneath my dignity. I can and will be a better person."

He would finish with his trademark call-and-response:

Jackson: "Repeat after me: I am."

Students: "I am."

Jackson: "Somebody."

Students: "Somebody."

Jackson: "My mind."

Students: "My mind."

Jackson: "Is a pearl."

Students: "Is a pearl."

Jackson: "I can learn anything."

Students: "I can learn anything."

Jackson: "In the world."

Students: "In the world."

Jackson: "If my heart can conceive it."

Students: "If my heart can conceive it."

Jackson: "And my mind can believe it."

Students: "And my mind can believe it."

Jackson: "Then I know I can achieve it."

Students: "Then I know I can achieve it."

Jackson: "Up with hope."

Students: "Up with hope."

Jackson: "Down with dope."
Students: "Down with dope."
Jackson: "Up with hope."
Students: "Up with hope."
Jackson: "Down with dope."
Students: "Down with dope."
Jackson: "Up with hope."
Students: "Up with hope."
Jackson: "Down with dope."
Students: "Down with dope."

Jackson: "[Fill in the blank] High School Number One! I love you very much. I love you very much."

He would leave the auditorium awash in cheers and tears.

For raw emotional effect, no speech he gave in 1988 topped his "I understand" refrain, in which he recounted the circumstances of his youth (with some poetic license) to those most in need of his ministering.

"You see Jesse Jackson on television, but you don't know the me that makes me me," he would tell black audiences in the inner city. "Jesse Jackson is my third name. I'm adopted. I never spent a night in my daddy's house. Never saw him shave in the morning. I really do understand.

"Born in my mother's bed. She couldn't afford hospital care. I really do understand.

"I am the son of a teenage mother, who was the daughter of a teenage mother. I understand.

"Born in a three-room house. Bathroom in the back yard, slop jar by the bed. I understand.

"We didn't eat turkey at three o'clock on Thanksgiving Day, because Momma was off cooking someone else's turkey. We'd play football to pass the time till Momma came home. Around 6 p.m. we would meet her at the bottom of the hill, carrying back the leftovers from Mrs. Marshall's table. I really do understand.

"All these experts on subculture, underclass. I got my life degree in subculture. Looked down on. Rejected. Low expectations. Told you can't make it. I was born in the slum, but the slum wasn't born in me. And it wasn't born in you. You can make it.

"Hold your head high. Stick your chest out. You can make it. I know it gets rough sometimes.

"Hold on, the morning comes.

"I know you get tired sometimes.

"Hold on, the morning comes.

"Suffering breeds character, character breeds faith, and in the end, faith will never disappoint. So hold on, the morning comes."

The effect of these speeches on black audiences—the cheering, the singing, the weeping, the swaying, the praying—was almost too powerful. Sometimes even Jackson was troubled by it. Once, as he and his entourage were boarding a bus after an event in Milwaukee, a middle-aged black man, missing half of his teeth, approached him as if he were the savior. "You got to do it for us, Jesse. You got to do it for us, Jesse. You got to do it for us, Jesse," he kept repeating.

Jackson took the man in an embrace, but was thrown by the beseeching tone. As soothingly as he could, Jackson squared up to the man and said, "I'll do what I can. But you got to do it for yourself, too."

After a speech in New Jersey near the end of his campaign, Jackson paused to ponder his impact. "Ten thousand people left their way to hear what one person had to say. What can you feel except responsible? What can you feel except obligated? I might be tired, but I'm a conduit. And they plug into me. And they shoot this electricity through me. Then my lights come on. And they get the heat! And they get the light! It's reciprocity. They give to me, I give to them. I give to them, they give to me. Reciprocity."[16]

Jackson knows better than anyone that his speeches don't reduce well to print, but he likes to tweak critics who accuse him of speaking in doggerel. "Y'all call 'em rhymes, I call 'em epigrams," he kidded a meeting of the American Society of Newspaper Editors in the spring of 1988. "These are shorthand ways to deliver messages. I could say, 'Down with narcotics, up with sobriety,' but I don't think I would be communicating very well."

JACKSON CAN be as charismatic in private as he is on stage. As an entrepreneurial rather than an institutional politician, he's always scrambling to sign on people to help him keep the enterprise afloat. His chief recruiting tool is the force of his personality. In 1988, his circle of advisers grew broader than it had ever been before. He was able to bring into his orbit, among others, California Speaker Willie Brown, Washington attorney Eleanor Holmes Norton, future party chairman Ronald Brown, former Democratic National Committee political director Ann Lewis, former Office of Management and Budget director Bert Lance and former Democratic National Committee chairman John White.

Jackson is a relentless suitor. "Jesse called me thirty-five or forty times," said California's Brown, explaining why he finally signed on as campaign chairman. No politician works the phones harder than Jackson—or at odder hours. He is famous for making his calls post-midnight and pre-dawn. "I'll tell you one thing my relationship with Jesse has done for me," Lewis once said. "When the phone rings in the middle of the night, I no longer worry that one of my kids is in trouble."

The night Bruce Babbitt dropped out of the race following his poor showing in New Hampshire, Jackson was all over him for an endorsement. "First Jesse called, then he had Bill Cosby talk to me, then he came to my hotel room," Babbitt recalled. "He kept reminding me how we'd both marched in Selma, that sort of stuff. The next morning, he called again at 7 a.m. We talked for a few minutes and he said, 'Wait a minute, Bruce. I'm over here at the CBS station about to do an interview. Turn on your television set. We'll continue our dialogue.' So I turn the TV on to CBS, and Jesse is being interviewed about the horse race, and he immediately turns the interview to day care and budget deficits—all the stuff I'd talked about in my campaign. And I say to Hattie [Babbitt's wife], 'This guy's doing my message better than I ever did.' I've never seen more of a virtuoso performance in my life." Babbitt didn't endorse Jackson for President. Nine months later, however, when Ron Brown declared his candidacy for DNC chairman, Babbitt was among the first aboard the bandwagon.

"My definition of a leader is someone who can make you fetch," John White once said, following a breakfast meeting at which he found himself holding a glass of orange juice for Jackson for several minutes while the candidate finished a thought. "I haven't done that for anyone since LBJ."

I T'S NOT JUST politicians he woos this way. It's also journalists. Over the years, Jackson has built up first-name relationships with all three network anchors and most major newspaper and magazine editors across the country. Although he is often disappointed by his treatment at the hands of the establishment press, there's no precinct he works harder. He doesn't hesitate to get on the telephone and play assignment editor. As in: "Dan, I'm going to Mozambique next week. CBS really ought to think about sending a camera crew." Or: "Ben,

I'm down here leading a protest outside the South African Embassy. I don't see any Washington *Post* photographer."

Most politicians wouldn't dare try anything so brazen. Jackson doesn't always get his way, but his batting average has been damn high through the years. Hurley Green, owner and editor of the Chicago *Independent Bulletin*, a black community paper on the South Side of Chicago, once described what it was like to be on the receiving end of the Jackson treatment.

"He can turn your head around. Just turn it around. I remember the first time I went down to one of those Saturday meetings [at Jackson's PUSH headquarters in Chicago]...I'm sitting in the audience and all of a sudden Jesse says, 'Hully'—he's always calling me Hully, he preaches in the Southern idiom—so he says, 'Hully, Hully Green. Are you here?' And I jump up in front of a thousand people and say, 'Yes, sir.' And he says, 'Now y'all give Hully here a hand.' And I'm thinking, daaammmnnn!

"And then later he's sermonizing away and says, 'Now ain't that right, Hully?' And you know he's sinking it in a little deeper, giving you prestige and strokes. Then he wraps it all up by saying, 'All y'all step back. Hully, come on up here. Now, Hully, I got some very important things for you to do and I want your phone number at home, at the office and at your girlfriend's.' And you know, by that time I'm hooked. I'm probably fifteen or twenty years older than this kid and I'm hooked."[17]

Walt Harrington, a white staff reporter for the Washington *Post* magazine, described "the treatment" in a long and flattering piece he wrote on Jackson in 1987:

"After only a few sitdown talks, when I have no strong sense of who he is or isn't, Jackson announces that I am a deeply spiritual person. I laugh and tell him that religion is not my best side; I'm something of an agnostic. No, Jackson says theatrically, not religiously spiritual, but still spiritual, filled with a special empathy found in people only rarely, especially white people. That, he says, is true spirituality.

" 'I say it,' Jackson says, 'only because it is true.'

"Take my word for it, I'm not immune to flattery. But this bit of buttering would be too obvious for even the most vain person to take seriously. Except for one thing: Jackson has inexplicably touched a piece of my identity that I don't believe I've ever talked about with anyone, a self-perception I consciously hide with a jocular cynicism, but which, nonetheless, is an important part of me. I am impressed, and intrigued. Jesse is working on me."[18]

Sylvester Monroe, a black reporter for *Time* who has covered Jackson over the years, recalled the first time he found himself on Jackson's infamous "call list":

"The phone rings about six-thirty in the morning and this vaguely familiar voice says, 'Hey brother.'

"I'm so tired I can't think straight. But I know this doesn't sound like my brother. I say, 'Huh?'

"The voice says, 'Vest, this is your brother.'

"I'm thinking: This *isn't* my brother. So I say 'Huh?' again.

"And then finally he says, 'This is your brother. Jesse Jackson.' "

"I say, 'Oh, hi, Reverend Jackson.' "

As someone who's been on that call list, as someone who's muttered "Daaammmmnnn!" once or twice as Jackson playfully called out his name to audiences, I too know how Jackson can turn your head. The best a journalist who finds himself in this situation can hope for is to recognize the charms that are at work and try to compensate. My guess is that no reporter—no matter how disciplined or dispassionate— who traveled with Jackson in 1988 will ever forget his campaign, and many of us will continue to have trouble keeping it in perspective. "These are the sorts of things you want to save for your grandchildren," David Rogers, *The Wall Street Journal's* congressional correspondent, mused to me once as we sat together on a Jackson bus. He was removing a cassette of that afternoon's Jackson speech from his tape recorder.

I have my own favorite memory. It is a speech Jackson gave in Philadelphia the night after he lost the bruising New York primary— and, with it, any fleeting hope he may have harbored of winning the nomination. He spoke before an all-black audience of civic leaders and politicians whose spirit seemed to have been broken by the racial undertow of the New York campaign. "We, the rejected, are like a bag of potatoes," Samuel Evans, a black community leader in his eighties, said in introducing Jackson. "They french-fry some, bake some, mash some, make potatoes au gratin out of some. We are all prepared for the master's table.... We must understand we are all victims of a racist society."

He got a big applause, but Jackson, on this particular night, would have none of it. "Hold your head high," he admonished his audience. "Expand your hope. Spread that hope, and let the children feel it. When the sun comes out in the spring, flowers blossom, eggs crack, chickens start talking chicken talk, and hope is alive. Everything in the universe moves when there is hope in the air. We're too poor to be pessimistic. Got too much experience to be cynical. We know there is honey in the rock. We know that joy cometh in the morning."

CHAPTER SEVEN

Dan Quayle:
Feeding Frenzy Devours
Fortunate Son

"IF IT'S QUAYLE, I'll eat my press pass," Bob Kaiser, the Washington *Post*'s assistant managing editor for national news, mused a few minutes before word shot through the media warren at the Hyatt Regency Hotel in New Orleans on the second afternoon of the Republican National Convention: It was Quayle.

Kaiser was astonished—but no less so than Walter Shapiro, a senior writer at *Time.* The previous morning, when *Time* had hosted Quayle for a group interview over breakfast, Shapiro's seat at the table was empty. "I figured, why bother getting up at that hour," he lamented, "when you *knew* it wasn't going to be him."

Shapiro was rueful—but no less so than Jack Nelson of the Los Angeles *Times.* The day before the announcement, he'd bumped into a friend who worked at a mid-level position in the Bush campaign, Ede Holiday. "Keep your eye on Quayle," she'd advised. Nelson smiled politely. In the front-page speculation piece he wrote for the next day's *Times,* he buried Quayle's name a few paragraphs from the bottom.

Thirteen thousand journalists converged in New Orleans that week to eat, drink, be merry—and chase exactly one unscripted political story. Twelve thousand nine hundred of them, give or take, were about as hot on the trail as Kaiser, Shapiro and Nelson.

When the name J. Danforth Quayle was sprung on this unsuspecting group, it was like "dropping a hot dog into a tank of sharks," recalled Roger Ailes, an ardent Quayle supporter. It produced a feeding frenzy that rocked the convention, tarnished the press, skewered

Quayle and—though this assertion is impossible to prove—still may have wound up as a net plus for Bush's presidential campaign.

Quayle took a press pounding unlike anything meted out to any running mate in recent history. In 1984, Geraldine Ferraro had to endure a brief but intense firestorm over her husband's finances, but, overall, Ferraro's press was adoring compared with Quayle's. In 1972, George McGovern's selection of Senator Thomas Eagleton had more disastrous political consequences: Eagleton was forced off the ticket when it was disclosed that as a young man he had received electroshock therapy for depression. But Eagleton, through it all, never became a national laughingstock.

Quayle did. He came under relentless attack, in part because (unlike Eagleton) he hung in and took it, and in part because there was so much raw material to work with—the avoidance of combat duty in a war he had vociferously supported, the use of family strings to ease his way through life, the mediocre academic and slender congressional record, the penchant for malapropisms, the male bimbo image. Once the attacks began, they were fed by another dynamic: Quayle lost his self-confidence. "He was like the hockey player who takes a hard body check early and loses his legs for the rest of the game," said Bush pollster Robert Teeter. For the next eleven weeks, the shell-shocked Quayle allowed himself to be muzzled and scripted by handlers he barely knew—handlers who sometimes had trouble concealing their contempt for him. The qualities that had made him a formidable campaigner in Indiana—the sunny disposition, the spontaneity, the youthful enthusiasm—were kept under wraps. He spent the fall wearing the dazed look "of a deer frozen in the headlights," in a memorable metaphor served up by *Time.* Everybody noticed.

"Nobody who's been through what I've been through can be accused of not having faced combat," Quayle said after the first few days of the media squall over his National Guard service. The quip was offered in the grand tradition of joking one's way out of a ditch, but like so much else he tried that fall, it fell flat. To complain about foul treatment by the press—even when most Americans sympathized with the complaint—was asking to be seen as a victim.

What most people saw when they looked at Quayle was someone rich, gorgeous, coddled and strawberry blond to whom life had been preternaturally kind. As a young man, he'd applied to DePauw University against the advice of his high school counselor, who didn't think he had the grades. He got in anyway; it couldn't have hurt that his grandfather, newspaper magnate Eugene Pulliam, served on the board. At college, his professors remembered him as a "crashingly mediocre" student who used to make his way "from the Deke house to the golf course without ever passing through a classroom." His grades didn't qualify him for admission to Indiana University Law School, but he talked his way in. He served his country during the Vietnam War by writing press releases for a National Guard unit in Indianapolis. When he graduated from law school, jobs awaited in state government or his family's newspaper empire. A few years later, when Republican leaders in Indiana's 4th Congressional District were looking for an attractive young man to challenge a lackluster Democratic incumbent, they turned to Quayle. He ran and won. Four years later, when the anti-tax, anti-government wave that elected Ronald Reagan was cresting, Quayle was one of a batch of relative unknowns who unseated prominent liberal senators—in his case, Indiana's Birch Bayh. And now, after all this good fortune and good timing, he was being given the chance to become the second-highest elected official in the land—chosen because Bush unaccountably bypassed dozens of other potential running mates whose names were better known and credentials more reassuring.

The zinger that Texas Agriculture Commissioner Jim Hightower had fired at George Bush earlier in the summer—"Born on third base and thinks he hit a triple"—never really connected, for Bush's every mannerism bespoke an appreciation of how much he'd been given and how much he owed back. But to many Americans, it was a perfect fit for Dan Quayle, a young man who seemed, at first blush, untested by adversity, unmarked by life, unreflective about the way he'd been indulged.

Even if it betrayed a tin ear, Quayle's complaint about flak from the press wasn't without substance. In the first twelve days after he was named to the ticket, ABC, CBS and NBC devoted a staggering combined total of ninety-three stories to him in their regular nightly news shows. In other words, there were nearly three Quayle stories per network newscast per night, or about a quarter of each newscast per night.* Quayle got more coverage on the network nightly news in those twelve days than Dukakis received during the entire primary season. And the spin of the coverage, according to the Center for Media and Public Affairs, was two to one negative.

---

*From a study published by the Center for Media and Public Affairs in September 1988. These figures do not include the prime-time convention coverage or the morning and weekend news shows, which also were dominated by Quayle stories.

What accounted for this "journalistic wilding"? Republican critics attributed it to a combination of liberal ideology and elitism—the same deadly combination they'd been complaining about for twenty years. One such critic was Dan Quayle.

"The media didn't know me, and I think there was a certain elitism in the media that said: 'By God, if I haven't sat down and interviewed this guy, he really shouldn't be Vice President,' " Quayle said in an interview in his West Wing office six months after the campaign had ended. "I think there was a certain sense [in the media] that if we don't know this guy, then is he really that good? George Bush obviously thinks so, but who else? And if you start from that premise and take someone like myself, who did not have a national reputation—I'd been in the Senate for eight years but wasn't the chairman of a major committee, did not really pursue a national profile and hadn't done extensive foreign travel, by desire—then you can have a field day, if you want to."

Quayle continued: "If you are a young conservative Republican, I know there is going to be some institutional bias to start with. Not that the press is going to do it unfairly—I mean, they try to be objective. But by God, if they can get it they're going to get it, and there's a little pumped-up feeling there."

Many of his campaign advisers had similar explanations.

"There is a particular delight the press takes in deflowering a virgin on the national scene," said James Ciccone, Quayle's domestic policy adviser during the campaign.

"The choice was an affront to most of the reporters in New Orleans," said Mitchell Daniels, a senior political adviser and friend of Quayle's, who had served as White House political director from 1985 to 1987. "For one thing it was a surprise, and the press hates to be surprised. But deeper than that, quite honestly I think that Quayle was unacceptable to many members of the working press on a cultural basis. They got the picture in their minds of a lazy dilettante. This was especially true among reporters roughly Quayle's age. Teeter said to me at one point that one problem Quayle has is that there are a whole lot of reporters who are his age and are saying to themselves that while they were down in the basement of the library studying to get their degree, Quayle was out in the sun, drinking beer and dating the homecoming queen."

The press corps, not surprisingly, has a completely different explanation for their rough coverage of Quayle.

"This was a simple and straightforward reaction to someone who had been thrust upon us very unexpectedly as a putative President of the United States," said the *Post*'s Kaiser. "We all had the same cynical, utterly predictable but healthy reaction—'Who is this guy?' This is where the cynical patriotism of journalists comes into play. Whatever else we are, we are the guardians of things that matter. The question raised by this choice was whether George Bush was toying with us."

As reporters began asking "Who is this guy?" the answers—especially from Republicans, who figured to be sympathetic and supportive—fueled the frenzy.

"The Republicans at that convention were just as astonished as the reporters," said the L.A. *Times*'s Nelson. "The fact that they reacted the way they did made us bore in all the harder." Nelson remembers having dinner at Commander's Palace in New Orleans' Garden District the night the choice was announced. Dan Murphy, Bush's former chief of staff at the office of the Vice President, was at the table next to him. "How do you explain it?" Nelson leaned over and asked. "It boggles the mind," Murphy replied. Virtually every reporter in New Orleans could tell a similar story.

"What was really so striking about that week in New Orleans was how many Republicans were willing to express their misgivings about the choice—usually in private, but sometimes in public," said Al Hunt, Washington bureau chief of *The Wall Street Journal.* "It was rampant. I remember bumping into John McCain [the Republican senator from Arizona] after he had just finished a TV interview saying that Quayle was such a good-looking guy that he would appeal to women.

"I said, 'Jeez, John, that was a dumb thing to say.'

"He said, 'Hey, when you get asked about Danny Quayle, what else are you going to say?'

"This wasn't a case of reporters going to ten people and only quoting the one who had something nasty to say," Hunt continued. "It was hard to find a Republican who could look you straight in the eye and express enthusiasm for the choice. I guess about the only one I can recall was Gordon Humphrey [senator from New Hampshire], and you can only carry Gordon so far.

"Now you can make the case that Quayle may have gotten hurt because he wasn't a real Senate insider, but the truth is, there are a lot of noninsiders in the Senate who are respected by their peers, because they demonstrate distinction in other ways—as issue raisers, idea people, whatever. Quayle didn't measure up on any scale. I happen to think peer review is valid, and it's certainly what drove a lot of that early coverage."

To be sure, some of these harsh reviews came from Republicans who were disappointed because they or their candidate hadn't been put on the ticket. But the crabbed judgments about Quayle weren't sour grapes alone. In the late spring, the Bush campaign had asked Senator Mitch McConnell (R–Ky.) to sound out his Republican Senate colleagues and assemble a list of senators considered to be vice-presidential timber. Given the custom of senatorial courtesy, McConnell's list was extremely long. Quayle's name was not on it.

Among former colleagues in the House, where Quayle had served an undistinguished two terms from 1977 to 1981, the reviews weren't any better. "I'm underwhelmed," Illinois Representative Henry Hyde, a Midwestern neighbor and ideological soul mate of Quayle's, said hours after the choice was made public.[1]

Bush political director Rich Bond spent the night of the announcement on the floor of the convention taking the temperature of the delegates. He encountered Representative Tom Tauke (R–Iowa), an old friend.

"Whaddaya think?" Bond asked.

"I'm disappointed," Tauke said.

"Why?"

"You don't want to know."

"Yes, I do."

"You want me to lie?"

"No, tell me the truth. I'll take it from there."

"Well, the guy's a lightweight."[2]

One possible lesson of Quayle's rude reception is that any time a presidential nominee puts a relative unknown on his ticket, he's borrowing trouble. "The one thing that politics can't abide is a surprise," said Lee Atwater, Bush's campaign manager. But Kaiser draws a telling comparison with 1968. "I remember when Humphrey chose Ed Muskie, Muskie was an unknown, and there was a tremendous wave of anxiety among Democrats that Humphrey had made a terrible mistake. But then very quickly, you had a series of very persuasive statements from elder statesmen in the party that Muskie was one of the finest young men in politics, and that Hubert had really done something very clever here."

If there could be no such tribal laying on of hands for Quayle, why did Bush—a creature of the Washington political establishment if ever there was one—choose him? Several theories overlap, and each contributes to a mosaic.

• Bush framed the choice as a kind of first-do-no-harm elimination contest, working from the truism that running mates rarely help you but often hurt you. Teeter's polling for the campaign reinforced that view; it did not make a persuasive political case for anybody. "The long-ball hitters weren't hitting very long, and the singles hitters who were supposed to get you a state weren't really getting you one," said Atwater.* California, with forty-seven Electoral College votes, was uppermost in the minds of all the geopolitical accountants in the Bush camp, but its governor, George Deukmejian, had been unwavering in his assertions of disinterest, and the California GOP feared that his departure would weaken its hand in the critical redistricting war that will follow the 1990 census. (After the election, Deukmejian chose not to seek a third term for governor in 1990 anyway.) The two presumed "long-ball hitters" on the short list were Dole and Kemp, both of whom had national followings, both of whom had had their closets searched and résumés scrubbed in the course of their own candidacies for the GOP nomination. But Bush eliminated them for having personalities incompatible with the office he was vacating. He wanted a Vice President like the Vice President he'd been: reticent, unfailingly loyal, the consummate team player. It is probably no coincidence that none of the recent presidential nominees who themselves were once Vice President—Nixon and Humphrey in 1968, Ford in 1976, Mondale in 1984, Bush in 1988—chose running mates who had sought the presidency before or who had built up a strong independent power base. Better than most, those who had served in the job understood its requirements and its limitations.

• Consciously or subconsciously, Bush knew he needed a running mate beside whom he could stand tall. One Democrat's cynical assessment of the criterion was that Bush wanted "a lapdog's lapdog." By whatever description, Bush's instincts served him well. For all the troubles the selection brought, Bush's assumption of the role of Quayle's protector helped him transform his own image from weakling to macho man. This change was launched at the convention, and it was the fulcrum upon which everything else in the campaign turned. Once Bush assuaged doubts about his strength of character

*The lone exception was Attorney General Richard Thornburgh, a former governor of Pennsylvania, who, according to Teeter's polling, improved Bush's prospects in the Keystone State, which at the time was considered a Dukakis stronghold. As it turned out, Bush carried Pennsylvania without him.

among voters in his own base, the Republican party's natural 54–57 percent presidential coalition became fully available to him.

• Bush was taken with generational arguments offered by Atwater— a political theorist as well as hardball tactician—who had given him a copy of *Left, Right and Baby Boom*. Published by the Cato Institute, a libertarian think tank, this slender book analyzed the political inclinations of the baby-boom generation, 76 million strong and comprising more than 40 percent of the eligible electorate. The collective argument of the book's fourteen separate essays was that baby boomers were susceptible to appeals from both economic conservatives and social liberals, were fiercely independent and anti-institutional and were still very much up for grabs by either party. No one argued—nor has it ever been demonstrated—that baby-boom voters are more likely to support baby-boom candidates. But Bush, who tends to think of voting blocs in conventionally linear ways, may not have known that—or, if he did, may not have believed it.

• Bush felt warmly toward Quayle, who was roughly the same age as his sons and for whom he'd campaigned several times in Indiana.

• The reviews Quayle drew from the national-security community— whose judgments Bush valued—were far better than those he got from House and Senate colleagues. Men like Henry Kissinger, Kenneth Adelman and Brent Scowcroft all spoke well of Quayle's grasp of the nuances of arms control.

• Bush was not heavily lobbied on behalf of anyone else by anyone in his inner circle of advisers, and Quayle emerged as a kind of least-common-denominator choice, unacceptable to no one. The lone important exception was campaign chairman James A. Baker, who opposed Quayle and who is thought to be responsible for a leak that led to a *New York Times* story on the Saturday before the convention that gave a boost to Quayle's prospects. (The presumed motive of Baker, who by then sensed Quayle was going to be selected, was to raise Quayle's profile in the hope that someone would shoot him down. This two-cushion shot didn't work for a simple reason: even after the *Times* piece came out, virtually no one considered Quayle a serious possibility.) When Baker, Atwater, Teeter, Ailes, chief of staff Craig Fuller and longtime Bush friend Nicholas Brady met on the Friday before the convention, Teeter went around the room asking people to list their first, second and third choices for Vice President. Only Fuller and Ailes made Quayle their first choice, but Quayle showed up somewhere on almost every other list. (Fuller listed Quayle as his first, second *and* third choices.)

• Bush liked the idea of surprising everyone, including his own people. "There was an infatuation with surprise, so as to produce for George Bush a bold move," recalled Fuller. It helps to remember the political context. In mid-August, just before the GOP convention, Bush was trailing Dukakis in the polls by 7 to 10 points, having been down by as many as 17 just after the Democratic convention. He was still viewed by many as a wimp and, increasingly, as a creature of his handlers. He was determined to make this decision on his own. Borrowing a technique from his days at the CIA, he broke the decision-making process down into separate cells. Teeter did the polling and headed a group that ran the political traps, while Robert Kimmitt, a lawyer with virtually no political background, conducted the background checks. Only Bush received all the information from both cells.

"I think that boring-and-predictable George wanted to show 'em," said Daniels, making it clear that part of the "'em" Bush wanted to show were his own advisers. "I'll never forget walking in on a scene on the thirty-eighth floor of the Marriott Hotel [the Bush campaign headquarters in New Orleans] the day after the announcement was made, and the National Guard story was just heating up, and all the strategists were racing around in a state of great anxiety. But there sitting in a corner, amid all the hustle and bustle, was Bush. He couldn't have been more serene. I think a big part of it was that he'd pulled off a big surprise."

He'd also pulled off a leak-free announcement—a matter of great pride. A few weeks before the convention, Bush had commissioned a campaign aide to review how the announcements of running mates had been handled over the previous twenty years, and he found—as he suspected—that in a majority of cases the story had leaked. He was determined not to have this happen to him. "Leaks drove him crazy," Teeter said. "Part of it was the handler idea. He was worried that if this was leaked, it might be seen as the handlers' choice. He wanted to be sure it looked like what it really was—his own choice."

Bush avoided leaks by telling no one in his inner circle of the choice until just a few hours before it was announced to the public. This deprived them of the chance they assumed they'd have to second-guess his selection and anticipate pitfalls that might lay ahead. It also meant they had virtually no time to do what they usually did so well—plan and choreograph media events.

The original plan had been for Bush to announce his choice

Thursday morning, the final day of the convention, with the option to move it up to Wednesday night. That timetable was a small break from a fairly recent custom, which called for a nominee who'd wrapped up his victory beforehand to announce his running mate early in the convention. Bush's strategists had wanted to wait, for a couple of reasons. First, they wanted to keep up some suspense. This was their only real news of the week, and they were frankly worried about declining television viewership.* In addition, they wanted to preserve what Fuller called the "natural flow" of the week. Monday was to be devoted to Reagan; Tuesday was the baton pass from Reagan to Bush; Wednesday, the broadsides against Dukakis; Thursday, the acceptance speeches and the uplifting, patriotic close. They figured the unveiling of the vice-presidential choice would fit in best with the Stars and Stripes finale.

That was the plan. During Bush's flight down to New Orleans from Washington on Tuesday morning, the plan was scrapped. Fuller recalled: "Sometime during that flight, George Bush and Jim Baker had a discussion about what was on George Bush's mind. . . . Having watched the convention on television the night before [at his residence in Washington] and having seen Bob Dole and others kind of publicly anguishing over this business of being out on a limb, George Bush felt bad.† And he felt that once he made his decision— which by then he had—he should act on it.

"So he and Baker got into a discussion of, well, what if we were to announce it upon arrival in New Orleans? And Baker came back from the stateroom of Air Force Two to the lounge, where Teeter, Ailes, Kimmitt and I were, and said, 'Okay, what's your judgment? I want everybody to think about this. If we can get everybody on the phone as soon as we land, what do you say we announce it when we get to New Orleans?'

"There were pros and cons, but we all ultimately agreed to recommend that he make the announcement early, on the theory that it wasn't going to hold and that [Bush] was going to be less and less comfortable with holding it. We all kind of agreed that it would be an electric moment to announce it when he arrived—and that we

---

*With reason: According to Nielsen ratings, a nightly average of only 18.5 percent of the nation's 88.6 million television households watched the GOP convention, and 20.2 percent watched the Democrats—both record lows. This despite the fact that, as usual, all three networks preempted their prime-time programming to carry the conventions live.
†Dole had said on television that he found the vice-presidential selection process "demeaning." Bush was furious. Not only did the comment speed up his announcement timetable, it buried whatever slender chance Dole may still have had to be the choice.

would just have to build other interesting items into the rest of the convention. We were all kind of taken with the whole notion of a bold move."

Fuller continued: "In retrospect, I wish we had not arrived at that judgment on the airplane, because I think that we should have built in more time, regardless of who it was but particularly because it was Dan Quayle, to prepare ourselves and the nominee for what was to follow. None of us knew it was going to be Quayle. I think it's safe to say that all of us, even those, like me, who were Quayle supporters, thought it was going to be someone who'd been around the track a few more times."

When Air Force Two landed, Bush greeted the departing Reagans at the Belle Chasse Naval Air Station just outside of New Orleans, whispered his choice into the President's ear during a brief, graceful baton pass on the tarmac, then assembled his team in the privacy of the base commander's home and told them. There was no time to react, to strategize, to anticipate. The public announcement was just a few hours away.

"At that point, there were only four or five of us who knew, and we began making the phone calls, getting the others on the phone, losers first," Fuller said. One by one, Bush thanked the finalists— both Doles, Kemp, Thornburgh, Danforth, Domenici, Simpson—and told them he'd picked someone else. Quayle and his wife, Marilyn, were walking back from lunch in the French Quarter when his beeper went off. He guessed the news would be good. Over the weekend, he'd had an eight-hour interview with Kimmitt, who had already questioned him twice earlier. This third interview ranged far beyond the seventy-seven-item questionnaire that all the hopefuls had been asked to fill out. Kimmitt asked about the nature of Quayle's relationship with Paula Parkinson, the voluptuous lobbyist who in 1980 had spent a golfing weekend in Florida with three House members, including him. He also asked whether, in 1969, Quayle had used any pull to get into the National Guard. Quayle said that nothing had happened between him and Parkinson, and no strings had been pulled in 1969.

When Quayle got back to his hotel room and returned Bush's call, Bush told him he was his first and only choice. After the thank-you's and congratulations, Bush turned the phone over to Baker, who instructed Quayle to be in the VIP area of a riverfront rally in downtown New Orleans, where Bush was scheduled to arrive in a few hours aboard the riverboat *Natchez.* "The decision is revocable," Baker deadpanned, "if you can't find it." Teasing though the quip

was, it marked the beginning of an awkward instructor-pupil relationship between the two that Quayle, by campaign's end, came to
resent.

Quayle found his way to the appointed spot, though not without
creating some anxious moments for the Secret Service—who were as
mystified as anyone about who he was and what he looked like.
When he bounded up on the makeshift stage, arms waving and fist
clenched, it made for an unsettling scene.

"I would never have put him on that riverside landing," said
Kenneth Khachigian, a speechwriter who had worked for Reagan
and spent the fall of 1988 writing for Quayle. "In retrospect, that was
one of the biggest mistakes. No one prepared him for it beforehand.
No one said to him, 'Here's how we propose you conduct yourself.'
So the poor guy gets up there and he was so exuberant. He hugs
Bush and yells, 'Let's go get 'em.' There was none of the decorum
you would expect of a new candidate for national office. I think this
was a case where we in the campaign did a terrible disservice to
Danny."

"He came up there looking like a contestant on *Let's Make a Deal*,"
agreed Professor Kathleen Hall Jamieson, an expert on presidential
image-making. "We have become so accustomed to colorful visual
choreography from the Republicans. For the life of me, I don't know
why they chose that setting."

The televised awkwardness of Quayle climbing all over Bush
didn't go unnoticed in the media work spaces at the nearby Hyatt.
Many reporters and editors who huddled around televisions—this is
how much of the convention is covered, even by journalists based at
the convention site—were beside themselves. In the Boston *Globe*
work space, Walter Robinson, the paper's Bush campaign correspondent, laughed so hard tears began streaming down his face. Over at
the Washington *Post* work area, Kaiser (his press pass still dangling
from his neck, uneaten) watched with a mix of astonishment and
alarm. "That incredible scene on the plaza had a big effect on the
early coverage," he recalled. "Here was this wild and crazy guy,
undisciplined, out of control—not just extremely boyish, but mani-
festing immaturity in his reactions."

The Quayle story was by then a tinderbox. The match that set it
aflame was tossed the next morning, when Bush and Quayle held
their first joint press conference. The twenty-ninth question in a
thirty-two-question session went as follows:

"Senator Quayle, there's been so much made of the fact that you're a baby boomer. Maybe you can give us a little picture of yourself. Graduating in 1969, the Vietnam era, you chose to go in the National Guard rather than to serve in Vietnam. Can you give us a little bit of what you were thinking during that time?" asked Susan King, then of WRC–TV in Washington, D.C.

"Well, growing up in Huntington, Indiana, the first thing you think about is education," Quayle began. "You think about what any small-town person would think about, eventually growing up, raising a family. I was fortunate enough to be able to go on to law school, meet my wife. We have, I'm blessed with my three beautiful children. We're very happy, very content and looking forward to a very exciting campaign. I did not know in 1969 that I would be in this room today, I'll confess."

King: "Why the National Guard rather than serving in the Army, Marines, the Navy before going to Vietnam?"

Quayle: "My brother and I, two years younger, both went into the service at the same time, about the same time. He went into the Marine Corps and I went into the National Guard. I went into the National Guard and I served six years there, from 1969 to 1975."

Bush: "We gotta go to this side of the room here. . . . "

Was Quayle expressing second thoughts about the choice he had made nineteen years earlier? Was he seeking atonement in his brother's service? The foreshortened exchange raised more questions than it answered. The press wanted to hear more.

That night, Quayle made the rounds of the network anchor booths inside the Louisiana Superdome, submitting to what Washington *Post* TV critic Tom Shales described as "trial by booth" and "ordeal by anchor." By then, there was a new and potentially more damaging angle on the story: had strings been pulled to get Quayle into the National Guard? Robert Squier, the Democratic media consultant who doubled as an analyst for NBC, was familiar with those allegations because he'd worked for Bayh in his 1980 loss to Quayle. He, among many others, pushed the story out onto the press grapevine.

In sequence, Tom Brokaw, Peter Jennings, Dan Rather and Bernard Shaw all peppered Quayle that night with questions about undue influence.

"You're going back twenty years," he told Rather. "And let me say this: I was very interested in getting into the National Guard. And I am sure that I let a number of people know that I was interested into getting into the National Guard."

Rather: "It wasn't the case of your father or someone in your family calling the governor or lieutenant governor?"

Quayle: "I'm almost certain the governor and lieutenant governor were not involved in that"—a formulation that, to some ears, suggested he knew more about who *was* involved than he'd let on.

Two of those ears belonged to Kaiser. "When he was first questioned about the National Guard issue, he started fibbing and using loaded language in a way that flashed a series of red lights that all said: 'Chase me.'

"My sense then was, and still is, that he was profoundly embarrassed by what had really happened—that he chose not to fight in a war he supported and that some strings were pulled to make sure that happened. I think he was struggling desperately to put it in a light that would be less embarrassing."

And so the chase was on. The Bush campaign high command bunkered in on the thirty-eighth floor of the Marriott Hotel, where they stayed awake through most of the night trying to get the facts and assess the damage. They summoned Quayle and Quayle's father, James, publisher of the Huntington (Indiana) *Herald-Press* and pumped them for their best recollections. They scrambled to track down officials who had served in the Indiana National Guard at the time. "One reason we were paralyzed is that we didn't want to comment on the story until we got to the bottom of it—but the bottom kept changing," Fuller recalled. "The rumors were flying in so fast, and it was taking all our effort to figure out what was real and what wasn't. There were times we felt like we were finally ahead of the news curve, but they seemed to happen around 3 a.m., so it didn't do us much good."

The following morning, Baker discreetly telephoned some of the reporters with whom he maintained close relations (he is well known in Washington for currying favor among journalists). "Are we ahead of you or are you ahead of us?" Baker wanted to know. He was in a jam. Bush would be giving the most important speech of his life that night—his acceptance speech. The last thing the campaign needed was a major distraction. Baker wanted to be able to go on television to throw cold water on the string-pulling story. His hurry-up investigation seemed to support a benign interpretation of what had happened back in 1969. But he feared climbing out on a limb only to have it cut off by a fact he hadn't uncovered. Meantime, he also knew he couldn't remain silent, for the convention was aflame with rumors that Quayle was about to be dropped from the ticket. Media heavies

like Nelson, David Broder and Evans and Novak were openly specu-
lating on that possibility. (This was never seriously discussed by
the Bush strategists, other than for everyone in the inner circle to
agree it was the worst option and that it was much too early to even
consider it.)

That Thursday morning, Baker went public with a lukewarm vote
of confidence in Quayle. He disclosed that in 1969 both Quayle and
Quayle's father had asked Wendell C. Phillipi, who was then managing editor of the Indianapolis *News* — one of the seven papers owned
by Quayle's grandfather, Eugene Pulliam — for help in getting into
the Guard. Phillipi was a retired commander of a Guard unit in
Indiana.

Though Baker cast the calls to Phillipi as routine and on the
up-and-up, there is nothing ordinary about the Pulliam family in
Indiana.* Eugene C. Pulliam, who died in 1975, was a publisher out
of the pulp novels: a two-fisted tycoon, archconservative, anti-
communist and anti–federal government, who used the front pages
of his newspapers to reward friends and punish enemies. The story
goes that when Martin Luther King, Jr., was assassinated, Pulliam
ordered the story placed on the bottom of the front page of the
Indianapolis *Star* because he felt King had been "a rabble rouser."
(His son intervened and moved the story back to the top of the page.)

The Pulliams and the Quayles were not the sort of people who
had to worry about getting their calls returned, certainly not in
Indiana. "Danny called me up and said he wanted to talk to me
about National Guard enlistment, and I said I'd be glad to," Phillipi
told CBS News on the final morning of the convention. "He wondered
if it was subject to call [into the war zone]," he added in an interview
with the Indianapolis *News.* (The only call-up of the National Guard
during the Vietnam War had come a year earlier, during a three-and-
a-half-month period in the spring of 1968. A total of 12,000 Guardsmen
out of a nationwide force of 400,000 were mobilized for active duty,
and of those, 7,000 — or less than 2 percent — were sent to Vietnam.
That order expired on June 30, 1968, and was never renewed.) "I
called the adjutant general's office and asked if they had a place for

*The company Pulliam built, Central Newspapers, was reported in 1988 to be worth $1.2
billion to $1.4 billion. A family trust, which has 120 stockholders, controls 55 percent of the
stock. Contrary to some of the initial news accounts that depicted him as fabulously
wealthy, Dan Quayle owns less than 1 percent of the company stock. He grew up comfortably upper-middle class, the son of parents who bought the Huntington *Herald-Press*
from his grandfather in 1964. The small afternoon paper run by Quayle's father, James,
has a circulation of just 8,500 and a staff of just seven.

Dan Quayle, who's a fine young man, and . . . eventually he signed up," Phillipi continued.

Within a few days, the Bush campaign tracked down several former Indiana National Guard officers who verified that the unit Quayle joined was under its assigned strength of 136 slots at the time — so no line-jumping had been necessary. The truth, in short, appeared to be a classic half-and-half proposition. Yes, strings had been pulled. No, it hadn't been necessary.

In those first days, however, subtlety and nuance and context got lost in the media stampede. The coverage was all pedal, no brake.

A headline in the next morning's New Orleans *Times-Picayune* blared: DRAFT DODGER QUESTIONS DOG QUAYLE.

NBC *Today Show* anchor Bryant Gumbel wondered aloud on Thursday morning: "Could we have an Eagleton episode?"

CBS *This Morning* co-host Kathleen Sullivan called Quayle a "draft dodger" in an interview with Marilyn Quayle. "He's not a draft dodger," she snapped back. Sullivan went on to suggest that Quayle was a hypocrite ("someone saying they're very pro-Vietnam, but meantime trying to get out") as well as a philanderer ("You know what I'm referring to, what happened with Paula Parkinson in that condominium in Florida eight years ago").*

Even the newspaper chain built by Quayle's grandfather joined in the clubbing. The Arizona *Republic,* a Pulliam paper, asked in a lead editorial: "Where was Dan Quayle [during the Vietnam War]?" It said that if the "ugly suspicions" about the use of undue influence to get into the Guard proved true, "Mr. Bush should have no qualms about giving him the boot." In the Indianapolis *Star,* a local columnist wrote that Quayle was a "war wimp."

"This is guilt by press," fumed Ailes. "We might as well have hanging by press. . . . We recognize journalists have to kill somebody each week, and Danny's it. You just hope the American people are fair."[3]

A Gallup poll taken during the week of the convention showed that, by a 55–39 margin, voters thought the press had gone overboard in attacking Quayle. This wasn't an overwhelming margin, but it gave the Bush strategists an opening. They launched their counterattack the day after the convention, at an outdoor rally in the courthouse square in Quayle's hometown of Huntington, a quiet

---

*Nothing happened. Parkinson was the date of another congressman that weekend, and though she claims that Quayle made a pass at her, their relationship apparently never progressed beyond a single slow dance.

farming community in the flatlands of northeastern Indiana. Bush and Quayle flew there directly from New Orleans and gave brief rally speeches to an enthusiastic crowd of more than 5,000. After the speeches, Quayle conducted a press conference on an open public-address system that allowed the crowd to hear both the questions and the answers.

This was an unusual arrangement—campaign press conferences are typically held in hotel meeting rooms or on airport tarmacs, because they aren't normally thought of as a spectator sport. Flying out from New Orleans that morning, however, the Bush strategists lit on the idea of staging an event that would cast Quayle as a David facing down the Goliaths of the media in front of a cheering home-town crowd.

"The press was more restless than I had ever seen them, and I knew we could not get through the day without making Quayle available," recalled Atwater. "I remember telling Baker and the others on the plane that we just had to do something in Huntington, because the press was shouting mad. Fuller said the conditions [in the courthouse square] were terrible. I said, 'Don't worry about it. Just set it up so the press can hear the questions.' "

Fuller came up with the idea of an open-microphone exchange—something Bush had done occasionally during the primaries. "That was a totally staged activity," Fuller said in an interview six months after the campaign ended. "Totally staged. I've never acknowledged that before. . . . I knew Quayle was going to have a tough time at this press conference, and I wanted to give him a chance to respond and also to have a friendly crowd behind him."

In addition to cheering Quayle, the crowd turned on the press—chanting "bor-ing, bor-ing" at the questions and yelling slurs at the most aggressive reporters.

"Have you offered to take your name off the ticket?" Quayle was asked at one point.

"It is not a yes-or-no question," Quayle parried.

"Yes, sir, it is," the reporter bored in, to a chorus of boos from the crowd.

"There is no reason for me to make that offer," Quayle said.

The testiest moment came when Quayle, after repeated questioning about the National Guard, protested that "the implication is that somehow Dan Quayle, by voluntarily signing up for the Indiana National Guard, was not patriotic, and I resent that. . . . "

"No," responded Ellen Hume, then of *The Wall Street Journal,* "the implication is that people were dying in Vietnam while you were writing press releases."

The crowd booed loudly. The visual—hometown boy, courthouse square draped in a huge American flag, local townsfolk rallying against the marauders from the press—dominated news coverage over the weekend, and marked the beginning of the end of the feeding frenzy. It was a classic piece of political jujitsu—putting an adversary's aggressiveness to work against him.

The Bush handlers watched the spectacle unfold with a mix of amusement and apprehension.

"I was laughing my ass off," recalled Atwater. "Never in my wildest dreams did I think it would take the kind of turn it did. I thought I was in the middle of a Rod Serling episode. As diabolical as I am, it would never cross my mind that we could get away with something like that. If I had planned it, I would be proud to take credit for it, but it was more serendipity than anything else."

Baker, who puts a high value on good press relations, took less delight in the scene. He worried that the Bush campaign had broken an unwritten code of behavior: it's okay to bash the press in the abstract; it's not okay to use working reporters as live props (and never mind that the reporters had done it to themselves—that only made the setup seem all the more Machiavellian). In recent times, only one national politician has broken that rule: George Wallace. In his 1968 and 1972 presidential campaigns, he used to point out the reporters in his press entourage from *The New York Times* or the Washington *Post* or the newsmagazines and tell his audiences that they were Eastern liberal elitists who were just dying to tell the good folks of the South how to run their lives. Wallace, who in off-hours enjoyed the company of these reporters, would make sure a state trooper or local sheriff was positioned nearby, just in case someone in the crowd tried to take a pop at one of his props.

After the Huntington rally, Baker addressed the traveling press while they were writing and filing their stories at a nearby airport. "I don't want to leave you with the impression that you were being manipulated, that we had set anything up," he said. "We were not playing with the crowd. We were just trying to increase accessibility."

Few believed him. "I think the general feeling in the press corps was not only that it was a setup but that it was a damn good one and we walked right into it," said Bill Peterson, who covered the event for the Washington *Post.*

Hume took some flak from within the craft for appearing to push aggressiveness over the line to rudeness. She makes no apologies. "The smoother that politicians become, the tougher the reporters have to be," she said in an interview after the campaign, shortly after she started a new job as director of the Barone Center for Press, Politics and Public Policy at Harvard's Kennedy School of Government. "These exchanges were conducted in a tone you hear all the time at the daily White House press briefing. The difference was that this was on live television, and it doesn't look very attractive. Well, it's not our job to look attractive."

Buoyed by the Huntington event, and by a Gallup poll which showed that, by 75 to 14 percent, voters didn't think less of Quayle because he'd served in the National Guard rather than the Army, the Bush campaign stepped up its counterattack. The following Monday, Bush told a Veterans of Foreign War meeting in Chicago: "He did not go to Canada, he did not burn his draft card and he damn sure didn't burn the American flag." The veterans jumped to their feet and roared their approval.

Was Bush implying that Dukakis or Lloyd Bentsen had burned the American flag? Not George! He simply wanted to remind voters that they were the nominees of a party that—at least in some quarters— had once winked at such behavior. Patriotism has been a winning theme for Republicans ever since the Vietnam War, and the GOP was only too happy to play "capture the flag" again in 1988. During the summer, Republican Senator Steven Symms of Idaho made headlines with an unsubstantiated charge (quickly withdrawn—once the damage was done) that Kitty Dukakis, as a young woman, had burned the flag at an anti-war rally. Meantime, Bush was pounding Dukakis for having vetoed legislation in Massachusetts that forced public-school teachers to lead students in reciting the Pledge of Allegiance. And in his keynote address at the GOP convention, New Jersey Governor Thomas Kean assailed the "pastel patriotism" of the Democrats.

When the Quayle/National Guard issue arose, the Bush strategists were smart enough to see an opportunity as well as a crisis. With the subtlety of tank commanders, they revived the nation's collective memory of the Vietnam War era. It hardly mattered that, by a lopsided ratio of nearly three to one, Americans in 1988 felt that sending troops to fight in Vietnam two decades earlier had been a mistake.[4] Or that even as early as 1969 Americans thought it had been a mistake, by a 52–39 percent margin, according to a Gallup poll. However deep the national ambivalence about that war, the political fallout from it in the ensuing two decades has been unambiguous: Republicans have profited for being remembered as the hawk party; Democrats have paid for being remembered as doves, defeatists and protesters. This paradox goes to the nature of patriotism, which organizes itself around a set of feelings rather than a set of policies. The U.S. involvement in Vietnam had been based on the premise that this nation is a righteous superpower—the last, best hope of mankind. Even if the premise proved faulty in the jungles of Southeast Asia, it remains at the core of our national self-image.

The catalyzing of these Vietnam-era patriotic issues helped the GOP in another way: it activated latent public animosity toward the press, especially among conservatives. "By turning the Quayle issue into a Republican-versus-press struggle, the Big Media did for the vice president what Mr. Bush failed to do for himself—it united, energized and activated the Reagan coalition," conservative columnist Patrick Buchanan, once an adviser to Presidents Nixon and Reagan, wrote a few days after the convention. "Thank you, Dan Rather." Poll numbers lent weight to Buchanan's analysis: on the eve of the GOP convention, the Gallup poll had Dukakis leading Bush by 49–42 percent. On the day it ended, despite the relentless press pounding on Quayle and the National Guard, Gallup had the Bush-Quayle ticket in the lead, 48–44 percent.

While the National Guard issue may have boomeranged to the benefit of the GOP, it never came back around far enough to help Quayle. Those who thought he was a hypocrite for not fighting in a war he supported may have represented just a sliver of the electorate, but their passions were deep and their vocal cords strong. Angry hecklers—carrying placards bearing such inscriptions as "Chickenhawk" and "He's Cute, But Can He Type?"—turned up at his events for the remainder of the campaign. Even some prominent members of Quayle's own party raised their eyebrows over the choice Quayle had made in 1969. "I must tell you, in my generation, you knew who was in the Guard and who was in uniform fighting for their country," Bob Dole, who had nearly lost his life as an infantryman in World War II, said on *Meet the Press* the Sunday after the convention.

Farm boys like Dole and bluebloods like Bush volunteered for the great war of their youth as soon as they could after they turned eighteen. Some young men of that era who had medical disabilities—like James C. Quayle, Dan's father—went to the length of having corrective surgery in order to pass the physical. World War II was an uncomplicated fight against the forces of evil, and—once the Japanese bombed Pearl Harbor—everyone in this country wanted in. The wealthy died in greater numbers in that war, proportionately, than did the poor.

Vietnam was different: the poor fought, and the privileged did what they could to stay home. Of the 27 million young men who turned eighteen during the Vietnam War years, only 2 million ever saw Southeast Asia. The other 92.6 percent struggled with a complex array of choices. "On the exquisitely calibrated moral scale of that period, Quayle fell somewhere in the middle," wrote *The New Republic*'s Hendrik Hertzberg. "The aristocrats were the fighters and the resisters—those who volunteered for combat duty and sometimes lost their lives in the war, and those who chose to go to prison to demonstrate their opposition to it. In the second rank were the draftees and the COs—those who accepted induction and obeyed orders, even if that meant going into combat (which in the majority of cases it did not), and those who, in obedience to religious conviction, did alternative service in hospitals or nursing homes. In the third rank were the joiners and the exiles—those who, like Quayle, signed up with some branch of service in a way that guaranteed they could discharge their military obligation without incurring physical risk, and those who moved to Canada or Sweden, placing themselves beyond the reach of army or jail but sacrificing home, and sometimes career and relations with friends and family, in the process. The fourth rank were the evaders—those who arranged their lives to correspond with one of the categories exempt from the draft. (Graduate school, marriage with children, and civilian defense work were the most common ploys.) Bringing up the rear were those who faked or exaggerated physical or mental infirmities with enough success to obtain 1-Y status (a temporary medical deferment) or, best of all, the coveted 4-F. Only those in this final category truly deserved the name of draft dodger. Outside this scheme of moral ranking were the genuine 4-F's with true medical disabilities."[5]

Quayle seemed to hint at an appreciation for the moral complexities of his choice with his comment at that first press conference in New Orleans about what he hadn't known nineteen years earlier. Was he giving voice to the genuine discomfort of a suddenly very public man whose views about the obligation to serve had matured with age? Or was he merely expressing a politician's regret that he hadn't had the forethought to get his Vietnam ticket punched? One waited, in vain, for Quayle to provide answers during the campaign. Instead, he remained defiant, defensive and demagogic throughout the fall—insisting that he was proud of his service, maintaining that his decision had nothing to do with a fear of combat and attacking his attackers for questioning his patriotism.

Six months after the campaign was over, I raised the subject with him in an interview, hoping enough time had passed to permit a more subtle exploration. I asked whether his initial comment at that first press conference had reflected a sense of moral ambiguity. His answer stunned me. The only reservation he had about the choice he'd made in 1969, he carefully explained twenty years later, was that it hadn't been calculating enough.

"At the time, there wasn't this moral ambiguity as far as supporting the war but not being willing to sign up and go there—certainly not in my mind," Quayle said. "What that statement reflected was the political ambiguity of my situation. I had done what I thought was right, what I wanted to do at that particular time, which was to get on with my education, without making any kind of calculated decision about a political career, because I really wasn't set on a political career at that time. I had been more oriented toward law and the newspaper business. I didn't have a burning desire to be President— that developed later. . . .

"If I had in fact known at that time that I really wanted to be President of the United States, then I could have calculated—like I think some of my generation thought about it in college and calculated for that reason—that . . . from a political point of view, it looks better on a résumé to have served in Vietnam."

ONCE THE National Guard flap subsided, Quayle's next big ordeal was his nationally televised debate with Bentsen. The memorable exchange of the evening in Omaha came when Quayle made an ill-considered comparison of himself and John F. Kennedy. Bentsen pounced like a cat.

Bentsen: "Senator, I served with Jack Kennedy. I knew Jack Kennedy. Jack Kennedy was a friend of mine. Senator, you're no Jack Kennedy."

Quayle: "That was really uncalled for, Senator."

I watched the debate in suburban St. Louis with three Republican voters who began the evening with serious reservations about Quayle, but who were prepared to "grade him on a curve," as one put it, because they found it so hard to swallow the idea of voting for Michael Dukakis.

It wasn't Bentsen's zinger that my tiny jury wanted to talk about afterward; it was Quayle's response.

"He was like a little boy saying, 'You can't do that to me,' " said Janet Frantzen, forty-six, an administrative assistant. "He's led a sheltered life. . . . I can't see him going into Bush and saying, 'We've got to rethink this, Mr. President.' George would probably say, 'Go out and play some golf, Dan.' "

"You could see him in a meeting with foreign leaders, and if things got tough, he would say, 'That's not fair,' and start to cry," said Charles Schroeder, forty-one, an attorney. "I mean, basically, he hasn't been hardened."

"You get the sense that he can't think for himself," said Marcia Coonley, thirty-one, a widowed single parent. "I kept looking for the microphone in his ear," she added, conjuring up the image of an unseen handler in a control booth somewhere, barking instructions at the next Vice President.

Figuratively, she wasn't far off the mark. Quayle had been over-coached for the debate, and it showed. On question after question, he would pause for a disconcerting split second before answering, as if to search his mental file cabinet for the rehearsed response.

"In the preparations," he recalled afterward, "the whole attitude drilled into me was: 'Just don't make a mistake. Concentrate on making factual statements. Don't get into areas you're not comfortable with. Because if you do make a mistake, that's the thing they'll repeat over and over again on the network news.' "

His handlers had cause to worry. They remembered the 1976 presidential debate in which President Ford oratorically freed Eastern Europe from Soviet domination. The polls taken immediately afterward showed that a majority of viewers thought that Ford had won. But a few days later, after a drumbeat of news reports focused on Ford's gaffe, the American people declared Jimmy Carter the debate winner.

To avoid that kind of screw-up, Quayle's keepers took him off the trail for five days and fed him policy briefings, "pepper drills" and two mock debates. When the question of his qualifications to be President came up in one of the mock debates, Quayle tried out the line he'd been using on the stump—comparing his experience favorably with Truman's (when he became Vice President) and Kennedy's.

"I told him, 'I'd stay away from that line,'" recalled Jim Ciccone, one of his advisers. "'It may work out on the stump, but you're going to be in an adversary setting, and Truman and Kennedy are Democratic icons. Bentsen knows you've been using it, and he's probably ready to jump on it.'

"Quayle nodded and said, 'Yeah, you're right.'"

Unfortunately for Quayle, he didn't remember the advice when it counted. His troubles at the debate began when Brit Hume of ABC asked: "Let us assume, if we can for the sake of this question, that you have become Vice President, and the President is incapacitated for one reason or another, and you have to take the reins of power. When that moment came, what would be the first steps you'd take, and why?"

"First," Quayle responded slowly, "first, I'd say a prayer for myself and for the country I'm about to lead. And then I would assemble his people and talk." And then? Quayle didn't say. He simply recited chapter and verse from his résumé.

At his next opportunity, Hume asked: "You said you would say a prayer, and you said something about a meeting. What would you do next?"

This wasn't exactly quantum physics. Quayle could simply have said he would carry forward the policies of the Bush administration—a commitment, he might have added, that Bentsen would have trouble making about *his* ticket mate, given their numerous policy differences.

"I don't believe that it's proper for me to get into the specifics of a situation like that," Quayle said. Then, like an overeager young job applicant, he reiterated his qualifications. "I've been to Geneva.... I've met with Margaret Thatcher, Chancellor Kohl; I know them, they know me...."

The veteran journalists on the panel sensed his defensiveness. They refused to let the subject drop. Moments later, NBC anchor Tom Brokaw asked: "... surely you must have some plan in mind if it fell to you to become President of the United States, as it has to so many Vice Presidents in the last 25 years or so."

"Let me try to answer the question one more time," Quayle said, exasperated. "I think this is the fourth time that I've had the question."

"The third time," said Brokaw.

"Three times that I've had this question, and I will try to answer it again for you as clearly as I can because the question you are asking is what kind of qualification does Dan Quayle have to be President ... and what would I do in this kind of situation."

Quayle took one brief, not-very-assuring pass at the what-would-I-do? portion of the question. "I would make sure that the people in the Cabinet and the people that are the advisers to the President are called in, and I would talk to them, and I will work with them. And I will know them on a firsthand basis. . . ."

Soon he was back to qualifications: "It's not just age; it's accomplishments; it's experience. I have far more experience than many others that sought the office of Vice President of the country. I have as much experience in the Congress as Jack Kennedy did when he sought the presidency. . . ."

A sly smile sneaked across Bentsen's face as he prepared to lower the boom.

A year later, Quayle's coaches were still trying to explain what had gone wrong. "The second time he got the question, he was too robotic," recalled Ciccone, "and I think he knew it. Then when he got hit with it the third time, he didn't want to repeat himself, so he came up with the Kennedy line. Later that night, he said that as soon as it came out of his mouth, he knew he'd made a mistake."

Quayle's recollection is slightly different. "I got through that debate without making any mistakes," he said. "You can say the Kennedy thing was a mistake, but Bentsen was going to use a line like that, whether I gave him an opening or not. . . . And when I walked out of that debate, the reaction of the people around me was that it had been just perfect. Everybody was very excited. It wasn't until they started getting the polls that a lot of people started jumping ship. And that's when I decided the hell with it. If that's the way we describe loyalty around here, forget it, fellas, I'm on my own. And that's when I went back to my own ways."

Quayle got angry when James Baker, in a post-debate interview, praised him and Bentsen equally for their performances. Coming from the Bush/Quayle campaign chairman, such evenhandedness seemed tantamount to a concession of defeat. "The spinners aren't spinning it right," Marilyn Quayle fumed that night as she watched a tape of the Baker interview on TV in their hotel room in Omaha.[6]

Stung by Baker's comments, by unattributed quotes from Bush campaign staffers calling him a drag on the ticket and by stepped-up ridicule of him in Democratic television ads and late-night monologues, Quayle telephoned Baker the next day to complain of nonsupport.

"I didn't realize until then how bad things had gotten," he said later. "Up until that debate, it was just go, go, go—always on the road. And after all the National Guard stuff, I just got to the point where I didn't turn the television on and didn't read the newspapers. I blocked it out. I guess I could feel it building, but when it really clicked was when they ran away from me after the debate. I said the hell with it. I've put up with this long enough."

A few days after the debate, Quayle staged a revolt against his handlers. "From now on, I'm going to be my own spin doctor," he told startled reporters on his campaign plane in South Dakota. "I'm just going to let 'er rip."

The emancipation proclamation was more apparent than real. "My wife read what he had said, and when I called her on the phone from the road that night, she got real excited and asked, 'Does that mean you get to come home?'" Ciccone recalled. "I had to disabuse her of that. That rebellion was a combination of planning and spontaneity. When he said he was going to be his own spokesman, we sort of helped him embellish it and turn it into an anti-handler thing." The following day, Bentsen's press secretary, Mike McCurry, sarcastically tipped his hat at Quayle's anti-handler revolt, calling it a "brilliant piece of handling."

It wasn't all sham, however. For weeks, tension had been building between Quayle and the veteran team recruited by Baker to run the vice-presidential campaign. The group was headed by Stuart Spencer, a profane, gruff, highly regarded California consultant who'd held senior positions in Reagan's presidential campaigns in 1984 and 1980 and Ford's in 1976. Spencer had accepted the VP assignment before he knew Quayle was going to be the candidate. The two never got along very well. The anecdote that best captures Spencer's scorn for his young charge appeared in *Whose Broad Stripes and Bright Stars?*, an account of the 1988 campaign by Jack Germond and Jules Witcover. "I want him to step on his dick, and then we'll own him again," Spencer reportedly told another Quayle handler, Joseph Canzeri, when Canzeri asked why Spencer had allowed Quayle to speak extemporaneously.[7] Canzeri's opinion of Quayle was no better. "He was like a kid. Ask him to turn off a light, and by the time he gets to the switch, he's forgotten what he went for. . . . We knew we were going to have to script him."[8]

Even the handlers who hit it off with Quayle were surprised by how poorly he coped with his first weeks in the national spotlight. "I was astounded that Quayle was thrown the way he was by the whole experience," said Craig Fuller. "I had a lot of confidence in him, and I figured he was a natural. But when people looked at him that fall, and they saw that look of the deer frozen in the headlights, there was no way we could shake it. In a very real sense, I think his confidence got shattered—he was a real battlefield casualty there for a while. I think he was extremely courageous for having hung in the way he did."

"He was like a guy who had been blindfolded, walked up to the 10-meter platform and thrown off," agreed Mitch Daniels. "He needed a couple of weeks to crash around and get his bearings."

The handlers' rescue effort had gone into high gear in early September after Quayle gave what was billed as a major foreign-policy address in Chicago. A text had been handed out in advance to the traveling press. Whenever this is done, candidates are schooled to deliver their speeches as written, so as to avoid the confusion that can arise from serving up two different wordings of the same policy speech—one written, one oral. But Quayle, a novice at the business of being a national candidate, was accustomed to speaking extemporaneously.

"On the plane to Chicago, he said, 'You know, this isn't really very good. Why don't I make some notes and just sort of follow along with the text,'" recalled David Prosperi, Quayle's press secretary during the campaign. "Then we had some downtime in Chicago before the speech, and all the reporters wrote their stories, based on the advance text. You can imagine their horror when he gets up on the stage and does forty-five minutes of free-lancing."

"It was a big mistake to hand out that text in advance," said speechwriter Ken Khachigian. "The reporters had written their stories, maybe they'd gone out and had a few beers, figuring this was going to be an easy day. Then when Quayle speaks, he's on his own, and the reporters start saying, 'Holy shit—what's wrong with this guy?'"

Prosperi and Khachigian remember the bulk of the speech as being quite acceptable. But the only thing that made the network news that night—and for several nights thereafter—was Quayle's wounded effort to paraphrase Indiana University basketball coach Bobby Knight on the subject of national defense: "Bobby Knight told me this: 'there is nothing that a good defense cannot beat a better offense.' In other words, a good offense wins."

Say what?

A few days later, Quayle got even more tangled when he was asked a question at a news conference about the Holocaust.

"It was an obscene period in our nation's history," he said.

A reporter suggested that perhaps he hadn't meant to say "our nation's history," whereupon Quayle explained—or tried to explain—that he meant "in this century's history."

"We all lived in this century—I didn't live in this century—in this century's history. We did not have—as a matter of fact, we fought Hitlerism. The Holocaust is a critical point in history that we as a nation should understand."

Say what?

It didn't take too many of these malapropisms for Spencer & Co. to put Quayle on a short leash and insist that he stay on text, avoid ad-libs and keep a stiff-armed distance from the press. The result was the robot that America saw at that debate.

Quayle was a better candidate after he staged his so-called revolt. He became so comfortable with reporters that on one flight in late October, they put up a "Spin-Free Zone" sign on their section of the plane—a deadpan plea to Quayle to stop smothering them with access. One night in Orlando in mid-October, Quayle sat down with about fifteen of the reporters who had covered him throughout the fall for a convivial off-the-record dinner. Everyone discovered—somewhat to everyone's surprise—that they got along just fine. "This is the Dan Quayle America should be seeing," one correspondent mused to Prosperi after the dinner.

On the stump, too, there began to be some glimpses of that more attractive Quayle. He was looser and more engaging—closer to the candidate who'd pulled off two big upsets in Indiana. By that stage of the campaign, however, he was no longer "a story." He'd been relegated to visiting safe states, making no news, rallying the faithful. The voters had taken a good look at Quayle, and seen an unbearable lightness. Their first impression would not shake easily.

The Dukakis campaign tried to capitalize on that impression, running anti-Quayle commercials right up through the end of October. But the political rule of thumb has always been that voters don't vote for Vice President. That rule held in 1988.

LOOKING BACK on the campaign six months after it was over, Quayle said he took satisfaction in having joined a ticket that was trailing by 7 percentage points and being a part of a ticket that won by 7.5 percentage points. He said he helped the cause by serving as a "lightning rod."

But he also acknowledged that he took a terrible beating, and he placed some of the blame on himself. "I made a significant mistake, and I have to accept responsibility, when I allowed myself to operate in this constrained, controlled environment. I mean, these people [his handlers] didn't want me talking to the press. They wanted me to be so-called error-free. . . . I made the mistake about not confronting all those questions about me that arose, of not going out front and saying, 'Here I am, I'll answer your questions.'

"I have to accept responsibility for that, because George Bush told me, he said, 'Look, if you want to change anything . . . you tell me.' He was very supportive. So I have to accept that as a mistake."

Quayle said the press bears some responsibility, too. "The thing that disappointed me the most, I guess, was the unanimity of the coverage. What it showed me is how much of a herd mentality there really is. My problem was that, even if there were a few who wanted to write something good, I didn't give them an opportunity, because I allowed myself to be completely controlled. I never communicated with them, never called them up on the phone and said, 'Hey, let me get out my side of the story.' "

As soon as the campaign was over, Quayle hired a new press secretary, former *Time* correspondent David Beckwith, and began holding a series of private background meetings with Washington bureau chiefs, columnists, editorial writers, opinion leaders. As Vice President, he has been a more active participant in the Bush Administration's internal policy debates than his critics would have guessed. On matters ranging from Soviet relations to Star Wars to Central America to abortion and drugs, Quayle has been a vocal advocate for the conservative agenda.

There's been a slight thaw in his treatment in the media, but the public's attitude appears to remain contemptuous. It is no easy thing to mount a rehabilitation effort as Vice President—the office itself has been the butt of jokes for two centuries. "You just kind of sit around waiting for something to happen," Jay Leno had quipped during Quayle's National Guard flap. "If that isn't training for the vice presidency, I don't know what is." Of Quayle, the comedian said: "A lot of people think he's too inexperienced for a do-nothing job."

A year after Quayle was elected, a Washington *Post*-ABC survey found that a majority of voters who had an opinion thought that Bush had made a mistake in selecting Quayle; that he wasn't qualified to be President; and that he should be dropped from the ticket if Bush runs again in 1992. A *Wall Street Journal*/NBC poll taken around the same time found that, by 40–39 percent, even *Republican* voters thought he should be dropped from the ticket in 1992.

Bush has said he intends to stand by his man, but that decision is likely to remain open until 1992. Meantime, the hazing never seems to stop. In the closing days of 1989, MTV announced the results of a viewer poll. In the "Nobody's Home: The Bimbo of the '80s Award," the winner—over such worthy competitors as Jessica Hahn, Rob Lowe, Brigitte Nielson and Vanna White—was the Vice President.

CHAPTER EIGHT

The Handlers:
Lee, Roger and Willie

T HE FIRST TIME Lee Atwater heard about Willie Horton's
furlough, he had an epiphany. "It was one of those things,"
said Atwater, a raspy-voiced South Carolinian with a quirky charm,
a keen political mind and a lurid (but carefully tended) reputation
as a political spitballer, "that had thirty-second spot written all
over it."

The issue floated onto Atwater's radar screen in April 1988, when,
during a Democratic debate in New York, Al Gore accused Michael
Dukakis of giving "weekend passes to convicted criminals." At the
time, furloughs were as inevitable a presidential campaign issue
as, say, fox trots. But politics is the art of seizing the right symbol
at the right time in the right way, and Atwater had found the one
he wanted. "If I can make Willie Horton a household name," he
would tell a Republican group a few weeks later, "we'll win the
election."

The only households where the name had been heard at that stage
of the campaign were in Lawrence, Massachusetts, an industrial
community north of Boston where Horton had committed the crime
for which he was originally imprisoned—the grisly 1974 murder of a
seventeen-year-old gas-station attendant during a robbery that net-
ted $276.37. He was sentenced to life in prison without chance of
parole. On June 6, 1986, Horton left the Northeastern Correctional
Center on an unguarded, forty-eight-hour furlough. He was appre-
hended ten months later in Maryland, after a high-speed chase with
police in a car he had stolen from an Oxon Hill, Maryland, couple

whom he had terrorized for eleven hours—pistol-whipping and stabbing the man, raping and beating his fiancé.

The ensuing public outcry in Massachusetts was led by the Lawrence *Eagle-Tribune*. The paper wanted an answer to an obvious question: what was a convicted murderer serving a life-without-parole sentence doing out on furlough? The main purpose of furloughs is to facilitate a prisoner's adjustment to life outside the prison. If a prisoner has no prospect of being released, the rationale collapses. Although thirty-eight states and the federal government have furlough programs, Massachusetts is one of fewer than a half dozen states where it is possible for an unparolable inmate to be furloughed— the result of a 1972 prison reform law enacted under the administration of Dukakis' predecessor, Republican Governor Francis W. Sargent.

When the Dukakis administration resisted the *Eagle-Tribune*'s requests to see Horton's prison records, the paper launched a crusade. It published 175 articles about the case over the next year. In one editorial that appeared on May 3, 1987, a month after Horton's Maryland rampage and four days after Dukakis announced for the presidency, the paper ran a "Clip and Save" coupon at the bottom of its editorial page. It read:

Gov. Dukakis: Please Tell Me Why:
- Killers go free on furlough
- Killers are paroled
- The state lies when it says killers are jailed for life

Write Me: Name _____

Address _____

_____

"We haven't been able to reach him," the editorial concluded. "Perhaps you will."

With the help of other newspaper editorials from around the state, the *Eagle-Tribune* eventually pressured the Department of Corrections into releasing Horton's prison records. It discovered that he had had nine previous furloughs and that unparolable lifers in Massachusetts routinely received furloughs because the expectation was that they would have their sentences commuted by the governor. (Dukakis, as governor, had commuted the life sentences of twenty-eight murderers.) The paper's articles inspired a citizens' petition drive, led by Donna Cuomo, the sister of the seventeen-year-old youth Horton had killed in 1974. They collected 57,000 signatures, enough to force an anti-furlough referendum to be placed on the November 1988 ballot in Massachusetts. The plebiscite never had to be held, however. In the spring of 1988, the state legislature—reading the public's outrage loud and clear—stepped in and passed a bill curtailing furloughs.

Dukakis kept at arm's length from the explosive issue during the year it bubbled and boiled in Massachusetts. "Unfortunately, nobody in the cabinet would walk the plank, take responsibility and call the policy a mistake. And nobody in the governor's office was whipping them to do it," recalled one high-level Dukakis staffer. "We were preoccupied with the presidential race." Even if he hadn't been distracted by pressing business in Iowa and New Hampshire, however, it's not clear Dukakis would have handled the matter differently. His views on crime and punishment were forged in the 1960s, when rehabilitation enjoyed a brief heyday among penologists, academicians and some politicians. In the ensuing two decades, as a rising crime rate had brought the values of punishment, retribution and victims' rights back to the forefront of corrections policy, Dukakis hadn't shifted with the rightward tide. The best bellwether of his increasing isolation was his position on the death penalty. It hadn't changed; the public's had. In 1966, Americans opposed the death penalty by 47 to 42 percent, and Dukakis was part of a slim plurality. By 1988, Americans supported the death penalty by 79 to 20 percent, and Dukakis was a member of a small minority.

In December 1987 Clifford and Angela Barnes, the Maryland couple Horton had terrorized the previous April, flew to Boston to testify before a state legislative panel that was considering changes in the furlough law. Dukakis declined to meet with them: he didn't like the idea of making public policy from the passions of personal tragedy. (This proved to be a mistake. The next fall, Barnes extracted his revenge by appearing in a television commercial about Horton and by making the rounds of nationally syndicated television talk shows.) The Barneses told the legislature that they had moved out of the house where Horton had brutalized them, in the hope of escaping the horrible memories—but to no avail. "I don't think any of you could understand how it is to listen to your wife cry out as she is violated and beaten," Barnes testified. "I wish you could enter our dreams at night. I wish you could be there when the heater goes off at night or something creaks and we jump up."

In late March 1988—two weeks before the *Eagle-Tribune* was awarded a Pulitzer Prize for its coverage of the Horton case—Dukakis told a news conference in Boston that he would sign the bill curtailing furloughs, which by then was on its way to passage by veto-proof majorities in both chambers of the legislature. This was a reversal of the position he'd taken in 1976, when he pocket-vetoed an anti-furlough measure, saying it would "cut the heart out of efforts at inmate rehabilitation." Asked a dozen years later if he still was in favor of furloughs, Dukakis snapped: "That's irrelevant. The fact of the matter is that the people of this Commonwealth and the legislature aren't." He added that he would like to have some alternative program that would allow him to commute the sentences of first-degree murderers.

In his response to Al Gore at the New York debate a few weeks later, Dukakis brought none of this up. He simply said that his state's furlough program was about to be tightened, making it sound as if he had initiated the change that he had, in fact, resisted until the last. Gore, whose candidacy was in its dying days, chose not to press the attack. Democratic presidential primaries are often fractious— New York's was especially so—but tagging an opponent as soft on crime has never been part of the intraparty arsenal. The brief exchange merited just a few lines in the next day's national news reports.

The Republicans proved to be less squeamish. "The only question is whether we depict Horton with a knife in his hand or not," Bush's media consultant, Roger Ailes, mused shortly after the case came to his attention.

AILES AND ATWATER were the junkyard dogs of the most experienced team of political consultants ever assembled to run a presidential campaign; it was their go-for-the-throat instincts that gave the campaign its snarling tone. (Bush, of course, could have kept them on a leash, but chose not to.) Standing side by side, the pair looked a bit like Laurel and Hardy. Ailes, fifty, is dark, rotund, bearded and balding. Atwater, thirty-nine, is wiry and blond. Ailes can be garrulous and charming, but frequently flew into (controlled) fits of rage during the campaign—usually with the intent to intimidate. Atwater came across like a jumble of raw nerve endings—eyes darting, knees bobbing, arms flapping. Atwater's father was an insurance adjuster in Columbia, South Carolina; Ailes's dad was a salesman in Warren, Ohio. Each has a keen ear for the hopes and fears of the middle class. Each is a master of his craft.

During the campaign, Atwater would get away from the pressure cooker of the Washington, D.C., campaign headquarters to spend a few days each month listening to the voters. (Between field trips, he would stay in touch by reading the *National Enquirer.*) On one such mission in the summer of 1988, he took his wife and two young daughters to Luray Caverns, Virginia, where a convention of motorcycle riders had gathered for a Fourth of July festival. These were no Hell's Angels; they were suburbanites with split-level homes, blue-collar jobs and just enough extra income to afford a relatively low-cost hobby. "I figured they were the perfect cross-section, the middle of the middle class," said Atwater, "because they had enough money to support a bike, but not enough for a boat or a second house." When Atwater had dinner with his wife and kids at a Chinese restaurant in Luray that Saturday night, they overheard the two couples at the table next to them discussing the Horton case, which had just been the subject of a long article in *Reader's Digest.* The conversation was peppered with incredulity and outrage—how anyone could let a man like that go on furlough! "I started to talk to 'em about it, and they got [even more] upset. Pretty soon the waitresses and the folks from other tables all joined in," Atwater recalled. "We kept going after the place closed. Afterward I said to myself, 'This issue has real life; this issue counts to Americans.' "

To Atwater and Ailes, politics, stripped down to its irreducible nub, is combat. Atwater is fascinated by professional wrestling ("It's the only honest game in town") and samurai warfare ("If you ever lose a fight, you die"). Losing, he says, "has made me physically ill at times—I'm not ashamed to admit it." Once, after his client lost a congressional race in Texas by a razor-thin margin, he had the dry heaves for two days.

Ailes grew up as a sickly child, the target of neighborhood bullies. His father gave him a piece of advice when Ailes was nine: "The worst thing that can happen to you is you can die. If you're not afraid of that, you don't have to be afraid of anything." Ailes said he's never forgotten it. "I've trained my mind to think that way. I suppose I give that off, and people think I'm hostile or crazy."[1] His credo in campaigns is to "hit the opponent at his weakest point, at the most opportune time, with the least loss to oneself," and he's mystified by critics who worry about the nastiness of campaigns. "If you don't have anything bad to say about the opponent," he says with a shrug, "why don't you just let him have the job?"

He came to politics from show business, where he worked as a gofer, assistant producer and finally producer of *The Mike Douglas Show*. His first political client was Richard Nixon, whose 1968 presidential campaign became the subject of a best-selling book about the art of image manipulation—Joe McGinniss's *The Selling of the President*.

Ailes is much more than a maker of TV ads; he is a speech coach, debate preparer, drill sergeant, confidence builder, amateur psychologist. "He's very supportive in the beginning—he bolsters them, reinforces their egos," said fellow GOP consultant Robert Goodman. "When he feels their confidence level is up, then he can be blunt to a fault. He'll say, 'You stink!'—and they listen."[2] A 1988 *Newsweek* profile of Ailes led with a snapshot of the wizard at work. "The client just happens to be Vice President of the United States and the Republican nominee for president: a certain deference is required. So who's this balding, paunchy, rumpled guy yelling at George Bush as he rehearses his next campaign appearance? 'There you go with that f---ing hand again,' the bald guy screams. 'You look like a f---ing *pansy*.' Bush, chastened but apparently appreciative, repeats his lines without a trace of hand waving, and the bald man smiles. The client is making progress."[3]

Atwater and Ailes were unlikely matches for Bush, a Connecticut Yankee who had been raised on the code of good sportsmanship, fair play and noblesse oblige. One of Bush's youthful nicknames was "have half," for his eagerness to share his goodies with his playmates. His parents drilled into him the importance of a category of achievement known in the family as "claims no more," shorthand for "claims no more than his fair share of credit." As a mature politician, he had climbed the ladder by the appointive route, quietly accommodating his bosses and constantly nurturing an ever-widening circle of friendships.* His record at the rough-and-tumble of electoral politics was much spottier. Coming into 1988, he hadn't won a race on his

*It is said of Bush that he writes more personal notes than any other politician in Washington—almost to the point of obsession. On the flight down from Washington to Winston-Salem the day of his first televised debate with Dukakis, the traveling press corps sang him some Christmas carols for the holiday season. The date was September 25. The gag was that this was Christmas on Bush's calendar, for a few days before, speaking to a group of veterans, he had commemorated September 7 as the anniversary of the Japanese attack on Pearl Harbor. Bush enjoyed the joke. Once his plane landed, he had some time for debate preparation—precious hours Bush should have been using to bone up on his answers. But first he had to do something he considered more pressing. Shortly before the start of the debate, as reporters were gathering in the pressroom, a Bush aide delivered handwritten Christmas cards, thanking each of the reporters who had serenaded him. Each note said something a little different.

own in twenty years. His lifetime won-lost record was 2–3, with two victories in U.S. House of Representative races in Houston (1966, 1968), two defeats in U.S. Senate races in Texas (1964, 1970) and a losing bid for the GOP presidential nomination (1980).

Atwater and Ailes had a theory that Bush's good manners were misconstrued by voters as a lack of spine. They knew he had a fiercely competitive streak that he didn't like to show, and they were determined to tease it to the surface. The best way to do that, they figured, was to make sure Bush mastered the "defining moments" of the campaign—those two or three memorable confrontations that seem to occur in every presidential race and get taken by the voters as parables about character. These moments capture the public's imagination precisely because they seem spontaneous. Ailes and Atwater thought they were too important to be left to chance.

Both had witnessed the impact of such moments before. During the New Hampshire Republican primary in 1980, Atwater was working for candidate Ronald Reagan when Reagan "won" the Nashua debate with his declaration: "I'm paying for this microphone, Mr. Green," during an argument with the moderator* over the debate format. In 1984, the defining moment came in Reagan's second debate with Walter Mondale, when the President—who'd been so wobbly in the first debate that the press had subsequently raised the question of senility—promised in a deadpan voice not to exploit the age issue against his younger Democratic opponent. Ailes had been Reagan's debate coach that year and Atwater was the political strategist who had come up with a contingency plan in case the quip did not go over well. "Create a fog machine," he wrote in a memo to the campaign staff. "If it's clear the President did badly, then it's our job to obscure the result."

In 1988, the first defining moment for Bush came in a live interview with CBS's Dan Rather—and there was nothing spontaneous about it. Atwater and Ailes had been leery about the interview from the moment it had been proposed by CBS in early January. They counseled Bush against doing it. "I just smelled setup," said Atwater. "Rather was a middle-aged guy with a sagging career who remembered what the Kennedy interview did for Roger Mudd."† Bush would hear nothing of it. "I feel comfortable with Rather," he scribbled on the letter from CBS producer Richard Cohen proposing the

*Whose name was actually Breen.
†In 1979, after Ted Kennedy bungled a TV interview with Roger Mudd, Kennedy's presidential campaign sputtered while Mudd's stock rose.

interview as part of a series of political profiles that Rather was doing on the *CBS Evening News*. "Make sure this guy gets reply soon."

In the weeks leading up to the interview, Tom Bettag, executive producer of the *CBS Evening News*, made it clear to the Bush camp that the focus of Rather's questions would be on the Iran–contra issue. Atwater's concerns mounted. "By the Friday before the [Monday, January 25, 1988] interview, we were hearing all kinds of rumors that CBS was out to do a number on Bush," he said. "I had been warning the Vice President to stay away, and he said, 'Lee, I know you're looking out for my best interests, but Dan has been a friend of mine for twenty-five years.' In fact, he sort of scolded me, in a friendly way, for being so paranoid."

On the Sunday before the interview, Ailes received a phone call at home from Peter Teeley, the campaign press secretary at the time. Ailes recalled: "He said, 'I think this CBS thing is going to be worse than we thought. You had better get down to Washington.' I started checking around. I had a source inside CBS News who went outside to a pay phone and called me and said, 'I'm sorry to have to tell you this, but they're running around the CBS newsroom saying they're going to take George Bush out of the race tonight. They have hired a Democratic consultant [Thomas Donilon, a strategist for Carter, Mondale and Biden] to work with Rather. They have created a five-minute [lead-in] segment which is going to indict him by putting him on the screen with some sorry characters who have some problems. Then they're going to hand him a blindfold and Rather is going to execute him. So you guys better be ready.' "[4]

At Ailes's insistence, CBS had agreed to conduct the interview live. That would give Bush an edge: he could evade or filibuster secure in the knowledge that no amount of pasting and editing could give his words meanings he did not intend. Moreover, if the tightly wound Rather came on too strong, Bush could play the counterpuncher. Ailes coaches his clients to view every human contact as an instant size-up, in which a person has just a few seconds to absorb a given situation and then control the atmosphere by projecting calm self-assurance. He's also a great believer in what he calls the "man in the pit" theory of political confrontation. "If a reporter is bullying you, the viewers at home may start to root for you," Ailes wrote in a book, *You Are the Message*. "The more inflammatory the journalist, the cooler you should be."

Atwater, too, was a student of the sweet uses of confrontation. He'd gotten his first lessons in the subject from the first of his several mentors—South Carolina senator Strom Thurmond, for whom he worked, initially as a gofer, eventually as a campaign manager. "I remember when we were at the Republican convention in Miami, 1972," Atwater once told Washington *Post* reporter David Remnick. "We were driving in a car and all of a sudden we see this huge demonstration, all kinds of cops and signs and shouting. Well, course, Thurmond was a big hawk, and some of the kids recognized him in the car. Some yelled, 'Hey, it's Strom Thurmond, power pig of the South!' We couldn't move and I thought, 'Oh, man, we're dead.' But, man, Thurmond didn't sweat. He said, 'I'm gonna talk with these people.' Jesus! Well, he gets out, and there's TV cameras all over the place, and this eighteen- or nineteen-year-old girl confronts him. She starts calling him a fascist pig and cocksucker and all sorts of stuff. And the whole time Thurmond is just smilin' and sayin', 'Little girl, do your parents know you're out here? Honey, you sure are a pretty thing.' The girl's still cursing at him, and Thurmond gets back in the car and we drive away. I say, 'What were you doing?' And he says, 'Young man, that'll be twenty-five thousand votes when we get home.' Boy, did I learn from that man."[5]

When Atwater heard about the phone call Ailes had gotten Sunday from his friend at CBS, he called up Bush. "I said, 'Mr. Vice President, I know how you feel about this interview, but just in case I'm right and you're wrong, I've asked Roger to come out and meet you at the airport to go over a few things,'" he recalled.

"And he said, 'God, Lee, you just don't give up.'"

On the drive in from Andrews Air Force Base to Bush's vice-presidential office, Ailes told Bush what he'd heard and fed him some lines to use. "He didn't believe it was going to be a political execution or an attempt at a political execution," Ailes recalled. "I said, 'Why don't we plan for it just in case?' Basically, we decided we weren't going to take it lying down."

The interview was conducted with Rather at his New York anchor desk and Bush in his Capitol Hill office. As Bush watched the taped five-minute introductory report on Iran–contra on a television monitor, he grew upset. "If that's all this is going to be about," Bush snapped to the CBS technicians in his office just before he went on the air live, "they're going to find themselves with a seven-minute walkout on their hands." Ailes stood a few paces away, off-camera, happily stoking his client's fire. Several times during the ensuing interview, he wrote out key words in big letters on a yellow pad to remind Bush what to say.

Rather's first question was on Iran–contra, and Bush started blazing away: "I find this to be a rehash and a little bit, if you'll excuse me, of a misrepresentation on the part of CBS, who said you're doing political profiles of all the candidates." He summarized the contents of the Cohen letter.

What happened over the next nine minutes was the spectacle of two ambushes colliding. Rather had anticipated a counterattack ("We knew it was going to be a brawl," recalled CBS's Cohen) and did not back off. The interview was all sparks.

Bush: "May I answer that?"

Rather: "That wasn't a question. It was a statement."

Bush: "It was a statement and I'll answer it."

Rather: "Let me ask the question, if I may, first."

And later:

Rather: "I don't want to be argumentative, Mr. Vice President."

Bush: "You do, Dan."

Two-thirds of the way through the firefight, Ailes scribbled the words "Not fair to judge career" on his legal pad to remind Bush of what they'd planned in the car ride in from Andrews.

"It's not fair to judge my whole career by a rehash on Iran," Bush immediately told Rather. "How would you like it if I judged your whole career by those seven minutes when you walked off the set in New York?" The reference was to an incident the previous September, when Rather had lost his temper and walked off the set because the start of his evening news broadcast had been delayed a few minutes by CBS's coverage of a match at the U.S. Open tennis tournament. The network was forced to go black for six minutes while producers frantically coaxed Rather back to his anchor desk. It was a breach of professionalism that some in the industry, including Rather's sainted predecessor, Walter Cronkite, considered a firing offense.

When Bush landed that blow, Rather initially was too stunned to respond. For the remainder of the interview, his questions took on a more biting tone, and his composure seemed shot. "Mr. Vice President," he hectored moments later, "you've made us hypocrites in the face of the world! How could you, how could you sign on to such a policy?"

The close of the interview was even more ragged. With a producer shouting into his earphone to bring the overlong segment to a close, Rather said: "I appreciate the straightforward way in which you've engaged in this exchange. There are clearly some unanswered questions. Are you willing to go to a news conference before the Iowa caucuses, answer questions from all ... "

Bush: "I've been to eighty-six news conferences since March, eighty-six of 'em since March ... "

Rather: "I gather the answer is no. Thank you very much for being with us, Mr. Vice President. We'll be back with more news in a moment."

"The bastard didn't lay a glove on me," Bush harrumphed into what was still a live microphone. "That guy makes Lesley Stahl look like a pussy." (These gamey post-interview comments didn't air live, but they appeared in print a few days later.)

Though Rather came under a great deal of criticism from viewers and station owners, his line of questioning had been much sounder in substance than in tone. For more than a year, Bush had been evasive about his role in the Iran–contra episode, using the claim of executive privilege to refrain from disclosing what advice he had given President Reagan. In a written response to a question from Washington *Post* columnist Mary McGrory, Bush had stated he had voiced "reservations" about the arms sale that "turned out to be well founded." But he didn't say when, or to whom. His critics wondered why Reagan didn't release him to disclose any privileged conversations, just as he'd released Secretary of State George Shultz to tell the Tower Commission how he had objected to the policy during cabinet meetings. Instead, both the President and Vice President stonewalled.

Had Rather been one of his own network correspondents, and had he posed his questions at a regular campaign press conference, hardly an eyebrow would have been raised. Reporters frequently badger politicians; it's part of the job description. Network anchors are different. Someone once described them as the secular equivalent of deities, for they come into everyone's home each night and explain the mysteries of the world. Rather got pounded not just by viewers but by colleagues in the media. "There was no excuse for him assuming the roles of judge and jury in a newscast," wrote Los Angeles *Times* TV critic Howard Rosenberg. "Who appointed him America's shrieking ayatollah of truth?" ABC's Ted Koppel observed more shrewdly a few days later that the problem was not that Rather had asked tough questions, but that he'd allowed himself to be maneuvered into serving as "a high priest in the ceremonial de-wimping of George Bush."

Bush was exhilarated by the exchange—if also a bit discombobulated. Over the next few days, he seemed so excited that he stepped on his newly acquired macho-man plumage a couple of times— gushing to an audience in Cody, Wyoming, that he deserved "combat pay" for the encounter and confiding to a group in Pierre, South Dakota, that it had been "Tension City" going head to head with Rather.

Ailes and Atwater were ecstatic. "I think it was the most important event of the entire primary campaign," said Atwater. "It was stronger than grits in the South. Rather is a guy people love to hate down there. I think it sealed Super Tuesday for us, and I think it was one of the reasons we were able to come back strong in New Hampshire after we took the hit in Iowa. It solidified our base." There is no polling to support Atwater's contention—in fact, the polls taken immediately after the encounter showed that most viewers disapproved of the way both men handled themselves. But that doesn't make Atwater wrong. The most significant political journey of 1988 was Bush's escape from the wimp image, and his dustup with Rather was one of its milestones. It helped in another way, too: after the fireworks of January 25, 1988, the media's curiosity about Iran–contra waned, and the issue never became a factor in the primaries or the general election.

T HE DE-WIMPING of George Bush was only one of several long-term strategic goals Atwater had brought to the campaign. From the day he signed on as campaign manager—a week before Christmas 1985—he assumed that the 1988 general election would have to be waged on the attack. His candidate was a quasi-incumbent running to retain an office his party had held for two consecutive terms and sixteen of the previous twenty years. There weren't a lot of bold new ideas left for a Republican to offer in 1988. "The strategic concept was developed way before we knew who the Democratic nominee was," Atwater said. "Whoever it was, we had to paint him as a frost-belt liberal not in tune with the values of mainstream voters. What we did was find the actual issues that allowed us to paint the picture." He added: "It was a hot-potato election. Whoever held the hot potato the longest, the mostest and the lastest was going to lose. We had to give Michael Dukakis the hot potato."[6]

Horton materialized in the nick of time as far as Atwater and Bush were concerned. The spring of 1988 had been a difficult time for both of them. Bush's early capture of the GOP nomination contest had proven to be a mixed blessing. There were no longer any contested primaries to keep his name in the headlines, and the front pages were dominated by revelations about drug-running Panama strongman Manuel Noriega's ties to the U.S. intelligence agencies; by Attorney General Edwin Meese's ethical problems; by Nancy Reagan's interest in astrology; and by kiss-and-tell books about the Reagan White House from former aides Donald Regan and Larry Speakes. (Atwater couldn't know it at the time, but this would turn out to be the last run of bad news the incumbent administration would have for the rest of the year.) Dukakis, meantime, was defeating Jackson every week in the final stages of the Democratic primaries and coming off like a moderate in the bargain. Republican polls showed that about as many people thought he was a conservative as thought he was a liberal. A Gallup survey taken in mid-May also showed that Dukakis' positive-to-negative ratio stood at 71–15 percent—a historic high for a major party nominee at that stage of the campaign year. Bush's stood at 52–41 percent—one of the lowest ever recorded. The same poll showed Dukakis leading Bush in a head-to-head matchup by 16 points.

Atwater consoled himself that the numbers were chronicling a false spring of popularity for Dukakis. But they landed with the clang of an alarm. Republicans around the country were getting restless and there was more than the usual grumbling and backbiting inside the Bush campaign headquarters.

Atwater decided it was time to muddy up the fresh new face from Massachusetts. This went against "the book." Incumbents aren't supposed to take the first punch, and campaigns are supposed to save their best shots for the fall, when the voters are finally paying attention. "I felt that Horton and some of these other issues would just be so incredible to the voters that it was going to take a while for them to sink in," Atwater explained. "Plus I was worried that if we didn't get the numbers down before the Democratic convention, Dukakis might come out of it 25 points up, and then we'd be looking at what Ford was looking at in 1976." (Ford fell 32 percentage points behind Carter after the Democratic convention that summer and was able to regain "only" 30.5 percentage points by election day.)

On the Thursday night before the Memorial Day weekend, Atwater headed up to the middle-class suburban community of Paramus, New Jersey, with the rest of the campaign brain trust—pollster Bob Teeter, adviser Nicholas Brady, chief of staff Craig Fuller and Ailes (James Baker was not with them; he had not yet left his position as

Treasury Secretary). Hidden behind a two-way mirror, they watched as a focus-group leader interviewed back-to-back groups of fifteen voters—all of whom were Dukakis supporters or leaners—about their attitudes toward the two candidates. She drew mostly blanks. "At one point I sent a note in to the group leader to have her ask whether the people felt guilty that they knew so little about the men running for President," Teeter recalled, "and the response from the group was: 'Hey, this is only May. By November, we'll know what we need to know.'" The voters were similarly out of touch with national issues. Atwater took this as an encouraging sign: "Peace and prosperity weren't on anybody's mind, which I viewed as a plus for us because I figured people would come around to thinking about those things, once the election got closer."

Midway through each group discussion, the leader told the voters about Dukakis' position on furloughs, the Pledge of Allegiance, the death penalty, Boston Harbor, taxes, national defense and gun control. When she took a tally at the end of the sessions, his support level had dropped by 50 percent—a staggering fall-off, given that it usually takes repeated exposure to negative information for voters to abandon even weakly held preferences. "After those sessions, I knew we had the wherewithal to win," Atwater said. "I realized right then and there that the sky was the limit on Dukakis' negatives."

Armed with a videotape and their own eyewitness accounts, Atwater, Ailes & Co. headed up the next morning to Kennebunkport, Maine, where Bush was on a working vacation. They proposed a strategy for the fall campaign: attack early, often and in person. Make the campaign a conversation about furloughs and flags.

Bush saluted smartly. He'd never been one for the "vision thing," anyway. The idea of using the campaign to build a mandate for a set of policies was alien to him. Policies weren't the point. Serving was the point. Striving was the point. Winning was the point. And if the focus groups and the handlers said that flags and furloughs could help him win, well then . . .

Ten days later, he unveiled a brawling stump speech at the Texas Republican convention, hammering Dukakis on the seven deadly sins market-tested in Paramus. From that day until election day five months later, he gave essentially the same speech—pausing only to change backdrops (the "sea of policemen" motif was a particular favorite) or to freshen up the one-liners. "They started picking Dukakis' pocket in the early summer, and they never had to stop," marveled Robert Strauss, the former Democratic National Chairman.

"Every morning for the rest of the campaign, they woke up and were able to say to themselves, 'Damn, this shit is still working.' "

When Atwater had asked his chief of opposition research, Jim Pinkerton,* to get the background on the furlough issue in Massachusetts, Pinkerton had come up with a bonus. "I called up Andy Card [a Bush aide and former Republican state legislator in Massachusetts], and he said if I thought the furlough issue was crazy, wait till I tell you about the pledge," Pinkerton recalled. "It was sort of like look-for a polio vaccine and coming up with a cure for cancer instead."

Like Willie Horton, the Pledge of Allegiance issue had had a tortured history in the state long before it was thrust onto the national scene. In 1977, Dukakis' state legislature had passed a bill requiring teachers to lead their classes in the pledge each day. There was opposition from civil libertarians and some teachers. The state attorney general wrote of one of the teachers' objections: "They believe the phrase 'with liberty and justice for all,' which is part of the pledge, is untrue." Dukakis sought an advisory opinion about the bill from his state supreme court. His court wrote that it believed the bill to be unconstitutional, citing a landmark 1943 U.S. Supreme Court decision, *West Virginia State Board of Education* v. *Barnette*, which held that requiring a student to recite the pledge under the threat of expulsion violated the freedom of speech and worship. Dukakis vetoed the bill; his veto was overridden; and the law has been on the books in Massachusetts ever since. But it's been held unenforceable by Dukakis' attorney general, and no teacher has ever been cited.

That was the case history. The Republicans had a field day with it. "Let's face it, my opponent was looking for a way not to sign that bill," Bush told cheering audiences throughout the summer of 1988. "I would be looking for a way to sign it." At the GOP convention, he jeered: "What is it about the pledge that upsets him so?" The next week the Texas Republican party printed a glossy, full-color, four-page brochure and mailed it to every swing voter in the state. HERE ARE THE WORDS DUKAKIS DOESN'T WANT YOUR CHILDREN TO HAVE TO SAY . . . read the bold type on the cover page. Inside, next to a picture of two small children with their hands over their hearts, was the caption: "I Pledge Allegiance . . . " Ailes prepared a thirty-second television spot along the same lines, which he held in reserve in case the race got close at the end. It never had to be used.

---

*Atwater fondly referred to Pinkerton's opposition research staff as "thirty-five excellent nerds."

Dukakis never understood the attack. He treated the pledge as a constitutional rather than symbolic issue, and he tried to fight brazen demagoguery with stiff-necked rationalism. "If the Vice President is saying that he would sign an unconstitutional bill, then in my judgment he is not fit to hold office," he said. In fact, the constitutional issues were less cut-and-dried than the lawyerly Dukakis had implied. The precedent-setting 1943 case involved requiring an oath of a student, not a teacher. It is conceivable that a court that construed the former to be an unacceptable abridgment of freedom would consider the latter an acceptable condition of employment. Either way, Dukakis knew full well that his state supreme court didn't have the power to declare the law unconstitutional; only the U.S. Supreme Court did.

Why did a nominee who had seemed so sure-footed in winning his nomination turn so lame once the general election began? "He didn't recognize that these issues could really put him outside the mainstream," said a high-level Bush adviser who asked not to be identified. "He comes from a certain parochial culture — Massachusetts, Harvard, liberal — where asking someone to salute the flag raises the case law on loyalty oaths. For most people, the Pledge issue went to the symbol of the nation; it essentially raised the question of whether Dukakis believed we were a special nation, with a special role and special responsibilities in the world." Bush was only too happy to supply an answer to that question on Dukakis' behalf. "My opponent sees America as another pleasant country on the U.N. roll call, somewhere between Albania and Zimbabwe," he taunted Dukakis at the GOP convention.

Dukakis was also a victim of overconfidence. When the flag-and-furlough attack began, he was still basking in the glow of his long-shot victory for the nomination. He had no sense of the shallowness of the voters' investment in him; no idea that his was still an empty vessel waiting to be filled. "At first, we used to read this stuff and laugh and say, 'How can this be? Why would people take this seriously?'" recalled Hale Champion, an old friend of Dukakis', who served as his chief aide in the statehouse during the campaign.[7]

On June 1, a week before the Bush attacks began, one of the Democratic party's smartest pollsters, Stanley Greenberg, sent a strategy memo to Dukakis headquarters in Boston. Based on focus-group interviews he had just conducted in Texas and California, it captured the surging sense of optimism within Democratic ranks. "An awakening independent electorate is developing an image of Michael

Dukakis comprised of the following elements," he wrote. " . . . steady and predictable . . . successful and competent . . . The contrast with Bush—aloof, flat, angry and puppetlike—reinforces the positive feeling about Dukakis that make him caring and approachable." Two pages later, Greenberg analyzed the opposition's potential lines of attack. "On being a Ted Kennedy-type liberal, I am not greatly worried. Their best bet is capital punishment and . . . the early-release [furlough] program, but I am not sure voters will find that a very convincing guide to a Dukakis presidency."

Although Bush was in far worse shape with the voters at that stage of the campaign, he and his handlers were far better attuned to the rhythms of modern McPolitics. They launched their attacks knowing it was a high-risk strategy. The customary practice in presidential campaigns is to leave the dirty work to surrogates. But Atwater felt that if Bush personally carried the attack, it would be a "two-fer"—the allegations would have more credibility, and Bush would acquire a fighter's image. To guard against the chance that Bush might come across as too strident, Atwater, Ailes & Co. came up with an improbable solution. They choreographed a schizophrenic fall campaign in which Bush alternated between George the Ripper and George the Kind and Gentle; between red-meat pronouncements about the death penalty and haunted musings on the plight of the deserving poor. Astoundingly—given the suspension of disbelief demanded of the voters—their client pulled it off.

The strategy worked because, as Atwater put it afterward, "we got an awful lot of help from the other side." Of the "amazing tactical blunders" he said the Dukakis camp made, the most costly by far was its failure to respond swiftly and forcefully to the attacks. They didn't seem to realize that in an age when voters are inclined to believe the worst about a politician, an attack ignored is an attack agreed to.

Eventually, Dukakis' handlers did try to fight back. They produced forty-nine attack television commercials during the fall, as compared with just fifteen attack spots produced by the Bush campaign.* When David D'Alessandro, a John Hancock account executive with no previous campaign experience, was recruited on Labor Day 1988 to take control of the badly mismanaged Dukakis advertising effort, he found a staggering collection of 1,200 scripts for ads that were never approved and never produced.[8] Twelve

*The tally is from Julian Kanter, director of the Political Commercial Archive at the University of Oklahoma.

hundred scripts, forty-nine attack ads—and does anyone remember a single Dukakis spot?

D'Alessandro acknowledged after the campaign that the ad effort has been a fiasco. "If this were Pepsi versus Coke, basically what Pepsi did was go into every region of the country to say something bad about Coke—real bad," he said. "They were saying up here that Coke has worms in it, they were saying down here that Coke is made with impure water. And Coke hasn't even introduced its product yet. And when Coke finally comes into the marketplace and says, 'We taste good,' the people said, 'No, you don't. You have worms.' We were sitting there naked with a big negative pasted all over us."[9]

Four months after the Bush attacks began, Greenberg penned another memo, this one spelling out in painful detail the distance voters had traveled from June to October. "The perception of Dukakis on the death penalty, prison furloughs and murderers is a fundamental blockage to voting for Dukakis," he wrote after conducting focus groups with swing voters in Texas. "Unless we address it directly, Dukakis will not begin to be heard by these voters. There is nothing else we have to say in this campaign—whether about Bush or Quayle—that competes with the credibility and emotional power of this perception.

"In their free associations with Dukakis, 'murderers' dominated the written comments and discussion: 'lets murderers out of prison without finishing sentence'; 'very upsetting to think of these days off for criminals.'

"These voters are looking for some way of understanding Dukakis' position. In the absence of an explanation, they are proceeding to imagine the worst. The Dukakis campaign has to muddy the water on this issue. That does not mean going toe to toe on crime—a fight we would almost certainly lose. But we need to give the voters some way of understanding or rationalizing the prison furloughs, so they can achieve closure and move on to other issues."

Not everyone in the Dukakis campaign headquarters had been quite as blind-sided by the furlough issue. Campaign manager Susan Estrich and pollsters Tom Kiley and Tubby Harrison all say they picked up its ominous potential in their polling and focus groups in the spring. They also knew that Dukakis didn't *have* a very good response—this was an issue he'd bungled as governor before he bungled it as a presidential candidate. Their best hope, they felt, was to try to get Dukakis to talk about crime in a personal way—to make it clear he cared about the rights of victims as much as the rights of criminals. In his acceptance speech at the Democratic National Convention, they wanted him to tell a national audience how his father had been robbed at gunpoint and his brother had been killed by a hit-and-run driver. Dukakis refused. He didn't want to exploit personal tragedy. Once his poll numbers plummeted in the late summer and fall, he did begin to refer to these family tragedies in his stump speeches—but never comfortably. When CNN anchorman Bernard Shaw opened the second televised debate by asking Dukakis whether he would support the death penalty if his wife were raped and murdered, Dukakis froze. He didn't use the brother–father response he'd rehearsed just hours before. He didn't respond at any emotional level at all. He spoke about the death penalty as if he were reading from a policy paper and then, inexplicably, he launched into a discussion of the drug issue. "When he answered by talking policy," said Susan Estrich, "I knew we had lost the election."

Estrich and others in the Dukakis camp believe the furlough issue worked for another reason: Willie Horton was black; his victim was white. "There is no more powerful symbol of racial hatred in this country than a black man raping a white woman," said Estrich, a former Harvard law professor who was herself raped by a black man while she was a college student. At a campaign managers' postmortem held by the Institute of Politics at Harvard's Kennedy School of Government a month after election day, she, Atwater and Ailes got into a heated exchange over the Horton issue.

Estrich: "There was certainly a perception, even among those of us who call Harvard home, that this was a very damaging and devastating attack, but an attack that went far beyond conventional terms of debate. . . . "

Atwater: "Good. I'm glad you brought this up because we needed to get it out in the open. . . . When I first heard about this issue, I didn't know who Willie Horton was. I didn't know what race he was. I was told a story about a guy—I didn't know the name—who had gone to a gas station. There was a seventeen-year-old kid there who was trying to work his way through college. The guy stabbed this kid twenty-four times, cut his sexual organ off, stuck it in his mouth, cut his arms and legs off and stuck the guy in a trash can.* This guy

---

*Atwater drew this grotesque account of Horton's 1974 crime from testimony given when Massachusetts' furlough bill was under consideration. The testimony was not accurate. Horton's victim was so badly cut up that only a pint of blood remained in his body when the police discovered it, but, according to police reports, his sexual organ and limbs were not cut off.

was then thrown in jail and received a furlough, and went out and raped and brutalized a woman.

"You know, it was sickening to me, but what was sickening was that it defied common sense. Let's think about it. Our specific quarrel with the furlough program was the specific situation in which murderers with no chance of parole got to be furloughed. That was the issue.

"What bothered me about it—as a simple man, and I really am and don't pretend to be any more—is it defied common sense. . . . What incentive did the guy have to come back? And what incentive did he have not to do what he did when he was on the furlough? Because if you don't have the death penalty, when you go back nothing worse can happen to you. That right there was what made the furlough issue click in my mind. . . .

"When it came to our attention that Willie Horton was black, we made a conscious decision—Roger was there at the meeting when I took the lead—not to use him in any of our paid advertising on television or in brochures. . . . The second decision we made was that the day we found any kind of brochure or television ad from an independent committee, we would denounce it publicly right off the bat.

"There was nothing racial about Willie Horton. We resent the fact that it was used racially in the campaign because we certainly didn't, and we were very conscientious about it. As a matter of fact—this has never been told before—when we first shot the furlough spot of the revolving door that we used on television, we used regular prisoners. Roger and I looked at it. Frankly, we were worried there were too many blacks in the prison scene, so we made sure that on the retake there were but one or two."

Estrich: "My point is that although you may not have mentioned Willie Horton by name in your furlough ad, George Bush mentioned his name regularly in his speeches. Each time he did—or at least often when he did—it would lead to a network story. We would have a little network recap and a bunch of newspaper stories that would show a picture of Willie Horton."

Atwater: "Let me tell you something. As a guy who has been in Southern politics for twenty years, there's no question in my mind that Republicans, Democrats, blacks and whites all reject racist politics. If there were any racist politics in this campaign, it would have backfired on us, on the party. That was a spurious charge, and I think the voters treated it as a spurious charge."

Ailes: "If Willie Horton were white, we would have used the furlough program."

Atwater: "We might have used pictures of him."

Ron Brown, chairman of the Democratic National Committee and Jesse Jackson's 1988 convention chairman: "Lee is saying, well, we trust the will of the American people. I know I trust them, too, but there's a lot of racism out there. We know it and we know the kind of divisions it caused in our society. . . . You knew what it [the Horton issue] was causing. Maybe you couldn't control everything, but nobody stepped up to the plate and said, 'It's divisive, it's dangerous, it's wrong.' "

Ailes: "So you're saying that because he's black, we can't use the issue?"

Brown: "I didn't say that, but there were a lot of things going on."

Estrich: "The question is what obligation a presidential campaign has when it flames such fires. To pretend that America has somehow overnight become a color-blind society is ridiculous. . . . Would being soft on crime be an issue for Mike Dukakis? Absolutely. Was it a more telling issue because it was personalized in this story? In my judgment, it was. Did that impose an obligation on the Bush campaign to somehow handle it differently? Make sure in this case, unlike others, your state directors didn't disobey you because it was so important? I never heard George Bush call for the Americans for Bush ad [on Willie Horton] to be taken off the air. You and I do know it wasn't technically a Bush campaign ad, but it looked a lot like a Bush campaign statement. Should he have stood up and said, 'I want to take the ad off the air because it personifies this in a racist way?' Maybe."

Under federal election law, independent expenditure groups such as Americans for Bush—which raise and spend money on behalf of (or in opposition to) candidates—cannot have any direct communication with the candidates their expenditures affect. But the political operatives who run these groups usually have a web of informal ties to the operatives of the campaigns they are trying to help, so it's impossible to know if there is collusion under the table. What evolved on the Republican side in 1988, whether by design or accident, was a classic good cop/bad cop arrangement. While the Bush campaign remained pristine by keeping Horton's face and race out of their ads, Americans for Bush (also known as the National Security Political Action Committee) showed his picture in an ad that ran in September. An announcer described how Horton had "murdered a boy during a robbery, stabbing him nineteen times," then "received ten weekend passes from prison" and eventually fled and "kidnapped a young couple, stabbing the young man and repeatedly raping his girlfriend." As the announcer gave these grim details, the words "Kidnapping," "Stabbing" and "Raping" flashed on the screen. The last picture was of Dukakis. The voice-over said: "Weekend prison passes. Dukakis on crime."

The ad was produced by Larry McCarthy, communications director for Bob Dole's presidential campaign and a former senior vice president of Ailes' communications firm. Americans for Bush raised and spent about $9 million. On September 10, a day after the commercial began running, the Bush campaign filed a complaint with the Federal Election Commission and the U.S. Postal Service stating its concern that the group's name falsely connoted a connection to the Bush campaign. On September 27, campaign chairman James Baker sent a letter to Americans for Bush asking them to take the ad off the air. At that point, it was scheduled to stop running in a few days anyway. "If they [the Bush campaign] were really interested in stopping this, do you think they would have waited that long to send us a letter?" Floyd Brown, a political consultant to Americans for Bush, told *The New York Times* on November 3, 1988. "Officially, the campaign has to disavow themselves from me," Elizabeth Fediay, founder of Americans for Bush, told the *Times*. "Unofficially, I hear they're thrilled about what we're doing."

In late October, another independent expenditure group, the Committee for the Presidency, began showing commercials that featured Clifford Barnes, Horton's Maryland victim, and Donna Cuomo, the sister of the boy Horton had killed in Massachusetts. The group was founded by a couple of California political consultants — Fred Karger and the late Bill Roberts, who had once been a business partner of Stuart Spencer's.

Around the same time, the Maryland Republican Party sent out a letter that had pictures of Dukakis and Horton side by side, above the caption "Is This Your Pro-Family Team for 1988?" Inside, it warned: "You, your spouse, your children, your parents and your friends can have the opportunity to receive a visit from someone like Willie Horton if Mike Dukakis becomes president."

When that flier triggered charges of racism from the Democrats, the Bush campaign denounced it and complained it had no control over what state parties and independent groups put out. Technically they were right, but as Michael Kinsley wrote in *The New Republic*, "People who play recklessly with powerful symbols shouldn't react with hurt innocence if their symbolism runs away with itself.... Hortonism is not a question of unintentionally giving offense to blacks. It's a question of knowingly, whether intentionally or not, feeding racial paranoia among whites. If that were an unfortunate by-product of the vivid presentation of some unavoidably central campaign issue, it might be excusable. When it's a spin-off of a highly optional issue manufactured from scratch in the campaign laboratory, the excuse that racial innuendo was not intended is hard to stomach."[10]

A WILLIE HORTON VIDEO ANTHOLOGY*

Weekend Prison Passes. Producer: Larry McCarthy for Americans for Bush (also known as the National Security Political Action Committee). The ad began to air on Sept. 9, 1988.

*Thanks to Michael Keegan at the Washington *Post* for help in producing these pictures.

Audio: *Bush and Dukakis on crime. Bush supports the death penalty for first-degree murderers. Dukakis not only opposes the death penalty, he allowed first-degree murderers to have weekend passes from prison. One was Willie Horton, who murdered a boy in a robbery, stabbing him 19 times. Despite a life sentence, Horton received 10 weekend passes from prison. Horton fled, kidnapped a young couple, stabbing the man and repeatedly raping his girlfriend. Weekend prison passes: Dukakis on crime.*

. . .

Revolving Door. Producers: Dennis Frankenberry, Sig Rogich and Roger Ailes for Bush-Quayle 88. The ad began to air on Oct. 5, 1988.

Audio: *As governor Michael Dukakis vetoed mandatory sentences for drug dealers. He vetoed the death penalty. His revolving door prison policy gave weekend furloughs for first degree murderers not eligible for parole. While out, many committed other crimes like kidnapping and rape. And many are still at large. Now Michael Dukakis says he wants to do for America what he's done for Massachusetts. America can't afford that risk.*

Context: To heighten its impact, this ad was presented in black and white and slow-motion. The announcer's voice is low, hoarse and urgent; the music has a chilling, murder-mystery beat. "What you try to do in an ad like this is cut through the clutter—that's why we went with all the dramatic effects," said Ailes. While accurate in its facts, the ad contains some false inferences. It encourages viewers to think that all 268 escapees from the furlough program were first-degree murderers. In fact, only four were; the rest were serving time for lesser crimes. It also encourages viewers to believe that a large percentage of furloughed Massachusetts inmates escaped. In fact, fewer than one percent did—and of those, only a tiny percentage committed violent crimes while they were at large.

. . .

Horton's Victims. Producer: Carl Haglund for the Committee for the Presidency. These ads began to air on Oct. 20, 1988, in California only.

Audio. Clifford Barnes: *"Willie Horton. He was serving a life sentence without chance of parole, until Gov. Dukakis gave him a few days off. Horton broke into our home. For twelve hours I was beaten, slashed and terrorized. My wife Angie was brutally raped. When his liberal experiment failed, Dukakis simply looked away. He also vetoed the death penalty bill. Regardless of the election, we worry that people don't know enough about Mike Dukakis."*

Audio. Donna Cuomo: *"Gov. Dukakis's liberal furlough experiment failed. We are all victims. First Dukakis let killers out of prison. He also vetoed the death penalty. Willie Horton stabbed my teenage brother nineteen times. Joey died. Horton was sentenced to life without parole but Dukakis gave him a furlough. He never returned. Horton went on to rape and torture others. I worry that people don't know enough about Dukakis's record."*

THE CAMPAIGN laboratory was a busy place in 1988. Never before in the television era had the commercials been so negative, so divorced from the real issues facing the next President or so important in setting the tone of the campaign.

"The name of the game in political advertising has become to convince people how bad the other guy is," said Malcolm MacDougall, an advertising industry executive and leading critic of political ads. "When you attack the other guy in a thirty-second ad, distortion almost has to be the rule. Because what political advertising does is find the one thing in a politician's career—and there is always going to be a Willie Horton, there is always going to be a Pledge, there is always going to be some dumb statement or some vote he cast—that is outrageous to a majority of the people. And you play up that one thing. You blow it up all out of context."

As MacDougall describes them, the politicians' attack ads bear a close resemblance to journalism's feeding frenzies. Both are driven by the same deconstructionist dynamic: Find the wart; make the wart stand for the whole. Both are products of a culture of disbelief. Both are fed by—and in turn feed—the cynicism of their audience.

But journalism, even in its worst moments, generally tries to place attacks in context. Thirty-second spots never do. MacDougall, who worked for President Ford in 1976 and, briefly, for Dukakis in 1988, offered a vivid analogy to explain why he thinks political advertising has become "fundamentally corrupt."

"Suppose I'm Lipton and I find out that once, way back in 1948, a watch strap got into a can of Campbell's Soup in a factory in the South somewhere," he said. "It was found and no one was hurt and it never happened again. If I ran an ad that said all that, no one would pay any attention. But suppose I ran an ad with eerie music in the background and I had some poor woman screaming as she discovers the watch strap and I had a grotesque close-up of the Campbell Soup can and my tag line said: 'Do you want a soup like this? Or do you want Lipton? We check every can.'

"It would be pretty damn effective. But of course there's no way in the world I could get an ad like that on television, thank God."

Before product ads can be shown on network television, they must be approved by the standards and practices departments of ABC, CBS and NBC. The network censors require that about one-third of the ads they review be substantiated and/or revised. If a competitor or consumer has a complaint with a product ad, he may seek relief from the Federal Trade Commission, a state attorney general or the ad industry's own review board. Political ads, on the other hand, are subject to no regulation of any kind. They are constitutionally protected as free speech and specifically exempted, in communication law, from review by broadcast censors. The only regulating body is the American public.*

This system of political discourse has its defenders. "I'm not sure this is a perfect way to run a democracy, but what has happened is that the whole system has adapted itself to the voters," said Charles Black, a leading Republican political consultant and a business partner of Atwater. "They have a short attention span. They don't follow government and politics every day. The more you try to inject it into their lives at times they're not interested, the more you're a nuisance to them, and you don't help your cause. They will not sit down around a kitchen table and read through both parties' platforms and make an informed family decision. They want it put simply. They like contrast. The less work they have to do to figure out the differences, the better they like it."

"The system has a lot of checks and balances," he continued. "It's an adversary proceeding. I sit down and plan a campaign like a lawyer planning a trial. I present my side of the case in the most favorable light, and I know the other side is going to do the same. The voters are going to serve as the jury. There's a third factor and that's the press. If you make a charge that you can't document, the press is going to call you on it, and it's going to backlash on you."

In the early days of political advertising on television, attack ads were used sparingly. Many candidates refused to run any at all; those who did typically insisted they be just a small fraction

---

*The political ad makers do have a trade association—the American Association of Political Consultants—with a code of ethics that admonishes members not to "indulge in irrational appeals" or "disseminate false or misleading information." But in its fifteen-year history, not one of its roughly 900 members has ever been disciplined. Recently, it has begun exploring ways to put more teeth into its guidelines.

of their overall mix of commercials. When they aired, the target often ignored them ("I will not dignify with a response my opponent's scurrilous . . . "). But as the cynicism of voters has mounted, so have the rewards of attacking and the demands for an effective counteroffensive. Since the beginning of the 1980s, many ad campaigns in statewide races have become rat-a-tat-tat electronic debates. Consultants are now so primed to produce a counterattack spot that they sometimes choose to hold it back for a few days so that the attack can sink in enough to provide a context for the rebuttal. Nineteen eighty-eight marked the first time that a presidential campaign was waged under these new rules of attack (though Dukakis didn't figure this out until it was too late).* It will not be the last.

Campaigns are like television series: a hit one season spawns imitators the next. In the statewide races in 1989 and 1990, the ads were as nasty and as trivial as ever. In New Jersey, one gubernatorial candidate used an ad to accuse his opponent of being a polluter because someone dumped an oil drum on his property. The opponent responded with a commercial accusing the attacker of being corrupt because his former law partner represented drug dealers. Each ad called the other candidate a liar; the visual gimmick used in both was a cartoon of Pinocchio with his nose growing. In Virginia, one gubernatorial candidate was charged with being in the pocket of his campaign contributors; the other was cited with being a slum landlord. In the ads in the Texas gubernatorial primary, one candidate was accused of taking bribes, another of taking drugs, another of enriching himself in office—and they all accused each other of lying.

"There's no question the ads have gotten meaner," said Eddie Mahe, a Republican political consultant. "They lack any taste of any kind. They lack any sense of even class. They're just like mud wrestling in a pigsty."[11]

Why don't the candidates "just say no" to this political kitsch? They are the ones, after all, who must govern once the campaign ends. Their ad makers merely move on to the next campaign, their professional standing and monthly retainers rising and falling with their latest won–lost record.

*Julian Kanter, the political commercial archivist at the University of Oklahoma, where the world's largest collection of political ads is housed, has collected a total of ninety-seven Dukakis spots from the 1988 campaign, of which forty-nine were negative, and forty Bush spots, of which fifteen were negative. That is a ratio of nearly one attack ad to every one positive ad produced—far more negative than ever before in a presidential campaign, Kanter said.

During his decade in the business, Democratic pollster Paul Maslin said he has seen candidates' attitudes toward negative ads evolve from revulsion to grudging acceptance to something close to "an addiction. . . . It's like taking a shot, because you can see the way they move the numbers. . . . The techniques have gotten so refined, the weapons so powerful, that if you don't use them, you'll lose them, because the other side will use them on you."

"I suppose you can say, 'I'm not going to use negative ads,'" said Republican senator John C. Danforth of Missouri, an Episcopal minister as well as a politician, who blew a fifteen-point lead and nearly lost a 1982 campaign because he resisted responding to attacks. "But campaigns are so volatile now, someone who isn't prepared to respond very, very quickly is likely to lose. You see massive shifts in the polls as the [negative] ads hit.

"You ask, who is in control? Really, it's your pollster and your media person. You're polling constantly to gauge what effect your opponent's ads are having, and if he puts on something that works, you instantly air-express it to your media man, and you hope inside twenty-four hours, he's got an answer ready. It's the opposite of a debate on policy. It's all very quick—and dirty. . . . [12]

"The effect this has on people who serve in the Senate is obvious. We come on the floor of the Senate and vote on somebody's amendment and the first thing that comes to our mind is, 'How is this going to be used in the next campaign in a thirty-second commercial?'"

In this age of attack ads, politicians have become increasingly dependent on the technologies of political market research—polling, ad-testing, focus groups, multi-variate analyses—to guard against ever uttering an unpopular word in public.* They have become risk-averse, defensive, even passive. All instinct for against-the-grain leadership is suppressed. But in their determination to speak only the words the voters want to hear, the politicians and their ads aren't animating interest in the political process. "The dialogue has become more sterile because the campaign ads are designed to repeat back to voters what they already know," said Stanley Greenberg.

Attack ads are also designed to selectively depress voter turnout, though most consultants are loath to admit it. "It is very difficult in

*Every time President Reagan gave a speech on television, his pollster, Richard Wirthlin, hooked up people in focus groups with hand-held devices that allowed them to indicate their feelings about the speech, second by second. This enabled Wirthlin to know—down to the sentence, the gesture, the word—precisely what had worked and what hadn't, and with whom. The information would be filed away for use in preparing the next speech. "I like to think I helped make a Great Communicator half a degree greater," he said.

a campaign to get a voter who supports the opponent to switch over and support your guy," said Neal Oxman, a Democratic media consultant. "It's less difficult to create enough doubt about the opponent that some of his supporters stay home."

When a presidential campaign is waged and won by these techniques, it's no surprise that the same instincts will prevail in the administration that follows. Though Bush has been highly popular in his first years in office, his critics accuse him of allowing the country to drift further behind in the world economic competition while he conducts a happy-talk presidency—a government "of the polls, by the polls and for the polls." In one of the only effective anti-Bush speeches delivered by a Democrat in 1989 or 1990, House Majority Leader Richard Gephardt recalled that when President Harry Truman launched the Marshall Plan in 1947, only 14 percent of the American people supported foreign loans and assistance, according to a Gallup poll. "Harry Truman lived by Sam Houston's maxim: 'Do right, risk consequences,' " said Gephardt. "The maxim of the Bush Administration seems to be: 'Do polls. Risk nothing.' "

This thraldom to public opinion polls is not a partisan phenomenon. Many Democrats believe it is one of the reasons their own party continues to be lost in an ideological wilderness. "If we never saw another focus group or poll in this city, we'd all be better off," said Representative Byron Dorgan (D–N.D.) "Most of us are here because we have some strong gut feelings about public policy. When we read the polls we stop trusting our gut. It's one of the reasons we have a President who doesn't lead and a Democratic Party that doesn't oppose."

IN THE WAKE of the 1988 campaign, Lee Atwater and Roger Ailes have emerged as the Darth Vaders of modern American politics. They are wearing their reputations differently.

Ailes bristles at his and blames the media. "What's changed is not the consultants, but the media's intense interest in the negative," he said after the campaign. "That's because the media is lazy, and instead of talking about the issues they'd rather talk about negative ads. The goddamn newspaper is negative. Television is negative. That's the reality of life. The fascination in the media with the negative is almost universal." Ailes spent 1989 reminding everyone who would listen that he'd also made positive spots in 1988, including an award-winning commercial of Bush lifting his granddaughter into his adoring arms.

Democrats, meantime, have been busy trying to turn Ailes' slash-
and-burn reputation to their advantage. In state after state where
Ailes had a client in 1989 and 1990, the Democratic opponent would
open the campaign by making Ailes and his "sleazeball ads" an issue.
"As far as I'm concerned, I'm running against Roger Ailes as much
as I am against [Representative] Lynn Martin," Illinois Senator Paul
Simon said when he announced for reelection. He used Ailes' name
in his fund-raising letters—and contributions shot up. "There is a
nationally orchestrated effort to take me out," Ailes said in early
1990. "But I'm not going to change my style. Has it hurt my business?
No. Has it hurt my income? No. Has it hurt my reputation? No. I
never had a good reputation to begin with. Is it likely to get me
pissed off and make me more effective? Yes."

For the first year and a half after the election, Atwater betrayed no
such sensitivity. He'd always reveled in his reputation as a political
spitballer, for the same reason that spitball pitchers revel in theirs: It
keeps the other side off balance. "I guess I sort of like getting under
people's skin," he's often said.

Right after the campaign ended, Bush tapped him to be chairman
of the Republican National Committee—thus turning over the reins
of the party that boasts of its devotion to traditional values to a man
who boasts he can summarize his philosophy of life and politics in
three words: "Bullshit permeates everything."

Atwater is an American original. In college he used to show
grainy black-and-white porno flicks to his fraternity buddies at fifty
cents a pop ("I'll guarantee you, they didn't ask for their money
back"). Until his recent illness, he consumed Tabasco sauce in
astounding quantities ("I'd put it in my iced tea if my wife would let
me"); ran fifty miles a week; worked twelve to fifteen hours every
day; practiced an hour daily on the guitar; smoked a pack of Marlboros
every Friday (then went cold turkey every Saturday through Thursday); and read at least one self-improvement book every week.
During his busy first year as party chairman, he somehow found the
time to play out every childhood fantasy, cutting a rhythm-and-
blues album with B. B. King and opening a barbecue restaurant
outside of Washington.

In December 1989, in a talk he gave to a class I was teaching at
Princeton University, Atwater described how he'd decided to get
into politics. "Politics was a great place for a guy who wanted to do
something bigger than learn how to play golf or be a big shot in an
insurance firm or a law firm," he told the students. "I knew from a

very early time that I had an obsession with the whole notion of individual freedom. I felt that the Democrat party was more of a collectivist party. Also, I was anti-establishment as a young man, and to some extent I still am. Down where I came from, all the young Democrats were dressed up like I am now"—he modeled his elegant double-breasted suit—"and I just didn't want to identify with them. So I started a Young Republican group on my campus. . . .

"I wanted to exercise the right to be an uncommon man and fulfill my own destiny and dreams. I also established some early goals for myself after reading *The Republic.* If you notice, Plato outlines very specific steps in the educational process. I kind of adapted them to myself and made the statement that I was going to spend from ages twenty to forty being educated. And if I happened to get anything else—fame, fortune or money—along the way, that would be fine. But I really wasn't going to decide what to do with my life until I was forty. I'm thirty-eight now, so I've still got two more years of the education process. But politics is the best way to get educated, because you need to know something about everything. You need to know about history, statistics, human nature, sociology, current events, political science, and if you're lazy like I was, it keeps you on your toes, because you gotta learn every day. You gotta learn every day. Root hog or die, as they say."

Atwater told the students about the year he had spent, immediately after graduating from college, as national executive director of the Young Republicans. "When I was filling out my paperwork to start my job there, I met a nice-looking middle-aged guy who shook my hand and said, 'Hi, my name is George Bush' [who was then chairman of the RNC]. And I said, 'Hey, great, I've got a few things I been wantin' to tell you.' And he says, 'All right, come on in.' So we went in and sat down in his office, which today is my office, and talked for twenty-five minutes, first time I ever saw him. And I've never forgot that, because for him to do that for me when I was twenty-two years old meant an awful lot. . . .

"In fact, the conversation inspired me to firm up my goals a little bit. I decided there were really two things I'd like to do from a career standpoint. And one is I'd like to manage a presidential campaign one day, and I'd love for it to be George Bush's. And secondly, I decided that one day I'd like to be chairman of the Republican party. Then the other, non-career goal I had was to make an album one day. It never even crossed my mind I would get to do that.

"So I made these goals for myself at the age of twenty-two and, just coincidentally in many respects, I have been able to reach them. But the thing I would point out to you as students is that clearly defined goals can pay off. I find a lot of people my age that went to school with me aren't happy. I just went home for Thanksgiving and, hell, they're listless. They were bright, ambitious, everything else, but they never really had goals. I did. And I gotta be honest with you, if I didn't meet them, I'd have been happier, because as far as I'm concerned, it's the voyage that makes you happy."

On March 5, 1990, Atwater was felled by a violent seizure while giving a breakfast speech in Washington, D.C., to a group of Republican contributors. Doctors found an egg-sized tumor in his brain. When he emerged from the hospital a few days later, he proclaimed himself a changed man: "I have a better sense of humanity, a better sense of fellowship with people than I've ever had before. . . . I can't imagine me getting back into a fighting mood. . . . I don't see how I'm ever going to be mean." He opted for the most aggressive treatment available, which involved drilling ten tiny holes in his skull and inserting radioactive seeds at the site of the tumor.

It remains to be seen whether Atwater will regain his health and rediscover his instinct for the jugular. But he already has legions of imitators in both parties who haven't lost theirs. A few weeks after the 1988 campaign, Democratic pollster Peter Hart observed: "The one thing you really hope is that every new kid who comes into the campaign consultant business doesn't take the Atwater and Ailes approach to politics as the way to get ahead."

At the moment, that's precisely the lesson that's emerged from 1988. As the 1990 campaigns got underway, veteran Republican operative Ed Rollins observed, "Right now every candidate wants to hire the Son of Atwater or the Son of Ailes."

CHAPTER NINE

The Voters: Low-Grade Fever

The perverse and unorthodox argument of this little
book is that voters are not fools.
— V. O. Key, Jr., 1963

ALL OF the public opinion surveys taken during the 1988 presidential campaign agreed on a few simple propositions. A majority of voters favored a change in the broad direction of public policy set by the Reagan administration. They wanted more government activism on a domestic agenda of schools, drugs, the environment and health care, less legislating of private morality and no further increases in the military buildup. They were even willing to pay higher taxes, so long as they were convinced that the money would be targeted to effective programs in their areas of concern. There is a word that roughly describes these attitudes: liberal. And, yes, it was tossed about with great effect in the 1988 campaign—but as a smear, not a rallying cry.

When political scientist V. O. Key, Jr., wrote that "voters are not fools," he meant that they are not putty in the hands of propagandists and demagogues. They are a "rational God" of reward and punishment, he wrote, whose votes are congruent with their public policy desires and their evaluations of candidate ability and performance.

In 1988, there was a disconnection between the voters' policy preferences and their presidential vote. Two possible explanations present themselves. One is that Key was wrong: this time, the voters really were duped. The other is that the polls were wrong: the voters in fact wanted a great many contradictory things (more services *and* lower taxes, for example) and that by the time they weighed them all, the rational choice was George Bush.

The first proposition does not seem plausible. The voters had plenty of exposure to both Bush and Dukakis over the course of a long campaign. Bush was far better served by his image makers, but in our video-literate society, voters know how to cut through what Key called the "buncombe" of campaigns. Even though they favored changes, they also felt good about the Reagan years. Caught between their satisfaction with the recent past and their desire for a different kind of future, they voted for the past. This is how elections usually work: voters make retrospective judgments, not prospective ones. The past is more knowable, and voters prefer to deal with what is real. In November 1988, the voters looked around and this is what they saw: a 5.3 percent unemployment rate, a seven-year run of low inflation, seventy-two consecutive months of economic recovery, a communist empire that seemed to be in terminal decline. They voted accordingly.

Nevertheless, when a presidential campaign fails to respond to what pollster William Hamilton has described as a "low-grade fever" for change, an important opportunity has been missed. The voters only get their hands on the rudder once every four years. As these polls make clear, they yearned to go places they knew George Bush wasn't taking them:

• In a nationwide survey by the Gallup Organization commissioned in the spring of 1987 by the Times Mirror Co., voters were asked which programs should be expanded in the federal budget for the coming year. Seventy-five percent favored increases in spending for the elderly, 72 percent wanted to raise spending on health care, 69 percent on education, 69 percent on AIDS, 67 percent on the homeless, etc. Only 24 percent supported growth in defense spending.

• In a nationwide survey for the American Federation of State, County and Municipal Employees taken two weeks after the 1988 election, pollster Peter Hart found that two-thirds of all voters said they would be willing to see their taxes raised to pay for long-term health care for the elderly and disabled, half would be willing to see taxes increased to pay for financial aid to college students from middle-income families; half would pay more taxes for programs making housing more affordable to young families. "Voters may have read George Bush's lips on no new taxes, but they did not cast their vote on that basis," Hart wrote. His poll found that more than three-quarters of the voters endorsed higher taxes on corporations and the highest income groups, and that 60 percent favored defense-spending cuts as a way to balance the budget.

• In a nationwide survey for the World Policy Institute taken in the spring of 1989, pollsters Stanley Greenberg and Celinda Lake reported that 63 percent of voters agreed that "our federal budget priorities are wrong: that we are spending too much on the military and shortchanging our economic, social and environmental needs." The poll listed a package of three major shifts in public policy direction and asked voters if they would support the entire plan:

1. Spending $200 billion a year more on research and technology, job training, rebuilding roads and railways, cleaning up toxic and nuclear waste dumps, investing in education, building low-income housing to reduce homelessness, fighting drugs and expanding care for the elderly.

2. Cutting $125 billion a year from the military budget by turning over to Europe and Japan greater responsibility for their own defense.

3. Raising $125 billion a year in new taxes on upper income households (over $80,000 a year) and corporations.

Eighty-one percent of the respondents favored this sharp change in direction, as against 16 percent who disapproved. In case anyone missed it, there *was* a candidate in 1988 who advocated this platform: Jesse Jackson.

• In a survey for Time/CNN in October 1989, Yankelovich Clancy Shulman found that even though George Bush's approval rating was running at an extraordinarily high level—75 percent—voters continued to support a public policy agenda quite different from the one he was offering. Eighty-six percent said they were willing to pay higher taxes for programs to feed poor children; 79 percent for a war on drugs, 75 percent for the elderly, 72 percent for schools, etc.

America's "rational God" could have voted for all these things in 1988 but chose not to. Why the disconnect? One clue was in the *Time*/CNN poll. The very voters who paid lip service to their support for *targeted* tax increases also opposed the general proposition of raising taxes. Plainly, these voters are cross-pressured; they doubt that government will use their tax dollars the way they want. By 73 to 19 percent, respondents in the *Time*/CNN poll said that Washington delivers "less value for the taxes you pay" than it used to.

Voters' confidence in government has dropped dramatically over the past quarter of a century, giving rise to an anti-government populism that has been the single most dominant strain of political thought in the modern era. In a 1982 book, *The Confidence Gap*, political scientists Seymour Martin Lipset and William Schneider took a close look at this loss of faith in government by reviewing survey research data collected over the span of several decades. Lipset and Schneider found that:

• Public confidence in American social and political institutions rose dramatically from the late 1930s, when scientific polling began, through the early 1960s. With the ending of the Depression, the winning of World War II, the sharp increases in income, education and standard of living in the 1950s and '60s, more and more people said that their political system was honest, effective and responsive.

• Since 1964, there has been a long slide in confidence. It, too, has been a reaction to a series of historical events—affronts to the nation's pride, sense of collective mastery and economic well-being. The list is familiar: assassinations, upheavals on campuses, riots in the inner cities, Vietnam, Watergate, oil shortages, inflation, stagnation, hostage crises, budget and trade deficits, a flattening out of growth in standard of living, an economy that seems in hock to Japan.

• Virtually all of the drop in public confidence occurred in the 1964–79 period. There was a brief revival in the early 1980s, but in recent years confidence has been drifting back down toward the lows of the 1970s. In 1977, Daniel Yankelovich spoke of the breadth and depth of the shifts that had occurred. "Trust in government declined dramatically from almost 80 percent in the late 1950s to about 33 percent in 1976," he said. "Confidence in business fell from approximately a 70 percent level in the late 1960s to about 15 percent today. Confidence in other institutions—the press, the military, the professions (doctors and lawyers)—sharply declined. More than 61 percent of the electorate believe there is something morally wrong in the country. More than 80 percent of voters say they do not trust those in positions of leadership as much as they used to. In the mid-1960s, a one-third minority reported feeling isolated and distant from the political process; by the mid-1970s, a two-thirds majority felt that what they think 'really doesn't count.' Approximately three out of five people feel the government suffers from a concentration of too much power in too few hands, and fewer than one out of five feel that congressional leaders can be believed. One could go on and on. The change is simply massive. Within a ten- to fifteen-year period, trust in institutions has plunged down and down, from an almost consensual majority, two-thirds or more, to minority segments of the American public."[1]

Schneider and Lipset wrote that while there were plenty of historical events that explain this sharp decline, there were also a number of "process effects" that made matters seem worse than they really were. They cited the proliferation of grievance groups—women, blacks, environmentalists, the elderly, gays, consumers—that do an excellent job of describing social inequities but have a hard time acknowledging progress, lest they lose their claim on public attention. They also blamed the bad-news bias of the media, especially television, which makes people more cynical about their political and social institutions.

Virtually no realm of the popular culture has been untouched by the virus of cynicism—not television, not art, not literature, not music, not movies. We live in the "era of the permanent smirk, the knowing chuckle, of jokey ambivalence as a way of life," *Spy* magazine, a jokey, smirky publication for hip Manhattanites, wrote during the 1988 campaign. Cynicism has even spread to (of all places) advertising. Two of the most successful advertising icons of the late 1980s were Joe Isuzu and Bartles & Jaymes. Isuzu, the oily TV pitchman, debuted in 1986 by offering cars that went 300 miles per hour, got 94 miles per gallon and sold for "just nine dollars." As he spoke, a scrawl ran across the bottom of the screen correcting all of his outrageous claims. Bartles & Jaymes, the deadpan country hicks, thanked people for their support before anyone had any idea there was a product to support. The ads were a parody of advertising; they worked because they let the viewer in on the joke: everyone lies. "Young people . . . are cynical as hell," said Jerry Della Femina, chairman of the ad agency that created the Isuzu ads. "They've been lied to before. They're amused by the shocking simple truth of the liar commercials."[2]

When fakery is a given, an entertainment, even a tool of salesmanship, cynicism has a firm grip on the popular mind. "The acceptance of a disparity between thought and conduct, between image and reality has become a mark of our sophistication," Louis Menand wrote in *The New Republic*. "One often heard the complaint in the '80s that the press was manipulated by images. But the press reported on manipulation night and day. Fakery was a virtual journalistic theme in the last two presidential campaigns. The point is how little it mattered. Americans know perfectly well that everything is packaged; the packaging comes, in effect, already discounted."[3]

It's no small irony that this "irony epidemic" would run amok in the 1980s. The decade opened with the election of Ronald Reagan, a great restorer of belief. As a tonic for our bruised national feelings, he offered a winning personality, a rebuilt military and a get-the-government-off-our-backs ideology. For a time, it worked. "He wrests from us something warmer than mere popularity—a kind of complicity," wrote historian Garry Wills. "We fable him to ourselves, and he to us. We are jointly responsible for him.... He has made pretending the easiest thing we do."[4] The nation suspended disbelief and had itself a patriotic bender. The TV ads were awash with red, white and blue slogans ("Miller's Made the American Way"; Chevrolet's "Heartbeat of America"; Chrysler's "Born in America"); the 1984 Olympics were ablaze in flag and country; Reagan's reelection campaign was a soft-focus collage of farms, station wagons, schools, churches, weddings, picket fences and puppy dogs, all framed by the tag line: "It's Morning in America."

Except almost no one really believed it. While Reagan himself floated above the cynicism (except for short periods during the 1982 recession and following the 1986 Iran–contra revelations), the sense of foreboding, distrust and declining expectation returned by the late 1980s. Consider three more polls taken during and after the 1988 campaign:

• Fifty-seven percent of Americans said they saw the next generation "bogged down by too many problems left behind for them," but only half of those interviewed in the same month—October 1988—said they thought a President, any President, could make much of a difference in their children's future, according to a *New York Times*/CBS News poll.

• By 71 to 26 percent, Americans agreed with the statement: "To win elections, most candidates for Congress make campaign promises they have no intention of fulfilling," according to a Washington *Post*/ABC News poll taken in May 1989.

• A majority of voters said they expected their lives to get better in the next ten years, according to a *Post*/ABC poll taken in January 1990. But their responses to a more detailed set of questions suggested they were merely giving lip service to traditional American optimism. Seventy-one percent said they thought it would be more difficult for young people to get a good job in ten years; 84 percent felt it would be more difficult for young people to afford to go to college; 86 percent believed it would be more difficult for young people to buy a house. By margins of at least two to one, they said that the problems of pollution, inflation, poverty, crime and homelessness would all get worse over the next decade, not better.

During the two years I covered the 1988 presidential campaign, I interviewed hundreds of voters in living rooms across the country.*

---

*A few of the following interviews were conducted by *Post* colleagues Dan Balz, David Broder or Haynes Johnson.

Everywhere I went, I found people who had lost faith in the American future, in American values and in American leaders. Here is how they expressed it:

ON THE FUTURE

"We're all pretty well set, but the kids behind us are not going to be able to afford the same standard of living. The economy is not there. We're eating our base, sending those jobs overseas. We're a consumer nation sucking stuff out of the rest of the world, and eventually we're not going to have the money to buy this stuff."
— Dale Harting, plumber, St. Louis

"I worry about the young people. Unless something drastic is done, they won't have the opportunities we did. We could buy a house, get an education, aspire to greater opportunities. Now we seem to be losing our lead in industry, trade, everything. I think it's going to be harder for our children and even harder for our grandchildren."
— Irma Woitesak, retired credit manager, Englewood Cliffs,
New Jersey

"I come from a family where my father worked and my mother was a housewife. I'm facing an economy where if I get married and I have a family, I'm going to have to go out and work. Hold down some kind of job so that I'll be able to have the same things financially that my parents did. That wasn't true 20, 30 years ago. And it worries me because I care about traditional kinds of things. I'd kinda like to be home when the kids come home from school. But I don't know if I'll ever be able to do that. I feel like I'm going to have to choose something to sacrifice — some of these traditional family values, or sacrifice financially. To live the way I want to live, I have to learn to play the game. I could have majored in music and been very happy. At the same time, I don't know that I could ever... Well, say I was to get married and have kids and something were to happen. Suppose I were to get divorced, which seems to be real popular these days anyways. What is it, over half now? I would not be able to support my family on what most musicians make. So that's why I'm headed for a business degree in grad school."
— Mary Siler, senior, University of Tennessee

"It's a time of uncertainty. I don't see any tragic times like the Great Depression, but there won't be big bucks made either. My parents always thought everybody would keep moving up, but it's not that way anymore. In a service economy like we're becoming, no one will make a big fortune. And someone is going to have to pay the bills for the deficits—us and our kids."

—David Flick, thirty-nine, state parole agent,
Penn Hills, Pennsylvania

"Yeah, and they're going to have to pay the bill for our Social Security and our health care, too. I don't envy them."

—Gloria Flick, thirty-nine, hospital billing clerk, Penn Hills,
Pennsylvania

"As far as the next presidential election, I'm sure nothing of consequence is going to be coming out of it. It's going to be a matter of merely riding an economic roller coaster and regardless of what person gets in there, basically there's not a whole lot that can be done. As far as how I view the standard of living and the economic future, I'm really resentful of the situation. Even in grade school you always thought that if you worked very hard and did all that stuff you would be better off than someone who did not. And here I find myself, not."

—Kelly Montileone, twenty-two,
graduate student, St. Louis

"I just don't believe in the American Dream anymore—the idea that you can have it all. I wish it were still out there, still around, but I don't think it is. You see people and they have something unfortunate happen to them, something catastrophic, and there are not the social programs to help them out. A family on a low income level has a child with some deformity, and that's it, that's the end of the line for that family. . . . My parents really went to town on the American Dream. I just don't think, even if we're very lucky, we're going to have that bulge of prosperity we had after World War II."

—Linda H. Green, twenty-seven, law student, Waco, Texas

"I think the gap between the rich and poor has widened tremendously. You see the guy in the BMW and the guy with the '59 Chevy with six kids in the back. As far as the middle class, I don't think there is much middle class now. The blue-collar guy is going down to the lower rung of the ladder now. It seems like there's a level that stepped up and a level that stepped down,

and there's not much left in the middle anymore."
—Harold Jones, refrigerator repairman, Akron, Ohio

"I think overall we've sort of gone over the peak as a national power and we're on the downslide of the slope now, the way Great Britain was the world power for so many years and then something happened. I think we've sort of gone over the hump. I don't know who's going to take over—Japan, maybe China." —Jean Prickett, St. Louis

ON AMERICAN VALUES

"The country is in poor shape. The foundation of morality has been destroyed. Everybody is lost. 'Made in America' is a joke now. It's what 'Made in Japan' was twenty years ago. Now everybody knows the Japanese products are better. The Christian work ethic has been laughed out of existence in this country. We're at a crossroads. There's a war going on between the liberal and conservative attitudes. It's a question of who wins. Before Reagan got in, the liberals had the upper hand. Now at least it's more of a fight."
—Gerald Schork, engineer, North Long Beach, California

"I have a Japanese car. That's a statement. What I'm trying to say to Detroit is: 'Build something better and I'll buy it.' I think we've gotten fat and happy over here. The Japanese stay in school longer and they work harder than we do. I think trade barriers are good, but they take our eyes off the main problem. We need to get our work ethic back." —Michael Keith, nineteen, college student, Knoxville

"Most of the individuals in the nation are in debt, so it's not surprising that the nation is in debt. We've created a monster and we're going to pay for it. We'll never solve the debt because we're too selfish. What will it take? Look at AIDS. That doesn't seem to have slowed anyone down." —Kathy Reid, thirty-six, housewife,
North Long Beach, California

"We've had exchange students from Japan live with us. They are awesome. Their schools are tough; they think ours are lax. If they're late three times, they get their head shaved. No wonder they're able to buy us out. They like to work; we like to play."
—Anne Blinkinsop, in her sixties, housewife,
San Bernardino, California

"After I got out of the Army I got my masters in education because I wanted to teach high school kids. Well, I spent six months student teaching at the local high school and it broke my heart what I ran into. I wasn't a teacher, I was a policeman. The classes were full of kids who didn't pay attention, who just disrupted things. I flunked thirty-seven kids in the first six weeks. I did that because I wanted their parents to come in and descend on me, because I wanted to tell them, face to face, how their kids were spending their time. But do you know what—and this is the part that really bugged me—not a single parent came in. To me, that said a lot about what's wrong with this country."   —James Brockmayer, retired Army colonel,
Titusville, Florida

"I blame a lot of our problems on Dr. Spock. The younger genera-tion today, they don't want to put out any effort but they want to reap all the profits. If you trace history and study the fall of Rome, you'll see it's pretty close to being the same as the fall of this country."
—James Wilson, fifty-five, retired New York City policeman

"The drug problem is absolutely horrible. It is taking our youth, it is stealing the soul of America. Unless we do something fairly rapidly, it's probably going to be the one thing that will defeat the United States.   —Irby Moore, fifty-three, NASA supervisor,
Titusville, Florida

"We're not Number One anymore. It scares me to see us losing that. We're so caught up in our Yuppie existence, we're letting it slip through our fingers."   —Barbara Greer, forty-seven, realtor,
San Bernardino, California

ON POLITICAL LEADERS

"I don't trust politicians. They're all crooked. They tell you we have to tighten our belts and they take care of their friends. And the middle man just gets stuck."   —Dominic Monfredi, fifty-seven,
machinist, Penn Hills, Pennsylvania

"We're losing our faith in our leaders. We don't vote for a person, we vote for an image he wants us to see."   —Wayne Spurgeon,
anesthesia coordinator, Knoxville

"I'll tell you why the people already in office keep winning. It's like, 'Let's keep the crooks we got. Why put new crooks in there?' Because in most cases it doesn't make a lot of difference."
—Larry Weaver, forty-nine, disabled plant manager, Dayton, Ohio

"I'm much less interested in politics than I used to be—basically because I don't feel like I'm getting the straight scoop. I feel that they do not want to answer the questions. Many times, they are confronted straight on and they don't answer the questions. They just say what they want you to hear, and that makes me very angry."
—Nyla Alford, fifty-three, Red Cross office manager, Waco, Texas

"My perspective is maybe a little bit different. I grew up during Watergate. I expect them to lie. I don't have any problem with them lying and not facing the issues because I just think that's built into the system and it's sort of a code. They say, 'We won't raise taxes,' and of course we're all sitting here and we really do understand that they will raise taxes, and they know, I think, that we understand. And the currency of the campaign are just these bright, shiny promises than can never be fulfilled."
                                          —Linda H. Green, twenty-seven,
                                              law student, Waco, Texas

O NE STRAIN that connects these laments is a belief that the moral bottom has fallen out of our culture—that Americans no longer work hard and delay gratification—because the standard of living is no longer rising. Until fairly recently, it's been taken as a birthright in America that each generation will do better than its parents' generation. Now the question seems to be on the table: Have 200 years of American upward mobility come grinding to a stop?

No. Real per capita disposable income rose by 21 percent from 1973 to 1987, according to the Bureau of Economic Analysis of the Commerce Department, and real family income rose by 11 percent from 1973 to 1986, reported the Congressional Budget Office. True, the rate of increase in the standard of living in this period was only half of what it had been in the 1950s and 1960s—the result of a parallel slowing in the rate of growth in worker productivity. But a slowdown in the rate of growth is one thing; an absolute decline is something else altogether.

Why, then, do so many Americans think they're living through a decline? One reason is that the effects of this slowdown have been

distributed unequally among different demographic groups. Young
men and women who joined the work force in the 1970s and 1980s
have been especially hard hit—in part because the cost of two of life's
big ticket items, a house and a college education, have risen dispro-
portionately. In 1970, the average annual cost of attending a four-
year private university ate up 29.6 percent of median family income;
by 1987, it took 40.4 percent of median family income. In 1973, a
thirty-year-old man earning the medium income for his age paid 21
percent of his monthly earnings for a median mortgage on a median-
priced home. In 1984, the typical thirty-year-old had to pay 44
percent of his income for such a mortgage. For the first time in
American history home-ownership rates—the great cement of middle-
class values—dropped nationwide, and fell rather steeply among the
young. In 1973, 23.4 percent of young adults under age twenty-five
owned homes. By 1988, just 15.5 percent did. Among those in the
twenty-five-to-twenty-nine age group, the rate dropped from 43.6
percent in 1973 to 36.2 percent in 1988, according to a study by the
Joint Economic Committee of Congress.

These declines occurred despite the entry of millions of women
into the job market. In 1970, 38 percent of the work force was female;
by 1989 the figure was 45 percent. It's a boomer cliché that today's
young adults need two incomes to enjoy the standard of living
that mom and dad managed on one. It's not quite true—mom and
dad didn't have the VCRs, the second cars, the designer jeans, the
glut of consumer gadgets so popular with their grown children. It *is*
true, however, that for certain demographic groups, there have been
some absolute declines over a reasonably long stretch of time. For
example, the median income of white males aged twenty-five to
thirty-four fell from $23,839 in 1979 to $20,962 in 1987 (in constant
1987 dollars); the median income of black males of the same age
group fell from $16,653 in 1979 to $13,650 in 1987, according to the
Census Bureau. The standard of living of the poorest quintile of the
population dropped by 9 percent from 1979 to 1987, while the standard of living of the wealthiest quintile rose by 19 percent in the
same period, according to a House Ways and Means Committee
report.* Meantime, the richest quintile of American families paid 5.5
percent less of their income in federal taxes (income and Social

*One way I measure this fraying of income equality is in the hair lengths of young men.
In the 1960s the children of the economic elites wore their hair long to express their
cultural alienation. Today the children of the working classes wear long hair, presumably
to communicate their economic alienation.

Security) at the end of the decade of the 1980s than they had at the beginning, while the poorest quintile paid 16.1 percent more of their income in taxes.

There's another reason so many Americans think that their standard of living has declined. Relative to the rest of the industrialized world, it has. In the 1950s, the United States was an economic, military and political colossus. It had been strengthened by World War II; its allies and enemies had been weakened. As political scientist Joseph S. Nye, Jr., has written, we were like the neighborhood bully who prospers while everyone else on the block has the flu. This anomalous condition could not last. The other nations were bound to recover, and our relative position was bound to deteriorate.

But to someone whose life-span happens to be measured by these past forty years, it's no surprise that this erosion should affect one's faith in the future. During the 1980s, a School of Decline came into vogue in this country. The best-selling book during the early months of the 1988 presidential campaign was Yale historian Paul Kennedy's *Rise and Fall of the Great Powers,* which argued that the United States, like great powers before it, was suffering from imperial overstretch—a failure to strike a proper balance between overseas military commitments and a maturing domestic economy. The University of Maryland's Mancur Olson analyzed decline from a different vantage point: he argued that entrenched interests—bureaucracies, unions, single-issue groups, grievance groups, entitlement groups—had gained enough power in our mature economy to protect the economic losers from what Joseph Schumpeter described as the "creative destruction" of capitalism. They've used their political muscle to tilt the market in uncompetitive ways, be it through closed shops or protective tariffs. Over time, such economies inevitably lose ground in the international footrace.

There was another theory of internal sclerosis that focused not on economic arrangements but on cultural and demographic ones. It surveyed the Me Decade(s) of the '70s and '80s and found a nation in which each demographically bound group lived within its own psychological ghetto, watched its own cable television stations, shopped at its own malls—and lost the glue of common purpose. "Narrowcasting" (as opposed to broadcasting) and "niche advertising" were the media and marketing revolutions of the past decade. Thanks to the explosion of cable TV, the average television household now receives twenty-seven channels. In 1988 alone, 491 new consumer magazines were started. If you're a bride from New Jersey, there's a magazine just for you.[5] "As a nation, we used to have a sense of manifest destiny," said Representative William Frenzel (R–Minn.). "Nowadays, everyone is chasing a different butterfly."

Ever since Tocqueville, observers of the American scene have warned against the excesses of individualism—though Tocqueville speculated they would be held in check by the "habits of the heart" that attract Americans to fraternal, religious and civic associations. In their 1985 book, *Habits of the Heart,* University of California at Berkeley sociologist Robert Bellah and four associates wrote that "we are concerned that this individualism may have grown cancerous—that it may be destroying those social integuments that Tocqueville saw as moderating its more destructive potentialities, that it may be threatening the survival of freedom itself." By 1990, record numbers of Americans weren't voting, weren't paying their taxes and weren't even filling out their census forms. While civic participation was breaking out all over the world, it was losing market share here.

It's beyond the scope of this book to untangle whether the Me-ism of the past two decades leaves us as impoverished and vulnerable as Bellah and his colleagues assert, or whether it's more accurately seen as a benign desire for control over one's own life in a complex world, as sociologists such as Herbert J. Gans argue.[6] Either way, it has consequences in the political arena. It has fueled the rise of interest groups, which focus on narrow issues; and the enfeeblement of political parties, which are broad, coagulating institutions. And it has also helped to create a political topography that has proven fertile to the Republicans at the presidential level. For when Americans turn away from civic purpose, they tend to vote Republican.

The 1980s are often compared to the 1950s and the 1920s—two other decades notable for what we now describe as yuppie greed. Each was followed by a decade of vast government activism and high civic purpose. Historian Arthur Schlesinger, Jr., among others, has theorized that politics in this country moves in cycles—from activism to retrenchment and back again—with each turn of the wheel lasting about thirty years. "The season of idealism and reform, when strong presidents call for active public interest in national affairs and invoke government as a means of promoting the general welfare, eventually leaves an electorate exhausted by the process and disenchanted by the results," Schlesinger wrote in late 1987. "People are ready then to respond to leaders who tell them they needn't worry unduly about public affairs; left to private action and self-interest in an unregulated market, our problems will solve themselves. This mood, too, eventually runs its course. Problems neglected become acute, threaten to become unmanageable and demand remedy. People grow increasingly bored with selfish motives and vistas, increasingly weary of materialism, and demand some meaning larger than themselves. This is what was happening at the end of the 1920s and the end of the 1950s and it is what is happening today." Schlesinger added that there is nothing mystical in the duration of each cycle. "Thirty years is the span of a generation. People tend to be formed politically by the ideals dominant in the years during which they attain political consciousness: roughly between their seventeenth and twenty-fifth years. When their own generation's turn in power comes thirty years later, they tend to carry forward the ideals they imbibed when young."[7]

Schlesinger was not alone in thinking the wheel was ready to turn in 1988. The polls seemed to support his thesis. And yet it did not happen. His cycles appear to have been thrown out of whack by an ongoing backlash against the intrusiveness of big government. We are a fiercely individualistic culture and our big government/high tax state is a fairly recent innovation. It was only after the Second World War that the federal government began telling people where they had to go to school, whom they had to accept into their neighborhoods and when they could not pray. Around the same time, it also began taxing them much more heavily than ever before. In 1981, the federal tax burden on the median income family of four was two and a half times greater than it had been in 1955. All of this produced a predictable get-the-government-off-our-backs reaction that helped elect Ronald Reagan in 1980. Despite Reagan's talk of paring it down, government spending as a percentage of GNP continued to rise in the 1980s. As political scientist Hugh Heclo has written: "Much as FDR and the New Deal had the effect of conserving capitalism, so Reagan will eventually be seen to have helped conserve a predominantly status quo, middle-class welfare state." But Reagan financed the welfare state (and the weapons systems) by borrowing, not taxing. So one legacy of his budget deficits is a political mind-set that says that the nation can't afford a new round of governmental activism because the cash register is empty.

This is a nation of voters, in short, who feel fundamentally blocked. They cannot vote for the changes they say they want because the government doesn't have the money to pay for them. And they don't have enough faith in government to pay more taxes so it will have more money. Moreover, neither party has the intellectual energy to yank the voters out of their box. The Republicans have been in power long enough to have put in place the core of their agenda — lower top marginal tax rates, deregulation, a military buildup, appointment of conservative judges. They are out of fresh ideas. In an era when the global rush to democracy has made the politics of the Cold War obsolete, the best they can hope for is to be invited by the voters to stick around for some fine tuning. The Democrats would seem to have more openings for a bold and affirmative message, but at the moment they can't get past the cynicism of voters. Democrats are still the party of government. Government — as Michael Dukakis found out in 1988 — is still the enemy.

Given the loss of vitality of the political center, it's no surprise that in 1987–88, the two preachers, Jesse Jackson and Pat Robertson, prospered, at least for a while, with the populist politics of grievance. Jackson's targets were big business and the greedy rich. Robertson's were big government and the meddling liberals. Part of Bush's political genius in the fall campaign was that he did a much better job of borrowing Robertson's themes than Dukakis did of borrowing Jackson's. "It was a brilliant stroke to run the incumbent Vice President, who was boasting of his own administration's success, as a candidate of grievance — of affronts localized in a liberalism that is soft on crime and defense, exotic as a Harvard boutique yet stealthy enough to win an election by misrepresenting itself to the American people," wrote Garry Wills. "The populism of power is a contradiction in terms. But Ailes and Lee Atwater and James Baker made it a contraption for garnering votes."[8]

Even as Bush found a winning appeal in contrived populism, however, he also became the first presidential winner in twenty-eight years whose party did not gain seats in Congress. The Democrats padded their margins by one in the Senate (to ten) and by three in the House (to eighty-five), giving Bush the smallest base of congressional support of any incoming President in history. As I noted in the first chapter, divided partisan control of different branches of government is a phenomenon unique to the modern era. In 1988, 45 percent of all congressional districts (196 out of 435) chose a presidential candidate of one party and a congressperson of the other. In only one presidential election prior to 1948 did more than 20 percent of the congressional districts split their votes this way.

Some political scientists find method to this madness. They argue that voters are resolving their contradictory wants from government — a high level of services, a low level of taxes—by deliberately hedging their bets. They elect a Republican President to project strength abroad and to keep a check on government at home; they elect a Democratic Congress to make sure that their government will take care of their needs and wants. Or, as Richmond *Times-Dispatch* columnist Charlie McDowell put it: "We elect Democrats to the Congress to give us stuff. We elect Republicans to the White House so we won't have to pay for it."

Others doubt that voters are so calculating. They say divided government is caused by congressional incumbents who have entrenched themselves and voters who haven't had the energy to object. In the past two decades there's no doubt that the electoral playing field has been heavily tilted toward incumbents: congressional staff size has doubled, the use of the congressional frank has quadrupled and incumbents now receive nine times more than their challengers in campaign contributions from political action committees.

As a result, the 1988 House races were the least competitive in U.S. history. Not only was the percentage of incumbent winners the highest ever (402 of 408 House members seeking reelection won, or 98.5 percent), but the margins of victory were the most lopsided ever. In 1988, an astounding 85 percent of the winners captured 60 percent of the vote in their district or more; that is, they won in a landslide.

Yet the same public that reelected so many incumbents by so many landslides also told pollsters—by a margin of nearly two to one at the end of 1989—that they disapproved of the way Congress was doing its job. There is more going on here than the familiar I-hate-Congress-but-I-like-my-congressman syndrome. What these near-100 percent reelection rates are measuring is ossification, not approbation. Voters don't care enough about politics to alter the standing arrangements. This doesn't mean they approve of the arrangements or that they disapprove. It means they have lost interest.

The clearest expression of this retreat from politics occurs every election day, when American voter turnout runs 20 percentage points or more below the rates in other advanced industrial democracies. There are several reasons. The bureaucratic obstacles are much greater here—it's harder to register (though it's been getting steadily easier in the last three decades); it's harder to stay registered; election days aren't holidays; absentee ballots are not easy to manage. In addition, political parties in other countries play a much more active role in commanding loyalty, communicating policy positions and getting voters to the polls.

Given these factors, it would be surprising if voter turnout here didn't lag behind other countries. What is more troublesome is that it has been declining sharply in this country, and that in 1988 it fell to its lowest level in more than six decades.

The nation has endured stretches of low turnout in the past. America's first five Presidents, from George Washington to James Monroe, won elections in which only 4 to 6 percent of the eligible electorate participated. Voting was a difficult enterprise in the early days of the republic: it was hard to get information about candidates or find out where polling places were. By the 1820s the infrastructure had grown more conducive to participation — better transportation and communication systems were in place. More importantly, populist Andrew Jackson was the nation's first presidential candidate who believed in mobilizing the masses. Turnout shot up to 57 percent in 1828 and reached 80 percent by 1840. For the remainder of the nineteenth century, the rates only once fell below 70 percent (69.4 percent in 1852) and sometimes exceeded 80 percent. Politics was highly partisan in this era, as the parties did what modern European parties do today — distributed propaganda, held torchlight parades, passed out sample ballots, rewarded supporters with patronage. At the turn of the century, voter turnout began to drop. This was the result of literacy laws and poll taxes enacted in the post–Civil War South, which were designed to keep blacks from voting, and registration laws adopted nationwide, which were designed to curb voter fraud. For the first half of the twentieth century, turnout in presidential campaigns ranged between 50 and 60 percent. In the 1950s, it began trending back upward, as Americans became better educated — a factor that has always correlated with higher turnouts. The rate reached its modern peak of 63.6 percent in 1960.

Since then, voter turnout has declined by more than a fifth, to 1988's 50.16 percent. The fall-off has occurred despite a rise in education levels and an easing of registration requirements — both of which theoretically should have led to higher turnouts. Voter-turnout expert Ruy Teixeira has calculated that about one-third of the drop is attributable to demographic factors such as the adoption of the eighteen-year-old vote, the decline of the traditional family and the increased mobility of the electorate. The rest of the slump is the result of the erosion of what he calls political efficacy — the extent to which people feel connected to politics.[9]

As Teixeira points out, the motivation to vote is based, at least in part, on a willing suspension of disbelief. Democracy's favorite aphorism—"every vote counts"—doesn't stand up to a cost/benefit analysis. For the overwhelming majority of voters, voting has never and will never "count" in the sense that one vote will change the outcome of an election. Moreover, the people who say they vote because it's their chance to affect public policy are engaging in benign self-deceit. In a democracy, you can be a "free rider"; the policy consequences of an election are conferred on voter and non-voter alike. Why, then, *do* people vote? Voting theorists say it's not so much that they want to get something from the system; it's that they want to say something about themselves. They vote in order to express their "sense of duty toward society, responsibility toward a reference group, commitment to a candidate, party or cause.... "[10]

As a result of the recent turnout declines, voting has become very much a "class act," just as it had been in the earliest days of the republic. Among the wealthiest fifth of the population, the turnout rate has ranged between 75 and 80 percent in the last three presidential elections; among the poorest fifth, the rate has hovered around 40 percent. The decline of the parties has caused the class gap to grow, for political parties have always been essential mechanisms for mobilizing lower-class citizens to participate. On the face of it, this trend would seem to be damaging to the Democrats, the "party of the little guy." However, a number of recent studies (including one taken right after the 1988 election) have shown that nonvoters are at least as Republican as Democratic.

The real problem with declining turnout is not the way it tilts the partisan playing field. It's the way it corrodes the playing field. "People are staying home as a conscious act of withdrawal," wrote historian James MacGregor Burns. "After the two-year hullabaloo of presidential campaigning, half of the audience fails to show up at the grand finale on election day, and two-thirds or three-fourths typically boycott state and local elections, the vaunted 'foundation of democracy.' They are not playing in our game of democracy, perhaps because they consider it only a game, a spectator sport."[11]

"I get so embarrassed when I see these Central American countries where people can get shot by the left or the right for voting, and yet they turn out to vote at twice the rate we do in this country," said Frenzel.

There are some who argue that this withdrawal from civic participation is a kind of happy apathy. They view voting as an inverse indicator of societal well-being: people are motivated to go to the polls when they're upset about something. There may be some validity to this Panglossian view, although it fails to account for the degree to which nonvoters are the least content members of society.

But even if we accept, at least in part, the explanation of happy apathy, there is still cause for concern. The less people participate, the less stake they feel in "the system," the more the fabric of democracy frays. Politicians grow accustomed to responding to special rather than public interests. The electoral system becomes, simultaneously, less accountable and more averse to risk. Leaders can't balance a budget, much less tackle larger problems.

None of this necessarily produces an immediate crisis. But over time, when a diverse and pluralistic society loses its glue, it loses its aspirations. Virtually everyone in America knows there are big challenges our society isn't facing; this knowledge explains their low-grade fever. The half of us who voted in 1988 elected a President who said the challenges were real but claimed we don't have the "wallet" to face them. What we don't have, of course, is the will. He urged us in his inaugural address to turn away from material self-interest and do what we could, on our own, to address the needs of the needy. The words were eloquent. But "it creates a very peculiar dynamic when the leader we elect to handle the tasks that are too large for any of us to take on by ourselves tells us these tasks are worthy but asks us to address them through our own altruism," noted Benjamin Barber, a professor of political science at Rutgers University. "I'm not going to be able to wipe out poverty by working in a soup line. The problems are structural, so the solutions must be structural. Altruism is not citizenship, and there is some harm when we confuse the two."

Perhaps we're counting on our children to face up to the challenges we're shirking. But when they try — if they try — what will they think of us, once they grow up and discover we have left them a pile of debt and a paucity of civic values?

CHAPTER TEN

Reporters in the Age of Television

MOMENTS AFTER the first debate between George Bush and Michael Dukakis ended, David Brinkley, who was anchoring ABC's post-debate coverage, and Peter Jennings, who had been on the panel of debate questioners, had this exchange:

Brinkley: "What did you think?"

Jennings (wryly): "I don't know. I didn't see it on television."

IN 1939, when television was still a curiosity of tubes and wires, E. B. White wrote: "I believe television is going to be the test of the modern world, and that in this new opportunity to see beyond the range of our vision we shall discover either a new and unbearable disturbance of the general peace or a saving radiance in the sky."

It would take another dozen years for television to come roaring out of the laboratory and into the fabric of the modern world. The stampede began in 1951, the year a coaxial cable was laid from coast to coast, enabling Americans in all parts of the country to see the same thing at the same time. Fewer than 10 percent of the population had a TV set at the time. By 1963, ninety-five out of every hundred American homes had one. That year the networks inaugurated their half-hour nightly news broadcasts and, overnight, television supplanted newspapers as the nation's most widely used and widely believed medium of information. It has remained so ever since.

Today, there are more televisions than toilets in American homes. The typical household keeps a set on for seven hours and two minutes per day. By the time a baby born the year the coaxial cable was laid reaches age seventy, he or she will have spent more than seven *solid years* in front of the television.

Television has changed almost everything about the way our society works, not least its politics. "Television *is* the political process," Theodore H. White once said. "It's the playing field of politics." [1] Media expert Michael Robinson has described the television audience for political information as a largely "inadvertent audience." The phrase suggests viewers who ingest the news with only one eye and ear, perhaps while eating dinner or romping with the kids or waiting for their favorite sitcom to come on. Robinson's vivid coinage may overstate the accidental nature of TV news viewing, but he's onto something important. Watching television is a passive, low-intensity activity — "chewing gum for the eyes" — which requires less concentration than reading a book or newspaper. The television audience, as a result, is broader, less educated, less sophisticated and less interested in public affairs than the readership of newspapers. Were it not for the ease with which television news falls into its audience's laps, its audience wouldn't take in as much news as television supplies.

"No matter how much some critics deplore the sketchiness of television's political coverage, the fact is that television gives considerably more attention to politics than most viewers feel they need or want," Austin Ranney wrote in *Channels of Power,* a 1983 book on the impact of television on American politics. In 1988, the three network news shows devoted a combined total of 2,201 stories to the presidential election — three times as much as to any other single topic, according to a study by the Center for Media and Public Affairs. Television inherited this disposition from print journalism. "In a sense, journalists are patrons of political life," wrote Michael Schudson.[2] " . . . the journalism of the national newsweeklies, most large metropolitan newspapers and network television news does not mirror the world but constructs one in which the political realm is pre-eminent."*

Question: Has television's fascination with politics produced an unbearable disturbance or a saving radiance?

Robinson, the coiner of the term "video malaise," was one of the

---

*Not all quarters of print journalism accept this construct. At *People* magazine, where circulation fluctuates by as much as 30 percent each week depending on the cover story, founding editor Richard B. Stolley established this rule of thumb for covers: "Young is better than old; pretty is better than ugly; television is better than music; music is better than movies; movies are better than sports; and anything is better than politics."

first academics to suggest the former. Using data from the University of Michigan Survey Research Center collected in 1964, 1968 and 1972, he found that the greater the dependency a person had on television news, the more likely he or she was to feel cynical, confused and estranged from government. Those who relied totally on television for their news about government or politics were 10 to 15 percent more cynical than nontelevision-dependent groups. When Robinson corrected for levels of education (television-news–dependent citizens are less educated than the nation as a whole, and the less educated tend to be the most cynical), the gaps narrowed but remained "statistically significant."*

All communication systems are seedbeds of disenchantment. They are forums for exchanging ideas, creating desires, challenging orthodoxies, fostering hopes, expressing disappointment. What makes the television revolution even more destabilizing to the established order than earlier communication revolutions, Robinson argued, is its ease of accessibility to the least politically sophisticated strata of society. When Latin was translated into common tongues during the Renaissance, when the penny press emerged in the nineteenth century, the availability of information expanded for all groups, but the increase was greatest among the social, economic and political elites. These elites served as a filter of political information; they explained government and politics to the masses. But with television, there is no need for intermediation. People can see with their own eyes.

Can anyone doubt the central role the television revolution has played these past few years in spreading the virus of democracy to corners of the globe yearning to be infected? "In the days of Goebbels, [dictators] could enslave people," James Reston said in a valedictory interview published upon his retirement from *The New York Times* in November 1989. "They could fill them full of such lies and deceptions. But then along came these new instruments, and they vault over boundaries and Iron Curtains. People begin to see that our standard of living is totally different. They see by television that tyranny is not inevitable but intolerable."

But television doesn't undermine only authoritarian regimes. It

*Robinson measured political cynicism by responses to the following three questions in the University of Michigan survey: (1) Agree or disagree: Sometimes politics and government seem so complicated that a person like me can't really understand what's going on. (2) Agree or disagree: Generally speaking, those we elect to Congress in Washington lose touch with the people pretty quickly. (3) Do you think that quite a few people running the government are a little crooked, not very many are, or do you think that hardly any of them are at all?

can take its toll on democracies as well. "Government [in the United States] has become weaker in the age of television, and the network portrayal of politics has played a role in that weakening," Ranney wrote in *Channels of Power*. Is it an accident that the dawn of the television news era roughly coincided with the flowering of an adversary political culture? Is it a coincidence that the first war this country did not win was its first "living room war," whose battlefield horrors were broadcast nightly into America's homes.* Is it a surprise that the first President to resign his office did so after watching the momentum toward impeachment gather force during televised hearings in Congress?

It's a chicken-and-egg proposition to untangle whether Vietnam and Watergate unfolded as they did because of adversarial television journalism or whether television journalism turned adversarial because of Vietnam and Watergate. It seems safe to assume that causation flowed in both directions but that—and this is not a small point—reality is more causal than reporting. The overriding historical reality of the late 1960s and early 1970s was that two successive Presidents pursued policies that were deceitful and unwise; that there was a great tugging at the social fabric as a result and that America is a more cynical nation because of it. The reality is also that television delivered the news about these policies in a medium—and to a unique new mass audience—where cynicism and anti-institutionalism tend to flourish.

Television, of course, did not invent anti-institutional journalism. Starting with Thomas Paine, who saw government as a "necessary evil," American journalists have always harbored a populist distrust of government and elected officials. "[T]o the extent that public life in America lacks a dignity and authority that might somewhat ennoble it, our populist heritage must bear a considerable portion of the blame," Irving Kristol wrote in 1972. "And when the press undertakes to see that government lives up to its responsibilities, but then gives these responsibilities the impoverished definition that populism prescribes, the press compounds the inertial movement of American politics toward permanent mediocrity. One cannot improve govern-

*According to then presidential aide Bill Moyers, President Johnson decided to stop the bombing of Hanoi and not to seek reelection in 1968 after CBS anchorman Walter Cronkite aired a battlefront report in which he expressed his grave doubts about the prospect of winning the Vietnam War. Until then, the tone of coverage on all three networks had been supportive. "It's all over," Johnson reportedly said after watching the Cronkite broadcast. David Halberstam would later write that this was "the first time in history a war had been declared over by an anchorman."

ment without having a superior notion of it. The adversary posture of American journalism, resting on populist principles, could have no such superior notion—and could not even know that it lacked one."[3]

Kristol argued that television exacerbated all these tendencies. "Television is the greatest disaster that journalism has ever experienced . . . [it] is the slave of that most superficial and unenlightening of perceptual instruments: the camera. Without the tyranny of the camera, television is a boring lecture or recital; surrendering to its tyranny, television news is an exciting, dramatic and grossly oversimplified presentation of events."

Some may counter: Television can't be any worse than the penny press of the early nineteenth century, when sensationalism and character assassination were the order of the day, and when presidential candidates were routinely denounced in print as traitors, atheists, adulterers. But journalism in those days was openly and proudly partisan—newspapers were often appendages of the Federalist or the Republican parties—so press broadsides could be discounted accordingly. The norm of objectivity did not develop within American journalism until the middle of the nineteenth century. Most historians date it to the invention of the telegraph in 1844 and the subsequent creation of the Associated Press in 1848. Because the AP gathered news for a variety of papers with different political leanings, its dispatches had to be free of editorial comment. Eventually, its objective style came to be adopted by the local papers as well. The Industrial Revolution and the acceptance of Darwinism nourished this new norm of objectivity, for they gave rise to a scientific belief system which held that truth was a clear, precise and quantifiable commodity.

This objective tradition has never had a completely free run, however. It's always bumping up against one countervailing journalistic tendency or another. In the heyday of "yellow journalism," publishing moguls didn't think twice about making up "facts" if they thought it would mean a few thousand new readers. An infamous exchange in 1898 between William Randolph Hearst, the great press lord, and Frederic Remington, then a budding young artist, epitomized the values of the age. Hearst had sent Remington to Havana to sketch pictures of hostilities supposedly underway there. Remington wired back: EVERYTHING IS QUIET. THERE IS NO TROUBLE HERE. THERE WILL BE NO WAR. I WISH TO RETURN. Hearst answered: PLEASE REMAIN. YOU FURNISH THE PICTURES AND I'LL FURNISH THE WAR."

In the early part of the twentieth century, a more wholesome threat to objectivity emerged in the form of muckrakers such as Lincoln Steffens and Ida Tarbell, who saw it as their journalistic duty to expose society's injustices and serve as a tribune of the powerless. Muckraking journalism has never been famous for telling all sides of a story. It is inherently unbalanced and often sensationalized—but, muckrakers argue, for the greater good. This progressive reformer strain runs powerfully through American journalism to this day— coexisting, sometimes uneasily, with the objective norm. The craft bestows its highest honors (Pulitzer Prizes, etc.) on stories that emphasize journalism's role as a crusader rather than an observer.

While this bad-news bias afflicts both print and broadcast journalism, it comes across in purer form on television. In their book *Over the Wire and on TV,* Robinson and co-author Margaret A. Sheehan compared the coverage of the 1980 presidential campaign on CBS News and UPI. They found that every candidate in both parties got more negative coverage on television than on the wire. The ratio of "bad press" to "good press" was 71–29 percent on CBS and 39–61 percent on UPI.* This bad-news bias in television coverage of presidential campaigns showed up again in 1984 and 1988.

• In 1984, according to Robinson's content analysis, which that year included all three television network news programs, President Reagan got 121 minutes of negative coverage and just twelve minutes of positive coverage—an extraordinary 10–1 ratio. His running mate, George Bush, did even worse. He received twenty-five minutes of negative coverage and zero (!) minutes of favorable coverage.†

• In 1988, according to a study by Robert Lichter, the coverage on the three networks was negative-to-positive by a ratio of two to one for both Bush and Dukakis. Lichter's research methodology was similar to Robinson's.

The bad-news bias of journalism is not a subject that journalists readily discuss. We see our job as a daily struggle to expose wrongdoing, watchdog power, right wrongs. Because we often come under counterattack from entrenched interests, we're cautious about

*Robinson and Sheehan measured only coverage that had a detectable spin; that is, they discounted the roughly 80 percent of the coverage on CBS and UPI that was neutral, or ambiguous, or was devoted to comments from partisans who were clearly labeled as partisan.
†Once again, all neutral reporting was discounted. To those who fear the power of the press, Reagan's 49-state landslide in the teeth of such negative coverage helps keep matters in perspective. Reagan ran in a year of economic recovery, the Grenada invasion and the Olympic victories. "Good news overwhelms bad press," Robinson noted.

laundering dirty linen in public. Nearly a decade ago, however, at an unusually candid symposium on television coverage of the 1980 presidential campaign at the Institute of Politics at Harvard's John F. Kennedy School of Government, several journalists shed their inhibitions and discussed their concerns about negative bias. What they had to say still rings true two presidential campaigns later:

Elizabeth Drew, political correspondent for *The New Yorker:* "[T]o bring up one more point that is very delicate—and I do it with some misgivings—I wonder to what extent the tone with which we cover campaigns affects the public's reaction to it. Politicians are far from perfect, and I believe very strongly in being skeptical about them and, when they say things that are wrong, correcting them.... But I wonder if sometimes the sum total of the coverage doesn't tip over to the point where the process is robbed of any sense of majesty, inspiration, where it does become very heavily an approach that runs down just about everybody who tries to get into it.... Again, this is a tough line to draw, but I wonder if we haven't had some effect on the public's reaction, which is: 'To the extent that I care, they're all a bunch of bums and fools.' "[4]

Robert MacNeil of PBS and Tom Brokaw of NBC both commented on the "smart-aleck close," the zinger that so many television journalists place at the end of their brief pieces, usually in an effort to expose the hypocrisy or manipulation of the candidate. MacNeil said it had almost gotten to the point where there was a "competition in bitchiness" in these closing comments.

MacNeil: "Television political reporters feel they have to express their detachment and distance from the material ... especially as they are given such an exceedingly brief amount of time, usually two sentences at the end of the piece, which is, after all, their face, their byline, their career involvement every night.... [They] compress into very few words what, I think, could easily be interpreted as cynicism."[5]

Brokaw attributed the smart-aleck tone to a combination of peer pressure and resentment: "We're on the airline, we're herded onto the bus, we're taken over to the setting of the day and told where our cameras will be set up. The pool cameras have been arranged for us, and so on. So the way to get back is to go out there and jab him quickly right at the end—get one quick shot and go. I think that's part of the problem, and I do think it is a major problem. I also think it is a major problem that television correspondents, present company included, too often succumb to the temptation to be very judgmental at the end of one minute and thirty seconds."[6]

Eight years later, at a press symposium sponsored by Ripon College, those same smart-aleck closes were provoking the same lamentations. "I sometimes wonder why we just can't end our pieces: 'And tomorrow the candidate flies to Cleveland,'" a wistful John Chancellor said.

Broadcast journalists haven't been alone in occasionally giving a public laundering to their concerns about negativism. In a controversial 1982 address marking the end of his tenure as president of the American Society of Newspaper Editors, retiring New York *Daily News* editor Michael J. O'Neill said: "No longer do we look on government only with the healthy skepticism required by professional tradition. Now we have a hard, intensely adversarial attitude. We treat government as the enemy—and government officials as convenient targets for attack and destroy missions. No longer do we submit automatically to the rigors of old-fashioned impartiality. Now, not always but too often, we surrender to the impulse of advocacy, in the name of reform but forgetful of balance, fairness and—if it isn't too unfashionable to say so—what is good for the country."

His comments provoked a great deal of churning within the journalism community. Michael Gartner, then the editor of the Des Moines *Register,* now the president of NBC News, led the chorus of critics. "That's marvelous language," he said at a press symposium that took up O'Neill's critique, "but what is good for the country? What's good for the country is truth and openness and aggressiveness and reporting what the news is. What is bad for the country is a press that becomes a handmaiden of government. Conspiratorial secrecy is what is bad for the country."[7]

O'Neill's speech also zeroed in on what he viewed as the destructive impact of television. Because it is "an impressionistic medium that marshals images and emotions rather than words and reason," because it provides incentives for public officials to create made-for-TV spectacles and react to the made-for-TV spectacles created by others, it reduces the dialogue of governance to "a confusing mixture of the real and the unreal, the important and the irrelevant." O'Neill said this works a special hardship on the presidency. "It [television] raises public expectations far beyond the President's reach and then, when he cannot satisfy them, it magnifies the perception of failure. By massive overexposure, the media also strip away the protective mystery of the Oval Office," he said.

Hodding Carter, a veteran of government service as well as of broadcast and print journalism, took dead aim at O'Neill. "I want you to think with me how totally and completely government has been able to seize the high ground in policy debate and maintain it simply by using television in a regular, intelligent and planned way. The most popular thing I know is for present and former government officials to complain about the distorting effect of television, about its superficiality, about its inability to put things in context, its lack of memory and all the rest. The dirty secret, from the government side, is that these are all assets for the government's presentation and the government's ability to do things."[8]

Carter's comments echoed a concern frequently heard in television's early days: the new medium would act as an electronic throne and lead to imperial presidencies. Given the reverses suffered by four of the first five Presidents in the television era—Johnson, Nixon, Ford and Carter—these fears waned. But Reagan's masterful use of television revived them in the 1980s.

In the past few years, press critics such as Anthony Lewis, Mark Crispin Miller and Mark Hertsgaard have argued that the press—weary from years of defending itself against accusations of a negative and left-wing bias, bedazzled by Reagan's popularity and a patsy for his photo ops—engaged in a "return to deference." Their complaints were directed in part at the malleability of the press and in part at the skills of the manipulators.

"This was a PR outfit that became President and took over the country," Hertsgaard quoted a former Reagan deputy press secretary, Leslie Janka. "Their first, last and overarching activity was public relations." Unlike their press-bashing forebears in the Nixon White House, Janka said, the Reagan image makers came to the realization early on that "the media will take what we feed them. As long as you come in there every day, hand them a well-packaged, pre-masticated story in the format they want, they'll go away." Theirs, in short, was a strategy of manipulation by inundation—just give the networks a stream of good visuals and snappy quotes, and the White House can become the de facto producer of the evening news. Michael Deaver, Reagan's chief aide for imagery, says his "secret" could not have been more simple: "I noticed how people who run TV news reduced things to sound bites"—so that's what he supplied. "The only day I worried about was Friday," Deaver told Hertsgaard, "because it's a slow news day. That was the day that bothered me most, because if you didn't have anything that day, they'd go find something."[9]

There is some truth in these self-congratulatory "confessions" of Reagan's image makers—but only a kernel. In an office as exposed as the presidency, where hundreds of decisions and public utterances are made and conveyed every year, and where actions most assuredly have consequences, images do not drive reality. Reality drives images. The handlers in the Reagan White House were maestros of the sound bite and photo op—and Reagan's approval ratings ran in the 50 to 60 percent range. The handlers in the Bush White House seem to go out of their way to keep their un-telegenic President off the evening news—and Bush's approval ratings have run from 70 to 80 percent. His secret? He's had the good fortune to be on duty when communism collapsed. Photo ops pale by comparison.

This still begs the question about journalism. Did the press pull its punches during the Reagan years? *The New York Times*'s Lewis summarized that argument in a speech he delivered three weeks after the 1988 presidential election:

"The established press in this country has to a large extent reverted to the symbiotic relationship with the executive branch. We are an adversary only at the margins, not on the fundamentals that challenge power. We have forgotten the lessons of Vietnam and Watergate. Think about the press treatment of the presidency in the 1970s and, by comparison, in the last eight years. In Ben Bradlee's phrase, there has been 'a return to deference.' We are all uneasily aware that something like that has happened. We are not sure why that came about, but we can place the change in the Reagan years." Lewis argued that the press was mesmerized by Reagan's popularity and intimidated by the press-bashing agenda of conservative groups. "Bullying has its effects," he said.

He cast an especially disapproving eye at the way the media covered the 1988 campaign, contending that reporters rewarded Bush for his inaccessibility, punished Dukakis for his openness and backed off prematurely on their coverage of Iran–contra. There is some substance to this critique, particularly the last part. Bush—who as Vice President had sat in on at least fifteen Oval Office discussions of the arms-for-hostages deal—was masterful throughout the campaign at evading an accounting of his role in Iran–contra, and the press was supine in letting him get away with it. For a time, some of the boys on the bus did try to hector Bush into being more forthcoming. The Washington *Post*'s David Hoffman went to the trouble of buying a bullhorn so he could shout questions at the scripted candidate. But to no avail. In the post–Labor Day

phase of the campaign, Bush said exactly what he wanted to say—
and not a word more. After a while, as the numbing boredom of the
campaign grind took its toll, the Bush press corps found itself whipped,
listless and full of mordant humor. "I love these cloverleafs," the
Dallas *Morning News*'s Mark Nelson remarked one sleepy October
morning as the eighteen-car Bush motorcade snaked its way onto a
highway in Columbus, Ohio. "It's the best view we get of George
Bush all day." Meantime, in a *Columbia Journalism Review* article on
the 1988 campaign, William Boot (a pen name for Christopher
Hanson, Washington correspondent for the Seattle *Post-Intelligencer*)
described a piece that aired on ABC the night Sam Donaldson and
crew were allowed onto Dukakis' bus in mid-October. After Donaldson
was shown asking a provocative question—"Did you see in the paper
that Willie Horton said if he could vote he would vote for you?"
—Dukakis was shown struggling ineffectually to close a window.
"He can't vote, Sam," Dukakis finally replied—face impassive, eyes
averted from Donaldson, and still struggling with the window. So
much for giving the media access.

In the 1960s and the 1970s, the prevailing ideological complaint
against the media had been the opposite of Lewis' and Hertsgaard's:
it was that television was the toady of liberal Democrats. In *The News
Twisters,* a book about the coverage of the 1968 presidential campaign,
Edith Efron wrote: "Network reporters in alliance with Democratic-
liberal politicians portrayed Hubert Humphrey as a talkative Democratic saint studded over with every virtue known to man. . . . Mr.
Nixon is not portrayed as a human being at all but is transmogrified
into a demon out of the liberal id. . . . If Richard Nixon is President
of the United States today, it is in spite of ABC, CBS and NBC.
Together they broadcast the quantitative equivalent of *The New York
Times*'s lead editorial against him every day—for five days a week
for the seven weeks of the campaign period."[10]

The flaw in Efron's case is the same as in Lewis'—they are imput-
ing ideological bias or intimidation to behavior that is more aptly
explained by journalistic tendencies, rhythms and operational
needs. As political scientist Paul Weaver wrote in a review of
The News Twisters: " . . . what Miss Efron's numbers measure is not
bias against Nixon himself because of his personality, party or
opinions, but rather bias against someone like Nixon for reasons of
his journalistically-defined situation and identity."[11] Nixon had
campaigned in 1968 on a secret plan to end an unpopular war—a
plan he said he couldn't reveal until after the election. That smacked

of deception and demagoguery, and the press saw it as its duty to point this out. Similarly, as the various content analyses of coverage of the 1980, 1984 and 1988 campaigns make clear, television was anything but "on bended knee" in its treatment of candidates Ronald Reagan and George Bush. On Iran–contra, there is no question that the media pushed hard on the story for a while and then rather abruptly abandoned it after the Bush-Rather fireworks. But this describes pack journalism, not ideological intimidation. The pattern is familiar. The media pursue a story aggressively— until they hit a wall, or sense a loss of audience, or begin to have second thoughts about their earlier enthusiasm. So they change direction. These start-and-stop rhythms are part of the behavior patterns of many institutions. What's surprising is not that they occur in journalism, but how swiftly and uniformly they occur in an institution that is supposedly pluralistic. In his *Columbia Journalism Review* piece, Boot compared journalists to fish swimming in a school: they all turn in one direction simultaneously because they are "oriented to each other. Any fish that gets out of school is vulnerable prey. There's safety in numbers."

This brings the debate back to the harder case—is there a bad-news bias against politicians, without regard to ideology? It seems to me there is. Washington *Post* editorial-page editor Meg Greenfield wrote a column during the height of the Dan Quayle feeding frenzy that does an elegant job of explaining why:

"[W]hat is driving much of the cynicism and inquisitorial zeal of the media is the fact that again and again—from Richard Nixon to Spiro Agnew to Tammy Bakker and Jimmy Swaggart, with stops in between for public bigwigs too numerous to mention—the history has been one of astonishing squalors routinely denied and subsequently confirmed. The most pious seem to be the first to fall. If you want to understand how skittish and self-protective we have all become about this, I ask you to imagine what it is like to (a) write a story or commentary giving the benefit of the doubt to some set-upon public figure and (b) have it appear on the day your subject is indicted or skips the country or holds a press conference to announce that he is an after-hours female impersonator who has defrauded the family-business pension fund and sold secrets to the Russians, but that he thanks his wife and children for their unfailing love and hopes to be treated for hypoglycemia, the proximate cause of his moral defects, while in prison.

"Professionally speaking, is there anything worse? Well, yes, I think so—just one thing. It is to have the story wrong the other way around. A lot of us old geezers who came along in the McCarthy era would in fact like to err in the other direction, though ideally we'd like not to err at all. But for us, it is more comfortable to have to say: 'I was wrong; the guy really is a rat after all,' than to have to run a correction saying he is not a terrorist or a felon and we regret any misunderstanding. It really comes down to what a journalist tries hardest to guard against (sometimes no doubt overdoing it). And this in turn reflects what embarrasses or humiliates him most: being wrongly taken in or wrongly doing someone in. . . . Neither type of failure is professionally pleasant. Both make you feel like hell."

We in the press have been in the throes of a long season of fretting more about being taken in than about doing in. In that disposition, we reflect—and in reflecting, we amplify—the cynicism of our readers and viewers. We are carriers, as well as chroniclers, of the prevailing disenchantment with public life. The more cynical the news reporters and news consumers have become, the more image-manipulating, demagogic and risk averse the newsmakers have become. And so our cynicism begets their fakery, and their fakery our cynicism, and so on.

But to leave the description of the relationship between reporters and politicians at that—a vicious cycle of deceit and distrust— is incomplete. There is another side to it—the camaraderie, the shared interests, the mutual admiration and, above all, the professional need to peacefully coexist. A generation ago, to be sure, these personal relationships were cozier than they are today. Some, such as John Chancellor, believe that something important has been lost because reporters and politicians no longer put their feet up after hours and break out the bourbon. He argues that those intimate glimpses—even if off the record—produced richer, more textured coverage. Others, such as David Broder, argue that they too often led to reporters being compromised or co-opted.

The after-hours camaraderie may have cooled over the years, but it hasn't vanished. Nor has the office-hours need to cooperate. Politicians have what reporters want—information; and reporters have what politicians want—ink and airtime. Each side can reward and punish, in response to the behavior of the other. The late Massachusetts Institute of Technology political scientist Ithiel de Sola Pool once wrote that the "relationship of reporter and politician resembles a bad marriage. They cannot live without each other, nor can they

live without hostility."* Media critic Edwin Diamond has described
the two as adversaries in the manner of professional wrestlers, who
know each other's moves, know there is a need for ritualistic combat,
but realize they must cooperate to perform their respective jobs. The
relationship alternates between "stroking" and "poking," wrote
Harvard political science professor Gary R. Orren.

I'm unable to resolve in my own mind whether it's good or bad
that this complicated relationship has been tilted so long in the
"gotcha!" mode. The reporter in me wonders how it could be
otherwise; the media critic counts the cynical voters and bland
politicians we have helped to create and wonders if there isn't a
better way. I've been conducting this internal debate for twenty
years. Rather than try to force some false resolution here, let me
pose a different question. Even if journalism wanted to change,
could it? Could we eliminate our bad-news bias? And could we—
especially the television journalists among us—overcome the tendency to present political news in a simplistic, moralistic, symbolic,
conflict-oriented, picture-driven language?

I am not optimistic. Our bad-news bias, as I have already suggested,
mirrors the populist righteousness of our readers and viewers. They
want us to have this bias—even though they complain about it. In a
nationwide survey that explored public perceptions of the media in
the summer of 1989, the Times Mirror Company (owners of the Los
Angeles *Times,* the Baltimore *Sun* and other newspapers) found that
63 percent of Americans thought that in stories about personal
scandals involving public figures, the journalists—rather than the
underlying facts—were driving the news. (Forty-nine percent of a
group of journalists surveyed agreed with this proposition.) However,
"the irony here is that they also say this kind of coverage weeds out
the people who ought not to be in office," said Andrew Kohut,
former president of the Gallup Organization, who conducted the
poll. "They see this as a legitimate area of reporting, but they are
[critical] of the nature of the coverage and the way it comes out." The
same survey found that 82 percent of the public regarded network
news favorably, 80 percent approved of local TV news and 77 percent
approved of daily newspaper coverage. "It's the watchdog role that

---

*Pool has also written that the very wariness of journalists to the seductions of co-option
fortifies their determination to be adversarial. "To do his job [the reporter] must grow
close to politicians and win their trust, but his job is also to publicly expose them."
Consequently, press behavior becomes "a reaction to the very compromises and concessions"
that the reporter must make—"a brave assertion that wards off guilt."

keeps the public favorability rating of the press up there," said Kohut.[12] It reinforces this point to remember that the most popular television news program in history has been CBS's *60 Minutes*, whose trademark is the bullying interview and the catch-a-thief tone.

As long as there is this kind of demand for press watchdogging, seasons of press hostility toward politicians are likely to outlast seasons of deference. Nor is this so merely because of audience pressure. It is also the product of the psychological make-up of most journalists. We see ourselves as "the societal conscience of last resort," in David Halberstam's phrase. What attracts us to our line of work is not only the chance to observe but the chance to expose. "For the most part, we do not first see, and then define, we define first and then see," Walter Lippmann wrote in his seminal work *Public Opinion.* Reporters strain mightily to see things clearly and whole. But we also define the world by its unfinished agenda, and in so doing we cannot help but see mostly bad news.

This leaves us to ponder whether improvement is possible along the second front of press transgressions—the tendency to oversimplify. Here, the market pressures are just as profound, if not more so. But here at least, in contrast to the bad-news bias, the internal norms of the press would have us resist these pressures. Elite newspapers, in particular, measure themselves on how much nuance, texture and complexity they can bring to their coverage, given the constraints of time and space. These constraints are not small. Lippmann, the most distinguished journalist of the century, made a famous distinction in 1922 between news and truth. "The function of news is to signalize an event. The function of truth is to bring to light the hidden facts, to set them in relation with each other, and to make a picture on which men can act." He worried that while the press could deliver the news, it was "too frail" to deliver truth. "[The press] is like the beam of a searchlight that moves restlessly about, bringing one episode and then another out of darkness and into vision. Men cannot do the work of the world by this light alone. They cannot govern society by episodes, incidents and eruptions."

The pressures to simplify are even greater on television than in print. Newton Minow, in criticizing what he famously referred to as the "vast wasteland" of television, once observed that even though readership surveys show that the comics and the personal-advice columns are the most popular features in a newspaper, newspapers don't turn over all of their columns to them. Broadcast journalism confronts these pressures from a different tradition. It is the stepchild of a medium devoted primarily to entertainment, and it has never been shy about incorporating entertainment values into its presentation of news.

For one thing, television news embraces the "value" of brevity. The twenty-two-minute nightly network news report does not contain enough words to fill the front page of most newspapers. This results in pressure for short sound bites, and the trends are not encouraging. In television's coverage of the 1968 presidential campaign, the average length of a candidate's sound bite was 42.2 seconds; by 1988, it was 9.8 seconds.[13] "In the 1970s, when we looked at commercials and advertising techniques, and the pacing of popular TV programs, we saw that the American mind was capable of handling a lot of different camera angles, quick shots and short bites, because Americans have seen commercials all their lives," senior CBS News political producer Brian Healy explained to the Washington Post's Lloyd Grove during the fall campaign. "So we have borrowed from the advertising techniques of commercial filmmaking to put our [news] spots together."

There's another reason television news yields more and more to the primacy of pictures. "With the advances in technology and satellites, we're able to get more footage more quickly," said former NBC News president Lawrence Grossman. "The result is that the news now is more 'show' and less 'tell.' In the early days of television, we had great chroniclers like Edward R. Murrow because we often didn't have the clips." This trend is not encouraging either. When journalists are forced to think pictures, write pictures and talk pictures, the net effect is high credibility (the camera never lies, or so the audience presumes) and abundant superficiality.

Finally, there are constraints of story format. In 1963, the year the half-hour news broadcast was launched, NBC News president Reuven Frank sent a memo to his correspondents: "Every news story should, without any sacrifice of probity or responsibility, display the attributes of fiction, of drama. It should have structure and conflict, problem and denouement, rising action and falling action, a beginning, a middle and an end."[14] NBC is by no means the only network with this instinct. "News stories at CBS tended to become two-minute morality plays, with heroes or villains and a tidy moral, to be summed up at the end," former CBS correspondent Fred Graham wrote in his 1990 book, Happy Talk. "For me," Roger Mudd said in the 1980 media symposium at Harvard, "the basic problem is the conflict between being an honest reporter and being a member of show business, and that conflict is with me every day. If you are dedicated to honest, unaffected, untrammeled reporting, you run up against the demands of making the news that evening interesting. I think over the last fifteen years, as competition has sharpened between the networks, none of us is content to let an event be an event; we have to fix it. We have to foreshorten the conclusions; we have to hasten the end. . . . We won't let the candidate lay out the issue on his own terms; he has to lay it out on our terms."[15]

In the decade since Mudd's lament, market pressures have gotten more severe—in both print and broadcast journalism. Total daily newspaper circulation dropped from 49 percent of the nation's adult population in 1980 to 41 percent in 1989. Large dailies in Los Angeles, Chicago, Philadelphia, Washington, D.C., Cleveland, Baltimore, St. Louis and Buffalo went under in the 1980s, continuing a long-term trend toward one-newspaper towns. By decade's end, a mere two dozen of the 1,525 daily-newspaper cities in America had more than one general circulation paper. "Newspapers are a waning presence in American homes, and even some editors admit their work is irrelevant to many people's lives," warned a 1989 article in the industry's leading trade journal, *Editor & Publisher.* To be sure, the surviving newspapers are highly profitable—on average, two to three times more profitable than businesses in general. But their minds have been concentrated by the recent hangings. The most widely copied innovation in print journalism in the 1980s was Gannett's *USA Today,* whose multicolor weather maps, news-you-can-use charts, bite-sized articles and happy-talk tone have become staples at many newspapers around the country. It calls itself McPaper, and the running joke is that if it continues to be a journalistic trendsetter, the Pulitzer Prize will have to include a new category—"best investigative paragraph." It's no accident that the paper is sold in vending machines that look like television sets or that so much of its coverage is about television. This is a newspaper for the television generation.

If print journalism had a bumpy decade in the 1980s, broadcast journalism was hit by a series of earthquakes. A new array of competing technologies shook loose huge chunks of its audience. During the 1980s, the percentage of households that subscribed to cable grew from 20 percent to 58 percent; the percentage of households that owned VCRs rose from zero to 64 percent; and the percentage of viewers who owned remote-control zappers increased from 29 percent (in 1985, the first year figures were kept) to 72 percent. Formerly loyal network viewers now routinely graze among up to a hundred broadcast and cable offerings on their set. They can watch recent-release movies on HBO or the Disney Channel, inhale sports day and night on ESPN, catch their City Council meeting on a local-access cable channel or bring home a rental movie—which the typical VCR owner does 4.3 times per month. As a result, the networks' prime time market share fell from 92 percent in 1978 to 68 percent in 1989.

The competition has sent network television entertainment programming into a downward spiral toward the simple, the shocking and the sensational. The phrase "trash TV" entered the vocabulary in the late 1980s, describing everything from shouting matches and real fist fights on "infotainment" talk shows to kinky sex and masturbation on made-for-TV movies. The news divisions of the networks haven't gone nearly that far, but they haven't been unaffected. In 1988 and 1989, NBC News aired pop documentaries about "Bad Girls" and "Women Behind Bars," which purported to be about the shocking new phenomenon of young female criminals but "whose true purpose—raw exploitation, was vividly revealed in the ads and promos for the show," wrote Peter J. Boyer, a television industry critic.[16] The line between news and entertainment was blurred still further in 1989 when ABC aired a dramatic re-creation on its nightly news show in which an actor portrayed Felix Bloch—a career diplomat suspected of having contacts with Soviet agents—exchanging documents with a Soviet contact.* Meantime, racy quasi-news shows like *Hard Copy* and *Inside Edition* gained wide syndication. Boyer posits, and many industry critics agree, that the takeover of all three networks by corporate titans in the 1980s—NBC by General Electric, CBS by Loews and ABC by Capital Cities—has undermined basic journalistic values. Of the three new corporate owners, only Capital Cities has a media background; the others, as former CBS president Richard Salant observed, come from "jet engines, light bulbs, tobacco and insurance." Their every-division-must-pay-its-way management philosophy resulted in the layoffs of 3,500 employees—from censors to reporters to technicians—at the Big Three from 1986 to 1988.

Inauspicious as these trends appear to be, there's another side to the story. The network news divisions, which had spent less than $100 million a year through most of the 1970s, were spending at the rate of $300 million by the mid-1980s, and there was fat to cut. Even with a smaller audience share, the nightly news shows remain the closest thing the networks have to a corporate symbol—

*ABC news executives subsequently called the incident an aberration and reprimanded the news employee responsible.

and no enlightened corporate owner, no matter how wedded to the bottom line, is interested in cheapening his imprimatur. Meantime, the decade also gave birth to public affairs shows like *Nightline* and *This Week with David Brinkley,* both of which consistently go behind the headlines with intelligence and nuance. In addition, PBS's *MacNeil/Lehrer NewsHour* and cable's C–SPAN and CNN provide the conscientious consumer with all the political coverage he or she could want.

So THEN, can media coverage of politics get better? The 1988 campaign left so many journalists feeling so sour that we've been awash in self-improvement vows ever since. Here are five of my favorites:

1. We should place less emphasis on polling. This is the most systematic way we oversimplify politics: we reduce it to a game of who's on first. Polling has an important place in campaign coverage and it's a wonderful tool to help us understand the electorate. But according to one study, there were three times more media polls taken in 1988 than in 1984. That's too much, for it drowns out issue coverage. A study by the Markle Commission on the Media and the Electorate, analyzing the content of all 7,574 campaign stories in 18 major media organizations (print and broadcast) from Labor Day to Election Day 1988, found that 36.1 percent were devoted to horse-race coverage, while only 9.7 percent were devoted to issue coverage. (The other categories were candidate conflicts, 20.8 percent; candidate qualifications, 19.2 percent; the electorate, 9.7 percent; and the media themselves, 4.4 percent.) During the last weeks of the campaign, we should do stories on the issues even if the candidates aren't talking about them. And if perchance the candidates do say something substantive, we should flood them with ink and air time.

2. We should worry less about what's going to happen tomorrow and more about what happened yesterday. There's something about a presidential campaign that brings out the seer in every journalist. I've already confessed my own foolishness on this front in Chapter 5, but to make it clear that this proclivity is widespread, here are some doozies served up in 1988 by fellow addicts:

"George Bush is a very weak front-runner. . . . My heart on the Democrats says Bruce Babbitt. . . . He'll take Bill Bradley [for a running mate]."   —Tom Oliphant of the Boston *Globe,* on *Agronsky and Company,* January 2, 1988

"[The big surprise of 1988 will be] the staying power of Pat Robertson, who's not going to just last for Iowa and New Hampshire, but for the whole course, all the way to the convention."   —Fred Barnes of *The New Republic,* on *The McLaughlin Group,* January 2, 1988

"I think Bush, if he's not dead, the pulse is very light. . . . This guy has great troubles as a candidate. I think he's going to lose New Hampshire. I think he's going to lose the nomination."   —Robert Novak on *The McLaughlin Group,* February 13, 1988

"I would say, Robin, the fact that [Dukakis] finished a weak third in Iowa . . . would raise the question whether, indeed, he is a national candidate."   —Roger Mudd on *The MacNeil/Lehrer NewsHour,* February 9, 1988

"Now [the GOP nomination battle is] looking increasingly like a Dole-Robertson line-up."   —Howard Fineman of *Newsweek* on *Washington Week in Review,* February 12, 1988

"I said several weeks ago that I thought there was a chance Jackson would be on the ticket [in] the vice-presidential spot. Now I'm fairly well convinced he will be on the ticket, and the question is: in the VP spot or in the presidential spot?"   —Sam Donaldson on *This Week with David Brinkley,* April 3, 1988

"I think Dukakis is formidable. He's steady. He can handle the heat. And I think Bush . . . is going to come unglued."   —Robert Scheer of the Los Angeles *Times* on *The McLaughlin Group,* June 13, 1988[17]

3. We should try, in our character coverage, to illuminate what is important rather than what is titillating. We should accept the

proposition that a politician is entitled to a realm of privacy and start from the premise that his or her private life remains private unless it impinges on public performance. (But the politicians, in turn, should understand that if they conduct their private lives in public or without discretion, their behavior may meet the test of newsworthiness.) We should press for more in-depth interviews of the candidates on the nightly news shows; more broadcast documentaries about them; more issue coverage in both the print and the broadcast medium.

At a press symposium in 1987, biographer Doris Kearns Goodwin put forward an excellent checklist of questions that political reporters should bring to their character coverage of presidential candidates. Her suggestions, as paraphrased by David S. Broder in an internal memo that circulated at the *Post:*

- How much physical energy does the candidate display? Does he keep humming, or does he run out of gas?
- How is he with people? Does he reach out and touch, or seem to shrink from physical and personal contact?
- How does he react to the experience of campaigning? What does he say he's learned from being out there? How, if at all, has he changed in the reporter's eyes?
- How does he deal with, and relate to, his staff? Is he a disciplinarian, a delegator? Does he play them off against each other? And who are they?
- What does the standard stump speech — or the changes and evolutions in it — tell us about the candidate? There's a reason he gives the speech over and over. What is it?
- Does he evoke emotion in his crowds? A leader is always in a relationship with his constituency. What relationship does he seek? What does he achieve?
- Does he have interests beyond politics? When he's not campaigning, can he talk about anything else?
- Does he have a sense of humor? Of irony? Of detachment? Is his humor always aimed at others, or can he kid himself?
- What kind of relationship does he have with his political peers? How open is he with them? How candid can they be with him? Who are they?
- How does he deal with setbacks, aggravations, frustrations? Can he bounce back? Does he scapegoat, shift blame? Is he overwhelmed with guilt?

• How truthful is his picture of reality? When recounting
stories, is he accurate, or does he embroider or shade reality?

4. We should become more aggressive about pointing out inferen-
tial falsehoods in political ads. As matters now stand, we blow the
whistle on outright lies but remain mute about half-truths that carry
false implications. Media consultants know this about us, and they
specialize in ads that contain no factual errors but still convey false
impressions. We need to find a journalistic grammar that allows us
to remain objective while we point out distortions that may be as
subtle as the sneer in the voice of the narrator of an ad. We also need
to be careful not to magnify the distortion we are trying to expose.
This can be tricky. As media expert Kathleen Hall Jamieson has
pointed out, Willie Horton's face got more exposure on the network
news than it did in any political ads. And, as my *Post* colleague
Lloyd Grove wrote during the campaign, the line between news and
ads can easily become blurred. Dukakis' infamous photo-op at a tank
factory in Michigan was the best case in point: first it was a pseudo-
event; then it was news; then because it was news it became an ad;
then because it had become an ad, it became news again. At each step
along the way there was media commentary about whether Dukakis
was viscerally anti-military, as his critics had charged. Perhaps he
was. But no media treatment of that question, no matter how
intelligent, could possibly have competed with the power of that
ridiculous visual. Jamieson dubbed the tank ride a "news-ad" and
warned the media not to play an unwitting role in the promulgation
of this dangerous hybrid of political communication. According to
a study by Kiku Adatto at Harvard's Barone Center for Press, Politics
and Public Policy, excerpts from political ads were shown as part
of network news coverage 125 times during the 1988 campaign, but
the veracity of the commercials' claims was addressed less than
8 percent of the time.

5. We should stop being so obsessed with playing the role of
theater critic. As Adatto observed, "The language of political reporting was filled with accounts of staging and backdrops, sound bites
and spin control, photo opportunities and media gurus."[18] She
reported that in 1988, 52 percent of all television campaign coverage
was devoted to stagecraft rather than substance; in 1968, by contrast,
just 6 percent of the television campaign reports were theater
criticism. Adatto vividly illustrated her point by reviewing some

of the television reporting before and after the first Bush-Dukakis debate.

Two days before the debate, ABC's Peter Jennings opened his coverage by noting, "Today, Bush and Dukakis have been preparing — read, rehearsing." He then turned to correspondent Brit Hume, who described a Bush meeting with Soviet Foreign Minister Eduard Shevardnadze as "unquestionably a campaign photo opportunity." Hume alerted his viewers to listen as the television microphones picked up the sound of Bush whispering to Shevardnadze, "Shall we turn around and get one of those pictures in?" Jennings noted that Dukakis had also found time for a "carefully staged photo opportunity," and turned to Sam Donaldson, who showed Dukakis playing catch with a Boston Red Sox outfielder, an event Donaldson described as "this morning's made-for-television, pre-debate photo opportunity."

After the debate, CBS's Lesley Stahl and Dan Rather engaged in the following exchange:

Rather: What about . . . the extraordinary jump in the perception that George Bush has very human qualities?

Stahl: Well, last night in the debate that was a very calculated tactic and strategy on the part of his handlers. They told him not to look into the camera. [She gestures toward the camera.] You know when you look directly into the camera you are cold, apparently they have determined.

Rather [laughing]: Bad news for anchormen, I'd say.

Stahl: We have a lot to learn from this. They told him to relate to the questioner, to relate to the audience if he could get an opportunity to deal with them, to relate to the opponent. Michael Dukakis kept talking right into the camera. And according to the Bush people, that makes you look programed, Dan [Stahl laughs]. And they're very adept at these television symbols and television imagery. And according to our poll, it worked.

Rather: Do you believe it?

Stahl: Yes, I think I actually do.

"Time and again reporters called attention to the politicians' use of television imagery," Adatto wrote. "And yet, for all their efforts, they did not escape their entanglement or recover their independent voice. Instead they became conduits for the very images they criticized. . . . This new relation, between image-conscious coverage and media-driven campaigns, raises with special urgency the deepest danger for politics in a television age. . . . It is the danger that the politicians and press become caught up in a cycle that leaves the substance of politics behind, that takes appearance for reality, perception for fact, the artificial for the actual, the image for the event."[19]

These are all noble goals and wise warnings. Many of my colleagues have their own lists that are equally high-minded. It's conceivable that our quadrennial self-improvement pledges really will make things better in 1992. But in all honesty, I'm not terribly sanguine. I suspect that we journalists just don't have the leeway to dramatically improve journalism in ways that our critics demand and that many of us would like. Bad habits don't become bad habits out of thin air. They are the product of who we are, of how we conceive of our role in society and of the tastes and appetites of our viewers and readers. These things do not change by decree.

If one thinks of a political campaign as a market in which a three-way transaction takes place between voters, candidates and journalists, it's clear that the market isn't functioning to anyone's satisfaction. I don't think the journalists can reform it from within. But I do think that a modest degree of regulation, imposed from without, might improve everyone's behavior.

CHAPTER ELEVEN

The Five-Minute Fix

A word is worth a thousand pictures.

—Anonymous

T HE ELECTION of a President is our democracy's crowning moment. It is the one time every four years that Americans hold a national town meeting, chart a common course and choose a leader who personifies our unifying myths. The exercise is part political transaction, part civic ritual. The way we conduct it matters—not just for the choice it yields but for the tone it sets for the ongoing enterprise of public life.

Yet despite the inherent majesty of the occasion, this country has never seen fit to establish ground rules to ensure that it unfolds above a floor of reason and dignity. We are devoutly laissez-faire when it comes to regulating political campaigns. Alone among the major democracies of the world, we do not set aside blocks of television time so that candidates can address voters in a setting and format designed to promote rational advocacy. Instead, we allow our candidates to "talk" in pictures, attack ads and nine-second news bites, secure in the belief that the voters will cut through the hokum. This confidence is, in the main, well grounded. American voters rarely get duped. It is not the argument of this book that they were duped in 1988.

Yet saying that our market of political discourse is efficient is not the same as saying it is healthy. Vast numbers of voters are dropping out of the market altogether: the dialogue doesn't interest them. At the close of our most recent national town meeting, a record 91 million adult Americans had nothing to say.

In the short run, it's hard to make a case that government works less well at a 50 percent turnout rate than at a 60 or 70 percent rate. But over time the depoliticization of our culture is surely harmful. It keeps talented people away from careers in public life. It makes government less accountable, voters more cynical and society more atomized. It creates a vicious circle of distrust, disengagement and declining expectations. Most important, it dilutes the glue any society must have in order to bind the hopes and fears of its citizens into a sense of common purpose. By my lights, the conversation of politics nourishes precisely to the degree that it defines public life as something larger than the sum of private interests.

There *is* a way to change the format of presidential campaigns so that they might more nearly attain this goal. The path to reform does not lie with proposals to eliminate or in any way restrict thirty-second attack ads, as some have suggested. Whatever one may think of these ads, they are democracy in action. They're on the air because they change votes and win elections. "If the American people thought George Bush ran a dirty campaign in 1988, there's a 100 percent chance he would have lost," Lee Atwater declared after the last election. He may be oversimplifying, but he's on to something. Either one believes in a free marketplace of political advocacy or one doesn't. If one does, under what theory of the First Amendment does one then tell George Bush—or any other politician—that he cannot appeal for votes in a manner that demonstrably works?

What I propose is that we add to the political conversation, not subtract from it. We need to create a new forum of communication on television—one that would compete with the thirty-second spots and the nine-second news bites, but in a format partial to words over images, reason over demagoguery, substance over trivia. It may seem paradoxical to try to revive our political dialogue by forcing more of it onto the medium that contributes so mightily to its anemia. But any serious reform proposal must go straight to the belly of the beast, for that's where the conversation "happens" for most Americans. The trick is to transform television into an ally of reasoned debate, not an enemy.

Here's my five-minute fix: Starting with the 1992 campaign, each major candidate for President should be given five minutes of free time a night—on alternating nights—*simultaneously* on every television and radio station in the country for the final five weeks of the campaign. If this plan had been in effect in 1988, George Bush would have had five minutes on Monday, October 3—at, say, 7:55 p.m.—

on each of America's 1,378 television stations and 10,337 radio stations, Michael Dukakis would have had the same five-minute time slot on Tuesday, October 4, Bush on Wednesday, October 5, and so on, right up through the final weekend before the election.

In return for this grant of free time, each candidate would agree to one simple format restriction: He (or his running mate) would have to appear on the air for the entire five minutes. No Willie Horton. No opponent. No surrogate. No journalists. Just the candidate, talking into the camera, making his best case to an audience of roughly 60 million viewers for five minutes a night.

Is there any guarantee this would elevate the conversation? Actually, no. Nothing in this format would prevent a candidate from blathering about puppy dogs and picket fences or from launching a barrage of slanderous attacks if he were convinced either of those approaches would win him votes.

But there are, embedded in this proposal, a number of dis-incentives to engage in that kind of discourse. First, there is the check of personal accountability. If a candidate chose to devote his five-minute presentation to mindless happy talk or distorted accusation, at least he would have to put his own face and voice on the line. Next, there is the certainty of a swift response. What Candidate A says tonight, Candidate B gets a chance to refute tomorrow night—same time, same stations. Next, there is the prohi-bition against images. Although an attacker can distort with words as easily as with images, a target always has a better chance to defend against words. Visual attacks operate in the realm of emotion, not reason. They are often unanswerable by rational debate, which is why—increasingly in political campaigns—they provoke not a defense but an equally scurrilous visual counterattack. Linguistic assaults, on the other hand, can be parsed, dissected, rebutted and refuted. In this sense, even sharply distorted verbal attacks are more conducive to reasoned debate than subtly manipulative images.

Suppose we were to achieve the goal of a more elevated campaign debate for five minutes a night. So what? Wouldn't it still be drowned out by the more potent, more visually stimulating thirty-second paid spots that would continue to dominate the airwaves? Perhaps. But there are three aspects of this free-time plan that would allow it to compete with—and perhaps even overwhelm— poisonous thirty-second political commercials: simultaneity, brevity and repetition.

Simultaneity* is by far the most important. It is a statement about the unique importance of the message and format. The idea that everyone in America who has a radio or television tuned in at 7:55 p.m. has to listen to the same thing would, in and of itself, concentrate attention. Millions of viewers and listeners would no doubt resent the nightly force-feeding of politics. Some would escape to a cable station,† or to a movie on their VCR, or to another room of the house. So be it—these are safety valves to coerced viewing. As for the opposite concern that remote-control zappers and other switch-off options make the roadblock too porous, it's hard to see a cause for complaint. No channel of communication can capture everybody, no matter how ruthlessly designed. What matters is not that millions would escape, but that tens of millions wouldn't.

If you are going to pass a law that tries to force political dialogue on viewers this way, you owe it to them to make it as palatable as possible. This is where brevity comes into play. The free-time pro-posals that have been advocated in this country over the years, as well as some of those in place in Western Europe and elsewhere, provide for time in fifteen- or thirty-minute segments. This is too long. Even when a gifted orator like former President Reagan gave a thirty-minute speech on television, the audience drop-off after the first few minutes was brutal. Five minutes is long enough to say something substantive, but short enough to keep most viewers parked on their sofas. In any half-hour format, the presentations would almost surely have to be limited to one or two per week; the market simply will not bear a half hour of political speechmaking night after night. This tradeoff—longer speeches but fewer of them—is unwise. Repetition is a powerful agent of marketing. Product adver-tisers live by this rule: it's not the first time a commercial airs that makes it sink in; it's the tenth, or the hundredth.

Ideally, these five-minute presentations, repeated night after night, would unfold as a serialized debate, with thrust and parry, charge and rebuttal, gambits and surprises, rising action and falling action—in short, the attributes of drama that journalism is always looking to superimpose onto campaigns. They would be replayed on the nightly news shows and reported in the morning newspapers (how much happier journalists would be to write about them and not about the

---

*By simultaneity, I mean simultaneous by time zone, as currently practiced by the networks. That is, whether you live in Portland, Maine, or Portland, Oregon, you would see the segment at 7:55 p.m. by your clock.
†It is not clear, legally, if cable operators could be compelled to provide the free time. If they could be, they should be.

thirty-second spots!). They might even be what voters talked about at the grocery checkout line or the office water cooler.

Here's one way it might work: Candidate A gives a speech about drugs in front of a courthouse in Miami, Florida, on a Monday morning in early October. When he's finished, his media team scurries off to the local television station with the footage, cuts and splices it down to five minutes and beams the finished product up onto the satellite in time for every local broadcaster in the country to pick it up for the evening free-time broadcast. On Tuesday morning, Candidate B attacks A's drug plan from a school yard in Columbus, Ohio. On Wednesday, A rebuts on drugs and opens a new dialogue on the environment from a beach near San Diego. And so on.

Candidates would probably want to tape some of their presentations ahead of time and have them in the can before the free-time season began. But I'd be surprised if they didn't find themselves discarding the canned stuff in favor of daily excerpts from stump speeches—which, in texture, immediacy and theatricality, would have it all over the notoriously inert talking-head or fireside-chat format. The other obvious advantage of waiting until the day of broadcast to tape is that it provides the flexibility to respond to whatever the opponent said the night before.

While there are no guarantees, there's a good chance that this debate would be both meaty and engaging. "The five-minute presentations would almost have to be substantive," said Atwater, "because if one candidate was smart enough to go the substance route, he'd get so many accolades in the press that the other candidate would have to follow suit." Over time, a dialogue of this nature is bound to inculcate in its viewers and listeners a new respect for politics—and thereby diminish the payoff for thirty-second paid spots that traffic in distortion and demagoguery. In other words, by reversing the spiral of diminishing expectations, it would elevate the political discourse across the board. This is a vital point, for the political conversation cannot be reformed in five minutes a night.*

If this is such a promising idea, how come no one thought of it before? As a matter of fact, lots of people have thought of it before. More than half a century ago, Frank Knox, the 1936 GOP nominee for Vice President, wondered aloud in a speech: "Why not . . . require that, near election time, both great parties be allowed, without

*Nor can it be reformed on PBS alone. To its great credit, PBS in the summer of 1990 began planning to offer blocks of free time for presidential candidates in 1992. But the PBS audience is tiny, and it's already getting a lot of political information. The only way to have a big impact on the political discourse is through the commercial stations.

expense, an equal amount of time on the air, to the end that both
sides of all issues be fairly and adequately presented to the people."
A few years later, just such a proposal was adopted nationwide. The
nation, however, was Great Britain. It instituted "party political
broadcasts" (PPBs) on radio in 1945 and on television in 1951. During national campaigns in England, which have always been mercifully brief, the two leading parties are given blocks of time to
make their appeals (lesser parties are given shorter and fewer blocks
of time, in proportion to their number of seats in Parliament).
British television permits no other forms of political advocacy—no
paid commercials. This model has been adopted by most democracies around the globe. A 1981 report by the American Enterprise
Institute found that of twenty-one countries studied, eighteen (all
except Norway, Sri Lanka and the United States) provided free
television time to political parties during campaigns. In seventeen
of the countries, free time completely supplanted all paid political
advertising: only Australia, Canada, Japan and the United States
permitted paid commercials.[1]

The length and format of these PPBs vary. Canada, for example,
provides five minutes a week to parties between elections, to allow
them to keep voters abreast of current affairs on an ongoing basis.
The British system has always favored the longer segments of fifteen
to thirty minutes and only recently have these portions been used
for anything more adventurous than talking-head presentations.*
Some countries, such as France, place severe format restraints on
how the candidates can use the time—neutral studio settings, no film
footage, no interviews, etc. Some countries have moved to shorter
periods of time, with Italy opting for five-minute programs and
Germany for segments ranging from two and a half to five minutes.
All countries make allowances for free time to minor parties, with
the amount of time generally proportionate to the number of seats
the parties hold in Parliament.[2]

PPBs have never taken root in this country—in part because we
have a weak party system, in part because our advertising/marketing
culture is so powerful, and in part because the idea of regulating
political speech in any way, shape or format cuts against the grain.
There have been several proposals in this country over the years,
however. The first comprehensive one was Newton Minow's 1969

*The Neil Kinnock speech that so dazzled Joe Biden was a clip of a stump speech that
was used in a party political broadcast. It was augmented by stirring music by Brahms and
vivid campaign footage, and represented a milestone in British adaptation of "American
style" political packaging—a development not universally hailed in England.

report for the Twentieth Century Fund Commission on Campaign Costs in the Electronic Era. It called for six prime-time thirty-minute programs to be made available to each of the major-party presidential candidates, with allowances for minor-party candidates as well. The report became the basis of a bill introduced by Representatives John B. Anderson (R–Ill.) and Morris Udall (D–Ariz.) in the early 1970s. It did not generate much public interest and in short order was swallowed by a more pressing congressional concern about campaign finance reform. In the 1980s, at least three free-time proposals were put forward by "good government" groups—the Democracy Project in 1982, the Center for Responsive Politics in 1988, and the Twentieth Century Fund, which in 1989 put out a monograph by University of Virginia political scientist Larry J. Sabato that updated the Minow proposal. Every congressional session, a handful of bills are tossed in the hopper, where they stay.

There is no question that Congress has the authority to pass a law requiring that broadcasters provide free time to presidential candidates—as a brief summary of the history of the broadcasting industry will demonstrate.

In the 1920s, when radio was an infant and an unregulated industry, it kept running afoul of an immutable law of scarcity: to wit, there are a limited number of frequencies on the electromagnetic spectrum, and therefore a limited number of stations that can broadcast in any given locale. Secretary of Commerce Herbert Hoover urged the broadcasters to work the problems out among themselves, but they weren't able to. New stations would continually come on the air and poach on frequencies already in use. The resulting babble all but threatened to kill the industry. Some governmental regulation clearly was needed. As the Supreme Court would later rule: "Regulation of radio was therefore as vital to its development as traffic control was to the development of the automobile."*

The Radio Act of 1927 and the subsequent Communications Act of 1934 established the airwaves as a federal resource—like a national park—and determined that the exclusive use of this resource be granted to licensees who agreed to uphold the "public interest,

---

*Some in the industry have argued that this "scarcity" rationale for regulation no longer applies, since there are now roughly as many VHF television stations in the United States as there are daily newspapers, and seven times more radio stations than daily newspapers. The Supreme Court, however, has always defined scarcity by the laws of physics, not the economics of the marketplace. "Unlike other modes of expression," the Court ruled in 1943 in turning down an NBC challenge to the government's right to regulate broadcasting, "radio is inherently not available to all. That is its unique characteristic, and that is why, unlike other modes of expression, it is subject to government regulation."

convenience and necessity." Licensees would be given local monopolies over a frequency, free of charge, along with a promise that the government would not censor broadcast signals. Thus, broadcast license holders have always had a hybrid status, possessing private rights as well as a public trusteeship.

It was not inevitable that the government adopted this model. Congress gave considerable thought to treating broadcasters as common carriers, obligated (in the manner of the phone company) to provide its basic service—the power to broadcast programs over the airwaves—to any and all who wanted to pay for it. Or it could have given more than one licensee the right to use a given frequency— splitting the time by hours of the day or days of the week—in order to ensure that a maximum diversity of programming got onto the air. Or it could have granted no licenses and created a quasi-public corporation to control all broadcasting, along the lines of the British Broadcasting Company (BBC). Or it could have auctioned off the licenses to the highest bidders, the way it auctions off mineral or offshore drilling rights.

Instead, Congress created public trustees with local monopolies.* To ensure that the stations bring a diverse range of ideas and interests to public attention, Congress and the Federal Communications Commission have also established standards to guide them in performing their public-trusteeship function—the equal-opportunities rule, reasonable access, the Fairness Doctrine. Given this half-century-old body of law and regulation, there is no doubt that Congress would be on firm legal ground if it were to enact a law which required that, as a condition of being granted a license, radio and television stations had to give up a few hours every two or four years (out of their annual inventory of 6,000 hours) for candidates seeking elective office to use as they wish.

There is also no doubt that the broadcast industry would oppose such a law, as it always has. The last time a proposal of this sort was broached on Capitol Hill, in a 1983 hearing by the House Task Force on Elections chaired by Representative Al Swift (D–Wash.), network executives protested that legislative remedies which "singled out the

*These licenses, granted free of charge, have acquired enormous value on the open market. In 1985, for example, according to the Center for Responsive Politics, independent VHF stations were sold for $450 million in Boston, $510 million in Los Angeles and more than $700 million in New York. The sale price includes the tangible assets of the broadcast station, but the most important asset is the license itself. While profit margins have dropped in the past decade as a result of competition from cable and VCRs, television stations remain much more profitable than most businesses.

broadcast media" (ABC) for an "inappropriate burden" (CBS) would be "both an unconstitutional restriction on speech and press and discriminatory against the broadcast industry" (NBC). Few legal scholars take these arguments seriously, but that doesn't keep the networks from clinging to them. Broadcasters have always chafed at the public trusteeship model and argued that they should enjoy the same First Amendment freedoms as print journalism. What rankles them about free time is not giving up a pittance of their inventory (about one-fiftieth of 1 percent per year)—it's being told by the government what to do and when. "You've got a great idea," former FCC counsel Henry Geller said in an interview in late 1989, "but the broadcasters will oppose it on principle. It doesn't have a Chinaman's chance."

That's certainly the conventional wisdom: free time faces the blind alley that looms before most good-government proposals. If they're not pushed by any particular economic or political interest, and they're opposed by one very powerful interest, the game is over before it ever really starts.

This need not be the case with free time, however. "As a general concept, we subscribe to your notion of more communication on television, rather than less," Edward O. Fritts, president of the National Association of Broadcasters, the industry's chief trade association and lobbying arm, said when I outlined the proposal to him and his senior staff in December 1989. "There would be a fair amount of resistance [among NAB members] to a mandated roadblock of time, but I suspect there wouldn't be unanimity, either against the proposal or for it." Many broadcasters—like many print journalists—feel vaguely implicated in the role their medium plays in delivering junk-food politics. They may sense a public service duty to—if not actively support free time—at least not go all out to kill it. Moreover, free time conceivably could become a grass-roots issue. Public outrage over political air pollution has reached new heights in recent years. "Political campaigns turn the stomach of the average voter," Senator John Danforth said on the floor of the Senate in March 1990 in a speech in which he proposed that free time be made part of a campaign finance reform bill. "Most people, by the time election day occurs, are sick of the whole process. I don't know what academics have concluded but I know what I have concluded just on the basis of talking to my own constituents. They are sick about modern politics and they are particularly sick about what they see on television." (In an interview for this book, Danforth added: "You hold a town meeting and ask people about campaign-finance reform proposals and two hands go up. You ask about what people think of campaign ads, and 150 people start talking all at once.")

Al Swift, who chairs the House subcommittee that would have jurisdiction over any free-time legislation, called it a "helluva" proposal and said that the "terrible emptiness" of the 1988 campaigns had made it timely. He raised the possibility of conducting hearings immediately after the 1990 election, with the hope of having a free-time law in place for the 1992 presidential campaign. "I really think the broadcasters have got to say no, but I don't think that alone can kill it," said Swift, himself a former broadcaster. "You could get the League [of Women Voters] and Common Cause and groups like that behind it, and you'd get Republicans on board because they're on a kick for more competitive races, and I think you'd get a lot of support on the Democratic side, too." He said he believed that no group is more fed up with the sorry state of political dialogue than incumbent elected officials.

That's not a unanimous view. The more conventional analysis from Capitol Hill is that the only group likely to be as vehement as the broadcasters in opposing a free-time proposal is incumbents. They're against any change in election law that would place challengers on a more equal footing with incumbents. "The political problem you run into," Representative Jim Leach (R–Iowa) noted drily, "is that laws are written by incumbents." While this proposal would affect the presidential race only, Leach observed that "Congress would be smart enough to see that if it worked at the presidential level, there'd be pressure to impose it at the congressional level."

He's right. There would be—and there should be. Free time, if it proves successful at the presidential level, ought to be quickly expanded to cover races for all levels of government. Otherwise, it is only a Band-Aid. The vast preponderance of air pollution emitted in the name of political advocacy these days comes not from the contest for the presidency, but from senatorial, gubernatorial and congressional campaigns. The 1988 Bush–Dukakis race was a milestone only insofar as the techniques of visual distortion perfected at the state and local level over the past decade bubbled up to the presidential level.

It is more complicated to fashion a free-time proposal that works for state and local races as well as for the presidency. But it is by no means impossible. The bedeviling problem is to figure out how a single, short-segment format could accommodate the thousands of federal, state and local races held every even-numbered year. To take the most challenging case, consider the New York City media market. It encompasses three states, forty congressional districts and hundreds of state legislative districts. If the New York television stations were forced to make available five minutes to every candidate at every level of government, they'd be running political broadcasts around the clock. No one would stand for that.

The solution is surprisingly simple. Don't guarantee five minutes to every campaign for every office. Simply allot five minutes of "local time" every other night to all the state parties in the country, and let them figure out how best to use it.

Here's how it would work. On the first Monday night in October, the New York State Democratic party would have five minutes of free time. The party executive committee might decide that in the New York City media market, the entire five minutes should be used by its gubernatorial candidate. In Buffalo that same night, the party might give three county commissioner candidates a minute apiece, an endangered state senator a minute, the candidate for U.S. Senate thirty seconds and a challenger for a state assembly seat thirty seconds. In Albany, the whole five-minute block might be given over to a challenger who has a good chance to knock off an incumbent congressman. The lineups would vary in all the other media markets in the state, according to local needs and circumstances. The next night, the state Republican party would get its five minutes—and make its chess moves. And back and forth the two parties would go for the final month of the campaign.*

By allowing the political professionals to allocate the time, it's a cinch that the most competitive races would get the most exposure. That's good for challengers, good for voters and good for democracy. During the decade of the 1980s, more than 90 percent of incumbents at all levels of government won reelections. It's difficult to measure whether this degree of job security breeds a loss of vitality among incumbents, but surely it discourages some bright, ambitious would-be challengers from launching a career in politics. The gridlock has

---

*There is a complication when media markets—such as New York City's—overlap more than one state. But if 70 percent of viewers of New York City TV stations live in New York, 20 percent in New Jersey and 10 percent in Connecticut, then those three state parties could divide those stations' blocks of time proportionately.

grown most acute in the House of Representatives, a body that now loses as many incumbents to death as it does to defeat. Not only did incumbents win a record 98.5 percent of their races in 1988, but the average House incumbent in 1988 enjoyed the most lopsided fund-raising edge in history over the average challenger—$427,117 to $128,024. There's an axiom in politics that the first dollars spent in a campaign are more cost-effective than the last dollars. If a challenger has something to say and a soapbox to say it on, he has a chance to win despite being outspent. Free time would give him the soapbox.

It would also revive the state parties by giving them something of value to parcel out each election season. No doubt, there would be knock-down fights in every state executive committee over which candidates should get how much free time. But this is the sort of strife that strengthens institutions. The decline of the political parties over the last thirty years is a long and sorrowful saga—and not the subject of this book. Suffice it to say that of all the factors that account for reduced voter turnout and increased voter cynicism, the loss of vitality of the parties is near the top of the list. Any proposal that enhances the parties' role enhances the electoral process. Moreover, there's a touch of symmetry to any proposal that would invigorate parties by giving them control over a chunk of television and radio time—for it was the television revolution that yanked the ground out from beneath the parties in the first place. Once, ward heelers and committeemen and sheriffs and county chairmen were the chief conduits of political communication between voters and leaders. Now television is.

In interviews for this book, Republican National Committee Chairman Lee Atwater and Democratic National Committee Chairman Ronald Brown both endorsed this proposal. "I'd be tickled to death to see something like this put into effect," said Atwater. "It's precisely the kind of reform we need. I can't see any down side. And I can't see why anyone would be against it, except for self-serving reasons." Said Brown: "I'm definitely for it, in principle." Moreover, the partisan considerations that often cloud the prospects for passage of electoral reform proposals might actually balance each other out in this instance. Democrats would be attracted to free time because it would place their 1992 presidential candidate on more equal footing in the presumed reelection campaign of George Bush.* Republicans

---

*One prominent Republican in Congress speculated that if such a law were to pass, Bush might veto it. "I can see Roger Ailes storming into the Oval Office and saying, 'Mr. President, you've got thin lips and a thin voice. You really want to give your opponent five minutes a night in a format that you're no good at?'"

would be attracted to any plan that gives congressional challengers a ray of hope. After thirty-four consecutive years of Democratic control of the House, they're ready for anything—even reforms that undermine their own safety as incumbents.

There would be some time-management problems involved in taking care of both the presidential race and the state and local races in the same year and still not intruding on the electorate for more than five minutes a night. But again, they're hardly insurmountable. One approach might be to have the free-time period run for six weeks in presidential years—to accommodate both the presidential race and the state and local races—and three weeks in the midterm years.

There's plenty of room for fiddling with these details, just as there is on several other matters that would have to be worked out in the legislative process—such as third parties, primaries and funding. My personal bias (and I assume that of Congress) is to tilt any free-time plan in favor of the two-party system. Free time should be made available to third-party or independent candidates only if they meet a fairly high threshold of political viability. In states where third parties are on the ballot, these parties should be allotted time proportionate to the percentage of the vote their candidates received in the previous campaign. In the presidential race, if a third-party or independent candidate emerges in the course of the campaign, he should face a stiff voter petition requirement in order to qualify for free time.*

Free time is probably not adaptable to primary campaigns—at least not in the model proposed here. In presidential primaries, there are usually too many candidates for the alternating-night approach to work. In state and local party primaries, one could not allow the party to allocate the time: primaries often pit insiders versus mavericks, and in races like this, the party leadership is usually not neutral.

The question of who should pay for the free time has been a source of lively debate over the years. The 1969 Twentieth Century Fund proposal called for the expense to be shared equally by the taxpayers and the broadcasters, but this drew sharp protest from industry critics. "An industry that is using public property, the

*For example, an independent candidate running in 1992 might be required to collect signatures totaling 5 percent of the votes cast in the previous presidential campaign (or about 4.5 million signatures) to qualify for a half-share of the free time, and 10 percent to qualify for a full share.

airwaves," should not "hold up the elected officials and make them pay to get time from public property," Nicholas Johnson, then an FCC commissioner, wrote of the 1969 proposal. Robert Squier, a leading Democratic campaign consultant who has long advocated free time, said in testimony before Congress that taxpayers should not have to pay a "double tax" to reclaim public property.[3] On the other hand, if reimbursing the broadcasters for part or all of their lost revenues were to soften their resistance, it might be worth it. One possibility is to draw on the presidential campaign fund, the same one that in 1988 provided $46 million in public financing to each of the two presidential finalists.[*] Another possibility: If the broadcasters are worried about the loss of a few hours of inventory every four years, how about an informal swap between the political parties and the networks? The parties would cut the televised portion of their conventions in half—from four days to two—thereby reducing by eight hours the prime-time coverage that the networks devote to politics every fourth summer. (This would be no great loss: in their current form, political conventions are dinosaurs that deserve the dwindling viewership they receive.) In return, the networks would drop their opposition to a five-minute fix.[†]

One final question is whether presidential candidates should be compelled to accept the free time. It seems hard to imagine that any candidate would turn down the offer of five uninterrupted minutes a night to such a vast national audience, but given the way candidates sometimes try to squirm out of debates, anything is possible. So in 1992, when each major-party presidential nominee will be given roughly $50 million in public funds to run their fall campaigns, the money should come with a string attached: recipients will be required to appear on the free-time segments and abide by the prescribed format. (As long as we're on the subject, let's add one more string: they should be compelled to participate in at least two televised debates, and their running mates in one.) Only a handful of states have public campaign-finance plans for state office, so this hook would not be available at the state and local level. But it wouldn't be necessary. If a given local candidate didn't want to avail himself or herself of the time, the state party would simply parcel it out to another candidate who did.

[*]It's worth noting, however, that, in yet another sign of the depoliticization of the electorate, the fund's surpluses have dwindled steadily during the 1980s, as a declining number of Americans have checked the box on their IRS 1040 form that diverts a dollar of their taxes into the fund. If present trends continue, it will run a deficit by the mid-1990s.
[†]A nonpartisan institute, the Center for Democracy, recommended a similar swap in a report on the national political conventions issued in May 1990.

FREE TIME is by far the most promising "process" cure for what ails our political campaigns. It is by no means the only cure. Briefly, here are three other important goals we should pursue:

1. Shorten the presidential campaign. If I were emperor, I'd decree the following change: On Labor Day of the odd-numbered year before the presidential year, the names of all states that would like to play host to the first primary are to be placed in a hat, from which a winner is picked. By not telling the candidates where the opening primary is going to be held until five months beforehand, we would (a) eliminate lots of mischief (see Chapter 5) that now occurs in the two years before the first primary; (b) break Iowa's and New Hampshire's hammerlock on the early action; and (c) spread the opening-night excitement around to less-jaundiced states. This is such a wonderful (if slightly Rube Goldbergesque) idea that it's a shame it would take an emperor to put it into effect. But it would. The political problem is that it would need the backing of an incumbent President, and what politician of sound mind is going to scrap the primary system that nominated him?

Even without an emperor's decree, however, it's already clear that the 1992 presidential season will be much shorter than the 1988 season—a happy development for which all candidates, journalists and their spouses and children should thank Representative Richard Gephardt. "After what happened to him, there ain't going to be a lot of folks camping out in Iowa for 140 days this time," noted Paul Tully, political director of the Democratic National Committee.

2. Make it easier to vote. While voter-registration requirements are not responsible for declining turnouts—otherwise, the turnout would not have been declining while registration requirements have been easing—it's still more difficult to vote in the United States than in most other industrialized democracies. We do this for a reason: we are a fiercely individualistic society, and people here have a way of doing what they can get away with. This includes engaging in vote fraud. That's why stiff registration laws were passed in the first place, and that's why I don't believe nationwide same-day registration proposals are a good idea. I do think states should be much more aggressive about registering voters— making mail-in registration universal (it's currently in use in about half of the states), placing voter-registration booths and forms on prominent display in all government buildings and any other public setting that will have

them and registering young people in high schools and when they apply for a driver's license. I also think we should make election day a national holiday, as they do in other countries. Call it Democracy Day. I have no idea how much this will increase turnout, but at the very least, it may force nonvoters to have a second thought.

3. Educate our children in the duties of citizenship. Pollsters Peter Hart and Geoffrey Garin conducted a survey and series of focus groups among teenagers and young adults in 1989 and found they had an impoverished view of citizenship. Being a good citizen, to them, was essentially a negative mandate: it meant not breaking the law. "Democracy is a kind of a fragile, complicated idea and unless it's passed from one generation to another with some degree of enthusiasm and commitment, it can get lost," said Sanford Horwitt of People for the American Way, which sponsored the survey. "It was very clear listening to these young people that they graduated from high school without the barest understanding of what democracy was about, where voting fits in, or where other forms of citizen participation fit in. I don't think the adult world has served them very well."

If youngsters in the Soviet Union and China can grasp the grandeur of democracy, surely our kids can too. Perhaps we should start with public-service spots on television that use the techniques of the media consultants to arm the young against the manipulations of the media consultants. Bruce Buchanan, director of a Markle Foundation study group that has been searching for ways to improve political campaigns, suggests: "How about a thirty-second spot where you see a bucket of paint being splashed onto a new car and hear an announcer ask, 'You'd be pretty angry if someone did that to your car, wouldn't you? Well, how would you feel if someone did that to your political process?' "

IT IS CONCEIVABLE that these "process" fixes will be unnecessary by 1992. Perhaps the sheer momentum of political change around the globe will spark a more robust political conversation here. Perhaps the widespread revulsion at the kind of politics that was practiced in 1988 will trigger a backlash into seriousness. Perhaps a recession will come along to concentrate everyone's mind. Or a leader to lift everyone's sights.

And even if none of this happens, perhaps things aren't as bad as they seem. We might complain about what we hear from candidates during presidential campaigns—but at least we hear something. In the early part of the nineteenth century, it was considered unseemly for someone who wanted to be president to confess his availability for office. Washington, Jefferson, Jackson, Madison, Monroe and the two Adamses never spoke a word in behalf of their candidacies. When Stephen Douglas became the first presidential candidate to make a nationwide tour during the 1860 election, he was roundly criticized in the press. Douglas "demeans himself as no other candidate has yet," complained one newspaper; "he goes about begging, imploring, and beseeching people to grant him his wish." It was only after the Civil War that candidates made a habit of "bloviating," to use Warren Harding's expression for moving one's mouth in front of the multitudes.

The challenge—when it comes to political campaigns—is not to re-create an idealized past that never was. It is to reinvent a present that isn't working. Now we have candidates who bloviate in a carnival of attack ads, sound bites, photo ops, feeding frenzies. The spectacle neither nourishes nor engages its audience, half of which has disappeared by the time the show is over.

Would the five-minute fix be a cure-all? Of course not. No mechanical fix can be. But while we wait for some force of history to raise the level of our public life, the least we can do is to try to array the rewards and penalties of political speech into a healthier alignment. The surest way to encourage better citizenship is to give citizens better political discourse. Presidential campaigns are the one moment every four years when every citizen in America—even the least interested— pays attention to the dialogue of democracy, at least for a little while.

The moment is too precious to squander.

Notes

CHAPTER 1

1. Of the 91 million nonvoters in the adult population in 1988, an estimated 9 million were aliens, convicted felons or mental incompetents—and therefore ineligible to vote. If one were to subtract them from the voting age population, the 1988 turnout would be roughly 53 percent, not the 50.16 percent figure used by the U.S. Bureau of the Census. Census figures are used in this book because they are the most commonly accepted and allow for comparisons from one election to the next.

2. *The Winning of the White House, 1988* (Signet, 1988), p. 13.

3. Harold M. Zullow and Martin E. P. Seligman, "How Presidents Speak Their Minds," Washington *Post,* January 29, 1989, "Outlook" section, p. 3.

CHAPTER 2

1. The account of the precautions taken in 1984 is drawn primarily from an article by David Maraniss, "The Character Issue: A Bomb Waiting to Burst," Washington *Post,* May 8, 1987, p. 1.

2. The account of the Miami *Herald*'s stakeout of Hart's townhouse is drawn primarily from an article by Jim McGee, Tom Fiedler and James Savage, "The Gary Hart Saga, The Story Behind the Story," Miami *Herald,* May 10, 1987, p. 1.

CHAPTER 3

1. *Time* magazine, May 18, 1987.

2. Ibid.

3. *Newsweek,* May 18, 1987.

4. *Time,* op. cit.

5. Ibid.

6. Ibid.

7. Ibid.

8. Washington *Post,* June 10, 1987, Op-Ed page.

9. Hendrik Hertzberg, *The New Republic,* June 1, 1987.

10. ABC–TV's *Viewpoint,* May 18, 1987.

11. *Newsweek,* op. cit.

12. John B. Judis, "The Hart Affair," *Columbia Journalism Review,* July/August 1987.

13. Ibid.

14. Hendrik Hertzberg, "Boston Diarist," *The New Republic,* June 15, 1987, p. 42.

15. Maureen Dowd and Alessandra Stanley, "The Bores on the Bus," *Gentlemen's Quarterly,* September 1988.

16. This account of press coverage of Celeste's alleged extramarital affairs is drawn from a 1988 Stanford honors thesis by Christopher A. Celeste, the governor's son.

17. *Newsweek,* December 28, 1987.

CHAPTER 4

1. Michael Kinsley, "TRB," *The New Republic,* October 26, 1987.

CHAPTER 5

1. A. M. Rosenthal, Op-Ed column, *The New York Times,* March 18, 1988.

2. Howard Kurtz, "Mario Cuomo: Told You So!" Washington *Post,* June 29, 1988, "Style" section, p. 1.

3. Thomas E. Patterson, *The Mass Media Election* (Praeger Publishers, 1980), p. 45.

4. Joe Klein, "Class of the Field," *New York* magazine, January 18, 1988.

5. Maria Laurino, "Mario, Italian Style," *Village Voice,* May 3, 1988.

6. Robert S. McElvaine, *Mario Cuomo, A Biography* (Charles Scribner's Sons, 1988), p. 418.

7. Ibid., p. 136.

8. Mario M. Cuomo, *Diaries of Mario M. Cuomo: The Campaign for Governor* (Random House, 1984), p. 121.

9. Ibid., p. 36.

10. Ibid., p. 320.

CHAPTER 6

1. Martin Plissner and Warren Mitofsky, *Public Opinion,* July/August 1988.

2. Michel McQueen, "Jesse Jackson Raises Spirits, Swells Pride of Black Brooklynites," *The Wall Street Journal,* April 13, 1988, p. 1.

3. Ibid.

4. David Maraniss, "For Jackson, Victory Is in the Crowd's Smiles," Washington *Post,* May 14, 1988, p. 1.

5. Ibid.

6. *Time,* April 11, 1988, cover story.

7. Patrick Welsh, "Young, Black, Male and Trapped," Washington *Post,* September 24, 1989, Outlook section, p. 1.

8. Carl Sessions Stepp, "Covering Jesse," *Washington Journalism Review,* March 1988.

9. Kirk Johnson, "Racism and the Young: Some See a Rising Tide," *The New York Times,* August 27, 1989.

10. Shelby Steele, "The Recoloring of Campus Life," *Harper's,* February 1989.

11. Leon Wieseltier, *The New Republic,* June 5, 1989.

12. Joe Klein, *New York* magazine, May 1989.

13. Ernest van den Haag, "Affirmative Action and Campus Racism," *Academic Questions,* Summer 1989, p. 68.

14. Harry MacPherson, "How Race Destroyed the Democrats' Coalition," *The New York Times,* October 10, 1988, Op-Ed page.

15. Ruy Teixeira, *Public Opinion,* January/February 1989.

16. Hendrik Hertzberg, "Jesse Is History," *The New Republic,* June 20, 1988.

17. David Maraniss, "Jackson Playing to the Camera: Snapshots of Candidate Change But Questions Remain the Same," Washington *Post,* December 27, 1987, p. 1.

18. Walt Harrington, "On the Road with the President of Black America," Washington *Post* magazine, January 25, 1987.

CHAPTER 7

1. Michael Kramer, *U.S. News & World Report,* August 29/September 5, 1988.

2. Ibid.

3. *Newsweek,* August 29, 1988, cover story.

4. Poll taken by Marttila and Kiley and Market Opinion Research in early 1989.

5. Hendrik Hertzberg, *The New Republic,* September 12, 19, 1988.

6. *Newsweek,* special post-election issue, November 21, 1988.

7. Jack W. Germond and Jules Witcover, *Whose Broad Stripes and Bright Stars?* (Warner Books, 1989), p. 436.

8. Ibid., p. 441.

CHAPTER 8

1. Margaret Garrard Warner with Howard Fineman, "Bush's Media Wizard," *Newsweek,* September 28, 1988.

2. Ibid.

3. Ibid.

4. From presentation by Roger Ailes at campaign managers' post-election

conference at Harvard University, John F. Kennedy School of Government, Institute of Politics, December 1988.

5. David Remnick, "Why Is Lee Atwater So Hungry?" *Esquire,* December 1986.

6. Thomas B. Edsall, profile of Lee Atwater in Washington *Post,* January 20, 1989, p. 1.

7. Robin Toner, "Dukakis Aides Acknowledge Bush Outmaneuvered Them," *The New York Times,* November 12, 1988, p. 1.

8. Christine M. Black and Thomas Oliphant, *All by Myself* (Globe Pequot Press, 1990), p. 245.

9. Lloyd Grove, "Attack Ads Trickled Up from State Races," Washington *Post,* November 13, 1988, p. 1.

10. Michael Kinsley, "TRB," *The New Republic,* November 14, 1988.

11. Michael Oreskes, " 'Attack' Politics, Rife in '88 Election, Comes into Its Own for Lesser Stakes," *The New York Times,* October 24, 1989.

12. David Broder, "Politicians, Advisers Agonize Over Negative Campaigning," Washington *Post.* January 19, 1989, p. 1.

CHAPTER 9

1. Seymour Martin Lipset and William Schneider, *The Confidence Gap* (New York: The Free Press, 1983), p. 15.

2. Barbara Lippert, "A Man for '87 — Joe Isuzu," Washington *Post,* December 28, 1986, Outlook section, p. 1.

3. Louis Menand, "A Farewell to the '80s," *The New Republic,* October 9, 1989.

4. Garry Wills, *Reagan's America: Innocents at Home* (Doubleday, 1987).

5. Examples drawn from article by Marjorie Williams, "The Eighties: The Fragmenting of Culture," Washington *Post,* December 19, 1989, p. 1.

6. Herbert J. Gans. *Middle-American Individualism* (Free Press, 1988).

7. Arthur Schlesinger, "America's Political Cycle Turns Again," *The Wall Street Journal,* December 10, 1987.

8. *Time,* November 21, 1988.

9. Ruy Teixeira, *Why Americans Don't Vote* (Greenwood Press, 1987).

10. Ibid., p. 6.

11. James MacGregor Burns. *The Power to Lead* (Simon and Schuster, 1984), p. 11.

CHAPTER 10

1. Dom Bonafede, "The New Political Power of the Press," *Washington Monthly,* September 1980, p. 24.

2. Michael Schudson, "The Politics of Narrative Form: The Emergence of News Conventions in Print and Television," *Daedalus,* Fall 1982, p. 107.

3. Irving Kristol, "Crisis for Journalism: The Missing Elite," *Press, Politics and Popular Government. Domestic Affairs Studies* (American Enterprise Institute, 1972), p. 49.

4. Martin Linsky, *Television and Presidential Elections* (Lexington Books, 1983), p. 50.

5. Ibid., p. 51.

6. Ibid., p. 64.

7. *The Adversary Press* (Modern Media Institute, 1983), p. 24.

8. Ibid., p. 52.

9. Mark Hertsgaard, "Did the News Media Go Easy on Reagan?," *Washington Post*, August 21, 1988, "Outlook" section, p. 1.

10. Edith Efron, *The News Twisters* (Nash Publishing, 1971).

11. Paul H. Weaver, "Is Television News Biased?" *The Public Interest*, winter 1972.

12. Quoted in Eleanor Randolph, "Though Viewed More Favorably than Bush or Hill, Media's Support Slipping," Washington *Post*, November 16, 1989, p. 15.

13. Kiku Adatto, "TV Tidbits Starve Democracy," *The New York Times*, December 10, 1989, Op-Ed page.

14. Michael Robinson and Margaret A. Sheehan, *Over the Wire and on TV* (Russell Sage Foundation, 1980), p. 222.

15. Linsky, op. cit.

16. Peter J. Boyer, "When TV News Must Pay Its Way, Expect Trivia," *The New York Times*, October 2, 1989, Op-Ed page.

17. Predictions all compiled by Martin Schram, "Kisses and Predictions," *The Washingtonian*, January 1989.

18. Kiku Adatto, "Sound Bite Democracy: Network Evening News Presidential Campaign Coverage, 1968 and 1988," Barone Center for Press, Politics and Public Policy, John F. Kennedy School of Government, Harvard University, June 1990.

19. Ibid.

CHAPTER 11

1. *Beyond the Thirty-Second Spot: Enhancing the Media's Role in Congressional Campaigns* (Center for Responsive Politics, 1988), p. 42.

2. Background on free time in other countries is drawn from a monograph by Howard Penniman and Austin Ranney, "The Regulation of Televised Political Advertising in Six Selected Countries," prepared for The Committee for the Study of the American Electorate, Washington, D.C.

3. *Beyond the Thirty-Second Spot*, op. cit., p. 64.

Index

A NOTE ABOUT THE AUTHOR

Paul Taylor has been a newspaper reporter since 1970, beginning with the *Twin City Sentinel* in Winston-Salem, N.C. After three years there he joined the staff of the Philadelphia *Inquirer,* and in 1981 he went to the Washington *Post.* In 1989, he served as Ferris Professor of Journalism at Princeton University. He lives in Bethesda, Maryland, with his wife, Stefanie, and their three children, Jeremy, Ben and Sarah.

A NOTE ON THE TYPE

This book was set in a typeface called Baskerville. The face itself is a reproduction of types cast from molds made for John Baskerville (1706–1775) from his designs. Baskerville's original face was one of the forerunners of the type style known to printers as "modern face"—a "modern" of the period A.D. 1800.

Composed by Superior Printing Company, Champaign, Illinois.
Printed and bound by Fairfield Graphics, Fairfield, Pennsylvania.
Designed by Peter A. Andersen.